Torah Lights
Bemidbar: Trials and Tribulations in Times of Transition

אור תורה סטון
OHR TORAH STONE
תורה ותיקון עולם

מגיד
MAGGID

Shlomo Riskin

TORAH LIGHTS

BEMIDBAR: TRIALS AND TRIBULATIONS
IN TIMES OF TRANSITION

Maggid Books

Torah Lights
Bemidbar: Trials and Tribulations
in Times of Transition

First Edition 2012

Maggid Books
An imprint of Koren Publishers Jerusalem Ltd.

POB 8531, New Milford, CT 06776-8531, USA
POB 2455, London W1A 5WY, England
& POB 4044, Jerusalem 91040, Israel
www.korenpub.com

ISBN 978 159 264 275 5, *hardcover*

A CIP catalogue record for this title is
available from the British Library

Printed and bound in the United States

To our beloved children

Batya and Eddie
Yosef, Mevasseret, Naomi, and Akiva

Elana and Menachem
Avishai, Amiel, and Elai HaKohanim

Hillel and Limor
Eden Barkai, Yaal David, and Saar Ari HaKohanim

Yoni and Limor
Shalev Hod Harel and Maayan Ivri HaKohanim
Nehora Yafit, Shoham Ahava, Carmi Rut,
and Adva Shirelle HaKohanot

in the hope that they receive from us
a fraction of what I received
from my parents and grandparents

In profound gratitude
to my beloved friend

BERNARD GOLDBERG

for having sponsored this edition
of biblical commentary
in memory of his beloved mother

ELSIE GOLDBERG

who graced the world
for well over a century of years

Contents

ḤUKKAT

BALAK

PINEḤAS

Tribute

I want to thank my revered teachers, Rabbi Joseph B. Halevi Soloveitchik, z"l, Professor Nehama Leibowitz, z"l and Rabbi Moshe Besdin, z"l for their many insights into the words and commentaries of the Torah. Much of what is written here is based upon lectures and discussions I was privileged to have had with them – as well as with the many great Torah scholars from whom I have learned throughout the years. Although I have attempted to give proper attribution so as to help bring redemption to the world, I am certain that there are insights I may have derived from others which I have come to think of as my own; suffice it to say that whatever may be worthy in this volume was inspired by my teachers, but I assume complete responsibility for whatever may not be deemed worthy.

I am most appreciative to Sheldon Gewirtz, who originally urged me to begin writing a weekly commentary on the Torah portion, and to Jacob Lampert, who helped in the writing of the columns during the early years of this activity. The congregations I have been privileged to serve as rabbi and preacher, Lincoln Square Synagogue in Manhattan and the many synagogues of the City of Efrat, Israel, as well as my students at the Ohr Torah Stone Institutions served as the original sounding boards for these commentaries, which were then written and distributed in weekly columns in *The Jerusalem Post* and some thirty Anglo-Jewish newspapers worldwide. Hopefully, each additional rendering has helped improve my formulation and understanding.

I am very grateful to my beloved and long-standing friend Matthew Miller, who encouraged me to publish these books in Israel and has overseen every aspect of this publication. His entire staff at Koren Publishers Jerusalem has been exceedingly helpful – especially Gila Fine, who supervised the final editorial stages.

Ayal Fishler, a young scholar and excellent linguist, was chiefly involved in the editing of the Hebrew translation, but has had a great influence over the final English version, as well. I am also grateful to Sue Epstein, a longtime resident of Efrat, who has always made herself available even for last-minute typing.

And, of course, everything of importance that comes out of my Efrat office has been started and concluded by my very faithful administrative aid, Micky Mirvis.

Lastly, my gratitude to my beloved and extended family – especially my cherished wife and life-partner, Vicky – who have not only heard these ideas around the Sabbath table, but have also questioned them, argued with them, and certainly refined them.

Most of all, I must give tribute to the Almighty, who has enabled me to labor in the vineyard of Torah during these last forty years as rabbi and educator, a calling which has made the Five Books of the Torah my constant guide and companion.

כִּי אִם בְּתוֹרַת ה׳ חֶפְצוֹ וּבְתוֹרָתוֹ יֶהְגֶּה יוֹמָם וָלָיְלָה

Introduction to Bemidbar

What makes a great leader? How can we understand the great success of a leader in one generation and the decline in his ability to lead the next generation? What causes a nation to descend from exalted commitment to destructive disaffection? How does a leader contend with resistance and rebellion in the ranks?

The book of Numbers deals with the uncertainties and complexities of transitions: from Egyptian subjection to desert freedom, from abject slavery to the possibility of redemption. Why do so many individuals and nation-states resist such a journey, seeming to prefer "escaping from freedom" over embracing responsibility? Why has almost every revolution on behalf of freedom failed dismally, allowing the new regime even greater powers of control than employed by the government it rebelled against?

These contemporary issues are explored in depth in the book of Numbers, and are textually, politically, and theologically analyzed in the pages of this commentary. Most importantly, we attempt to provide a glimpse into the complexities assailing the greatest leader in world history: *Moshe Rabbenu,* a fierce freedom fighter and passionate lover of God, a towering persona who fashioned a way of life to secure a sacred nation and forged a moral guide to ensure human survival – but who left the world tragically frustrated and disappointed, having failed in his primary mission to bring the People of Israel into the Promised Land.

Ultimately, God's greatest prophet has been resoundingly vindicated by Jewish history. I hope this commentary will demonstrate that our return to our homeland was only made possible by the teachings of God's chief spokesman, and that the legacy Moses left for posterity contains the best blueprint for human redemption.

Bemidbar

Desert, Divine Word, and Divine Habitation

And God spoke unto Moses in the wilderness of Sinai, in the tent of meeting, on the first day of the second month, in the second year after they were come out of the Land of Egypt.

NUMBERS 1:1

B*emidbar,* or "In the Desert," is the name by which this fourth of the Five Books of Moses (Pentateuch) is most popularly known – an apt description of the forty years of the Israelite desert wanderings which the book records.

Indeed this desert period serves as the precursor of – as well as a most apt metaphor for – the almost two thousand years of homeless wandering from place to place which characterized much of Jewish history before the emergence of our Jewish State in 1948.

The Hebrew word for desert, *midbar,* is also pregnant with meanings and allusions which in many ways have served as a beacon for our Jewish exile. The root noun from which *midbar* is built is D-B-R, which means leader or shepherd. After all, the most ancient occupation known to humanity is shepherding, and the desert is the most natural place for the shepherd to lead his flock: the sheep can comfortably wander in a virtual no-man's land and graze on the vegetation of the various oases or their outskirts without the problem of stealing from private property or harming the ecology of settled habitations. And perhaps D-B-R means leader-shepherd because it also means *word*: the shepherd directs the flock using meaningful sounds and words, and the leader of people must also have the ability to inspire and lead with the verbal message he communicates; indeed, the "Ten Words" (or Ten Commandments, *Aseret HaDibrot*) were revealed in the Sinai desert, and they govern Israel – as well as a good part of the world – to this very day.

Moreover, it must be noted that wherever the Israelites wandered in the desert, they were always accompanied by the portable desert *Mishkan*, or Sanctuary, which is derived from *Shekhina*, Divine Presence. However, God was not in the Sanctuary; even the greatest expanse of the heavens cannot contain the Divine Presence, declared King Solomon when he dedicated the Holy Temple in Jerusalem (I Kings 8:27). It was rather God's *word, dibur*, which was in the Sanctuary, in the form of the "Ten Words" on the Tablets of Stone preserved in the Holy Ark, as well as the ongoing and continuing word of God which He would speak (*vedibarti*, Exodus 25:22) from between the cherubs on the ends of the *Kapporet* above the Holy Ark. It was by means of these divine words that even the desert, the *midbar* – a metaphor for an inhospitable and even alien exile environment which is boiling hot by day, freezing cold by night, and deficient in water which is the very elixir of life – can become transformed into sacred space, the place of the divine word (*dibur*). And indeed those words from the Desert of Mount Sinai (*diburim*) succeeded in sanctifying the many Marrakeshes and Vilnas and New Yorks of our wanderings! God's word can transform a desert – any place and every place – into a veritable sanctuary; indeed the world is a *midbar* waiting to become a *dvir* (sanctuary) by means of God's *dibur*, communicated by inspired leaders, *dabarim*.

Postscript: A Story

Allow me to share with you a story from my previous life (in the exile of the West Side of New York City) which taught me how the word can bring sanctity to the most unlikely of places. In the early 1970s, a disco opened up in a window storefront building on 72nd Street and Broadway. Despite the fact that it was called the Tel Aviv Disco and was owned by Israelis living in New York, it remained open every night of the year, even *Kol Nidrei* night. I must have placed at least two dozen calls to the owners to try to persuade them to close at least on the night of Yom Kippur, only to have finally received a message from their secretary informing me that the owners would not speak to rabbis!

During this period, Rabbi Yitzḥak Dovid Grossman – a beloved and respected friend who is the rabbi of Migdal HaEmek – spent Shabbat with us at Lincoln Square Synagogue. A recipient of the Israel Prize, he is a charismatic religious leader who is well-known for the many prisoners and other alienated Jews whom he has brought back to religious observance. After a delightful Friday evening meal at my home, replete with inspiring Hasidic melodies and words of Torah, he suggested that we go for a "*shpatzir*" (Yiddish for leisurely walk). I tried to explain that the general atmosphere of the West Side streets of Manhattan were hardly conducive to Sabbath sanctity – but to no avail. His steps led us in the direction of 72nd Street and Broadway, right in front of the window revealing the frenzied disco dancers. "Did you ever see a mosquito captured in a glass jar?" he asked me in Yiddish (our language of discourse). "The mosquito moves with all sorts of contortions, and appears to be dancing. In reality, however, the mosquito is gasping for air. That is the situation of those 'dancers' in the disco. They are really gasping for air, struggling in their search for a real Shabbos. Let's go in and show them Shabbos."

Before I could say "Jackie Robinson," he was inside the disco – and as a good host, I felt obliged to follow him. He sported a long beard and side-locks, and was wearing a *shtreimel* (fur hat) and *kapote* (silk gabardine), and I was dressed in my Sabbath Prince Albert, kippa and ritual fringes out. As we entered the disco, the band of Israelis immediately stopped playing. I recognized three young men from the synagogue, who seemed totally discombobulated; two ran out covering their faces, and the third tried to explain to me that he wasn't really there, that his mother had had some kind of attack and he thought that her doctor might be at the disco.... Rabbi Grossman began to sing Sabbath melodies. Almost miraculously, the men danced on one side, the women on the other. After about twenty minutes he urged me to speak to them in English. I told them of the magical beauty, the joy, and the love of the Sabbath, and they listened with rapt attention. Rabbi Grossman led them in one more song – and we left.

I cannot tell you that the miracle continued; it didn't take five minutes, and we could hear the resumption of the disco band music. However, before the next Yom Kippur, the Tel Aviv Disco closed down. I don't know why; perhaps because the owners wouldn't speak to rabbis. And for the next two years, at least a dozen young singles joined Lincoln Square Synagogue because they had been inspired by our disco visit, because God's words had the power to transform even a disco into a sanctuary, if only for twenty minutes of eternity...

The Message of the Census Counts

Count the heads of the entire witness community of the children of Israel.

NUMBERS 1:2

The book of Numbers opens with a most optimistic picture of a nation poised for redemption. The Israelites have been freed from Egypt with great miracles and wonders; they have received the Revelation at Sinai, which provided them with a moral and ethical constitution for a soon-to-be established sovereign state, along with a commitment of faith to be a holy nation and a kingdom of priests, which is their mission for the world; the twelve uniquely endowed and individually directed tribes, each with its own flag, are united around a common Sanctuary dedicated to divine service; a standing army is organized; the tribe of Levi is trained to teach Torah and fulfill all the requirements for the sacrificial service. The only missing ingredient is the necessary obligatory war to pave the way for our settlement of the Promised Land of Israel!

But what follows instead is a total degeneration, a descent from the heights of an exalted rooftop down to the depths of a muddied pit. The Hebrews become involved in petty squabbles and tiresome complaints; the reconnaissance mission decides against the attempt to conquer Israel; Koraḥ, Datan, and Aviram stage a rebellion against Moses; a prince of the tribe of Simeon defies Moses' leadership by publicly fornicating with a Midianite woman; the entire desert generation dies in the wilderness; and only Moses' successor, Joshua, and the newly-born generation will get to live in the Promised Land. What happened and why? How could a nation so committed that it pledges "Whatever the Lord has spoken we shall do and we shall internalize" (Exodus 24:7) completely lose their sense of purpose and idealism and "gang up" against the very individual who was their great liberator and law-giver?

I believe that the reason for the change is hinted at in the midrashic name of this fourth book of the Bible, *Sefer Pikudim* – the "Book of Censuses" in Hebrew, or the book of Numbers (number counts) in English, after the two censuses, or number counts, of the population, which are taken between its covers. Indeed our book (and this portion) opens with the command to count the Israelites, stipulating as follows:

> Count the heads of the entire witness community of the children of Israel, by their families, by their parents' houses, with the number of names of each male body, from twenty years of age and above, all that are able to go forth to war in Israel.
>
> Numbers 1:2–3

Such are the details of the census given at the beginning of the book, when the Israelites are still imbued with a vision of mission and "manifest destiny," and when we still expect them to wage a war for the liberation of the Land of Israel.

However, twenty-five chapters later, after the scouts' refusal to attempt to conquer Israel, after the various rebellions against Moses culminating in Prince Zimri ben Salou's shameful public adultery with the Midianite Kozbi bat Tzur directly in front of the presence of Moses himself, a second census is ordered:

> Count the heads of the entire witness community of the children of Israel, from twenty years of age and above, with their household parents, everyone eligible for army conscription.
>
> Numbers 26:2

It is clear that the identification of each Israelite for the purpose of the census is radically different in the second census from the way it was in the first census. The first time the count included "the families [proving everyone's tribal affiliation harking back to Jacob, Isaac, and Abraham], the household parents, and the individual personal names"; the second time, the tribal affiliation and the personal names of each were missing, with only the names of the household parents of each individual provided!

Clearly, herein – between the lines of the significant omissions – lies the secret of the degeneration of the Israelites. This is apparently why the Midrash names this the "Book of Censuses" (*Sefer Pikudim*) rather than the Book of the Desert (*Bemidbar*): in order to point us towards the solution to our presenting problem by highlighting the different stipulations of each census respectively. In the first census, taken during the heyday of the generation of the Exodus, each individual Israelite felt connected to his tribal parent, to his biblical patriarchs and matriarchs; by the second census, however, that connection was woefully gone, and the individual only related to his immediate biological parents. Allow me to explain.

The book of Exodus, our birth as a nation, is built upon the book of Genesis, our origins as a very special family. The patriarchs and matriarchs were originally chosen by God because of their commitment to "compassionate righteousness and moral justice" – traits which would make them "a blessing for all the nations of the world" (Genesis 12:3) and ideals to which they were to "command their children and their households after them" (Genesis 18:19). This unique Hebraic culture was to be nurtured and developed within a special land, the Land of Israel, which is the very "body" and the national expression, the physical matrix, of our eternal covenant with God. Only against the backdrop of their land and state would Israel be able to teach compassionate righteousness and moral justice to the other nation-states. The towering personalities of the book of Genesis develop, falter, repair, sacrifice, persevere, and ultimately prevail on these twin altars of commitment to land and law, to sensitive humanity and sovereign nationality; these founding parents established the foundation for the continuity of an eternal people through whom the entire world will eventually be blessed by the peace of ultimate redemption.

"*Yiḥus*," lineage or pedigree, has little to do with privilege and special rights but has everything to do with responsibility and ancestral empowerment. Grandfather Jacob blesses his grandchildren, the sons of Joseph, that "they shall be called by his name and the name of his ancestors, Abraham and Isaac" (Genesis 48:16); this does not only mean naming them Abe and Ike and Jackie but rather means linking them to their patriarch's ideals, to their values, to their commitments. It also means endowing them – and empowering them – with the eternal promise they received from God that their seed would inherit the Land of Israel and would eventually succeed in conveying to the world the message (and blessing) of divine morality and peace.

Tragically, the desert generation lost its connection with the book of Genesis, with the mission and empowerment, with the dream and the promise of the patriarchs and matriarchs of their family. As a consequence, the second census no longer connected them to the tribal children of our patriarchs and matriarchs. And the loss of connectedness to Abraham and Sarah resulted in a disconnect from the God of our forebears, from the promise and the covenant of that God, from the unique message and mission of Israel provided by the DNA and idealistic life-models of our ancestors. That generation lost faith in itself, became in "their own eyes as grasshoppers, and so were they in the eyes of their enemies," and lost the courage to conquer the land, despaired of the dream to teach the world. By disconnecting from their past they lost their future; and so they did not even merit individual names, names which would count and could only be counted if they were linked with the proud names which founded Jewish eternity. Herein lies the secret of the dissolution of the desert generation. Are we in Israel today not faced with a similar disconnectedness from Abraham, Isaac, and Jacob, from Sarah, Rebecca, Rachel, and Leah, patriarchs and matriarchs of our past who must always remain paradigms for our future?

The Importance (or Lack Thereof) of Yiḥus

...by their families, by their parents' houses.
NUMBERS 1:2

Early in the book of Numbers the Torah records the first census in the history of the Jewish people: "Count the heads of the entire witness community of the children of Israel, by their families, by their parents' houses" (Numbers 1:2). Certainly a census is a momentous event – not only as a profile of a nation's most important natural resource – its people – but also as a means of enhancing each national with a sense of pride in his newly acquired significance as a member of an important nation.

At the end of the day, when all the counts of the various tribes were added up, the total number of those twenty years and above was 603,550 (Numbers 1:46). The census tells us – in more ways than one – that each person counts. Again and again we encounter the phrase in connection with the census: "by their families [*lemishpeḥotam*], by their parents' houses [*leveit avotam*]."

This particular term is repeated with each of the tribes and families, except for two instances wherein the phrase is inverted – in the case of the Levites, as well as the sons of Gershon. In these two instances, instead of the order of being "by their families" and "by their parents' houses" we find "by their parents house and by their families" (Numbers 3:15).

In contrast, Levi's other sons, Kehat (Numbers 4:2) and Merari (Numbers 4:27) are presented in the book of Numbers in a manner similar to the presentation of the rest of the tribes – first by their "families" and only afterwards by their "fathers' houses." Why should there be such a reversal in phraseology in the case of Levi and the children of Gershon?

In our last commentary, we rendered the phrase "*lemishpeḥotam*" to mean "by the family of their tribal forebears," and "*leveit avotam*" to mean "by their immediate parental names," in accordance with the interpretation of Rashi (1040–1105). However, the earlier Aramaic translation of these phrases, *Targum Onkelos*, which is generally placed alongside of the biblical text as a demonstration of its authoritative position, render "*lemishpeḥotam*" as "*lezarayaton*" – "by their seed, by their children."

Thus the usual formulation, found no less than seventeen times in our passage, is rendered to mean that each individual is numbered by their children and by their parents' house. The message of the *Targum* is clear: an individual is to be counted first by whom he or she has produced – by his or her children – and only afterwards and secondarily do we pay attention to his or her forebears, to the *yiḥus* which comes from one's parents and the parental forebears; perhaps *Targum* would include the tribal background as well in "*leveit avotam*."

From the perspective of this definition, we can also readily understand the reversal of the phrase regarding the tribe of Levi. Ordinarily individuals are defined first by whom and what they have produced – their children first. However, a kohen (priest) or Levite serves in the Temple and performs special ritual duties not by virtue of merit but only by virtue of ancestry: I am a kohen only because my father was a kohen. Hence in accordance with this reality, the Bible insists that their census is "by their parents' house and by their children" – the parents coming first!

And in addition to special ritual functions, the care and maintenance of the Sanctuary (during the years of wandering in the desert) was divided amongst the three scions of the house of Levi. The duty of Gershon, as described in the previous portion, focused on the curtains, the hangings, the various coverings inside the Tabernacle. According to the midrash, this was the easiest job in the Sanctuary. It is therefore assumed that the children of Gershon were satisfied to rest on their laurels; they remained in essence Levites, dependent on their "parent's house" for their status and function.

In contrast, the children of Kehat were in charge of the much heavier items, such as the Menora and the Ark. In *Bemidbar Rabba* (5:1), we read the following description: "When the Jews were traveling, two sparks of flame came out from the two poles of the Ark of the Tablets of Law." The Kehatites volunteered to put their lives on the line and risk the fire in order to bear the Holy Ark. And their brothers the Merarites learned from their example, volunteering to transport the heaviest wood and metals. These children of Levi were anxious to be their own people, to establish their own *yiḥus*. As a result, the Torah counts them in accord with "their children and their parents' house" – themselves and their children coming first!

What we've gathered from the overview is that a seemingly slight difference in word order may reveal a world of attitude and psychology. When each of us is counted and assessed when the Almighty conducts His census, the most important criterion in our judgment will not be who our parents were, but who and what we and our children have developed into. All too often, the descendant has descended too far down! And when we ponder the question of "Who is a Jew?" as we so often do within the context of necessity for conversion and the "right of return," it is important to note that at least from a sociological (rather than a halakhic) perspective, a Jew is defined more by his children than by his parents; indeed, I would argue that sociologically speaking, a Jew is he or she who has Jewish grandchildren!

Postscript

The Maggid of Mezritch (eighteenth century, Ukraine) was a great disciple of the Ba'al Shem Tov, and heir to his leadership of the Hasidic movement. It is told that when the Maggid was still a child, a fire broke out in his family home. Although the family was rescued from the flames, his mother was weeping hysterically. When he asked her why she was so upset at the loss of mere physical objects, the mother explained that she was crying for the loss – not of the home or its furniture – but of the record of their family pedigree, which had been destroyed in the flames. This record had traced back their familial roots to King David himself! "You don't have to cry over that," said the young Maggid, comforting his mother. "I will begin a new record of our family pedigree; from me will begin a new *yiḥus*. Subsequent generations will trace their lineage back to me."

Removing the Bar from the Mitzva: An Educational Proposal to Link Diaspora Jewry to Israel

Count the heads of the entire witness-congregation of the children of Israel, by their families, by their parents' houses; with the number of names of each male body, from twenty years of age and above, all that are able to go forth to war in Israel, you and Aaron shall number by their hosts.

NUMBERS 1:2–3

Is there any ceremony in contemporary Jewish life more vulgarized than the bar mitzva? Back in America giant sculptures of chopped liver baseball gloves graced the smorgasbord, and here in Israel, in circles where the event has nothing to do with mitzvot, the occasion has turned into a huge party with a disc jockey playing the latest hits with as many friends as one can pack into a catering hall. When the State of

Israel was young and innocent, the only beverages that graced the tables were fruit drinks, with the occasional bottle of sweet wine symbolizing the religious nature of the event, but now Manhattans and Gin and Tonics are part of the local landscape. Here Israel's newly designed catering establishments can also point to well-stocked liquor bars, suggesting that it's the "bar" and not the "mitzva" that will be remembered most about such rites of passage.

The origin of the bar mitzva stems from a Mishna in the *Ethics of the Fathers*, "At thirteen, one is obligated to perform the commandments" (5:24). And even though the social norms of Mishnaic times were certainly different from ours, it is difficult to imagine that even in those days every twelve-year-old girl and thirteen-year-old boy was mature enough to throw away slingshots and dolls and accept all the obligations and responsibilities inherent in the Torah.

Certainly the typical twelve- and thirteen-year-old girls and boys in our society are hardly to be considered mature adults ready to commit themselves to the Jewish traditions with proper seriousness and devotion.

If we look at the text of *Bemidbar* in the Torah reading quoted above, we find that it includes the laws that mandate a census of all Jews. However, we only begin to count them – and hence they begin to be considered mature adults – at age twenty, which was the biblical age of conscription to the army.

Thus we begin to realize that Jewish tradition recognizes two distinct ages of majority. The first occurs at twelve and thirteen when the young woman or man begins to grow physically mature enough to parent his or her own child and – God forbid – wreak acts of violence. According to Jewish law, the jurisdiction of courts over this age group is a necessary concession to society's need to protect itself from possible harm.

But it's not until age twenty that the individual may be considered emotionally and intellectually mature enough to be regarded in the heavenly courts as truly responsible for his or her deeds – the heavenly courts symbolizing the realm where final judgments are delivered (for the person's soul). Twenty is generally the age of independence from one's parental home and hence the understandable starting point of individual responsibility. Hence, the Midrash praises our matriarch Sarah by comparing her state of sinfulness at age one hundred to her state of sinfulness at age twenty: just as she was blameless at age twenty (for until that age she would not be considered culpable by the heavenly court), so did she remain blameless at age one hundred (*Bereshit Rabba* 58:1; Rashi on Genesis 23:1).

I also believe that the traditional blessing made by the parents at the advent of the bar and bat mitzva of their son/daughter – "Blessed is the God who has freed me from being punished because of this [child]" – is not a removal of the parent from responsibility for the child; it only removes the parent from exclusive responsibility. Before age twelve and thirteen, the parent alone is responsible for his or her children's actions; from age twelve and thirteen to age twenty, responsibility is shared by parent and child jointly; at age twenty, with maturity, the child must assume complete responsibility and cease blaming the parent! Indeed, my son Hillel maintains that true maturity comes when you stop blaming others – your parents, your teachers, your society – for failures and shortcomings, and recognize that you can only blame yourself!

So then why does our universal Jewish community not consider celebrating two ages of majority, the first being the bat/bar mitzva (son/daughter of commandment) at twelve or thirteen and then a second, being a ḥatan/kalat mitzva (groom or bride to the commandment) at twenty? The first would be a rite of passage into puberty and the beginning of an intellectual and emotional odyssey, and the second would be a much more heartfelt gathering, the individual having spent seven or eight intensive years receiving instruction in Jewish history, culture, and civilization in the pursuit of a more mature and sensitive Jewish life.

After all, until the age of thirteen, what a typical child who does not have the benefit of an intensive day school education absorbs is pediatric or mother-goose Judaism at best. But Judaism is far more than a series of miracle stories, the pap of the typical Hebrew school education. Judaism is Bible, twenty-four books which include our origins, earliest laws, mission to the world, prophetic vision, and exalted poetry. Judaism is the Talmud, Judaism is the Hebrew language, Judaism is the philosophy of Maimonides, the poetry of Rabbi Yehuda Halevi, the mysticism of the Ramban and the Ari, the Hasidism of the Kotzker Rebbe. Most of all, Judaism is a unique way of life, which includes the rhythm of summer, fall, winter, and spring, replete with the Sabbaths and the festivals, days of celebration and days of mourning.

And finally, Judaism is a history beginning with Abraham and Sarah encompassing the entire range of Jewish experience, from Persia to Poland, from Morocco to America, each with unique sounds of music and special spices and foods. In sum, Judaism is a total civilization, or rather a sum total of many civilizations, with a sacred literature and a unique life-stage at its core.

How can anyone expect children between the ages of eight and thirteen to genuinely appreciate the totality of the amazing culture they were born into? And if thirteen marks the end of Jewish education, it's much more than a fifty-fifty shot that they will have lost it before ever being truly exposed to it. The very least our tradition deserves is mature minds and independent spirits to explore their birthright.

If you've followed me thus far, let us go one step further. Diaspora Jewish leadership has already established an excellent Birthright opportunity for Jewish university students to spend some time in Israel. Why not register each Jewish child at birth with their local JCC – and begin collecting birthday gifts towards that special birthright trip at age twenty? And why not use the bar/bat mitzva experience to "twin" a Diaspora child with an Israeli child from his or her local *matnas* (center of culture, youth, and sport) – and gently, lovingly engage them both during the intervening years with nuggets of Jewish culture and civilization, the many gifts Judaism has given the world? Perhaps the Jewish Community Center in the Diaspora and the *matnas* could be responsible to teach these universal "trans-denominational Jewish civilization" classes. And then, at age twenty the ḥatan/kalat mitzva will receive a degree as a Knowledgeable Jewish Adult in front of the Western Wall, joining hands with our eternal tradition as well as with his or her Israeli counterpart. Only Jews who have been accepted to their heritage can ultimately be counted as part of the eternal Jewish people – and truly "lift up their heads" as members of the eternal Jewish census.

The House as the Original Sanctuary: Redemption of the Firstborn Revisited

Take the Levites instead of every firstborn among the children of Israel... and the Levites shall be Mine.

NUMBERS 3:45

Does Judaism establish a clear-cut and absolute division between the sacred and the secular, the Temple and the household, the priest (kohen) and the commoner (Israelite)?

Conventional wisdom and commentary would suggest that a single, central national sanctuary with its precise, priestly establishment was indigenous to biblical Judaism, and that it is only because of our history of destruction and exile, dispersion and fragmentation that localized houses of worship and family-centered religious rituals became the operative vehicles of Jewish continuity.

However, a careful study of the Torah portion of *Bemidbar* reveals that the initial biblical vision offered a far more complex, inclusive, democratic, and family-oriented religious expression and experience, demonstrating that the Creator of Heavens and Earth could neither be contained in one structure, no matter how grandiose, nor be properly served and invoked by an establishment clergy, no matter how professional.

Let us begin our Torah study by posing several questions. First of all, our portion describes the first census taken of the Israelites, cataloging the number of each of the tribes, excluding the tribe of Levi. It then establishes the special sanctity of the Levite, commands the redemption of the firstborn of the Israelites from their original sanctity by a kohen from the tribe of Levi, and finally describes the special tasks of Levi within and around the Sanctuary. The next portion of *Naso* concludes the tasks of the various Levite families and then describes the gifts to the Sanctuary of the various tribal leaders. Would it not have been more logical to have included the entire description of the Levite families in this Torah reading of *Bemidbar*, and then to have devoted the next portion of *Naso* exclusively to the dedication of the Sanctuary? Why carry over the census and sanctity of the Levite families into the next reading of *Naso*, which really deals with the Sanctuary?

Secondly, our portion of *Bemidbar* ordains the redemption of the firstborn (Numbers 3:40). It turns out that in the earliest days of our existence as a nation, religious leadership was vested in the firstborn son of each Israelite family; it was only when these firstborns joined in the desert worship of the Golden Calf – and the kohanim (of the house of Levi) did not – that the leadership was transferred to the kohanim.

Apparently residual sacredness still resides in the firstborn; therefore, these eldest sons must be redeemed, or divested of their sacred character, by a kohen when they reach the thirty-first day after their birth. As a kohen, I often have the privilege of participating in such redemptions and, at the central moment of the ritual, receiving the equivalent of five silver shekalim in exchange for the baby.

The kohen – usually while holding aloft a silver tray upon which the firstborn baby is placed – asks the parents a seemingly foolish and even obnoxious question: "What do you desire more, your firstborn son, or these five shekels of silver which you are biblically required to give me in exchange for the redemption?"

Phrased this way, the question creates an either-or situation: will the firstborn retain his sanctity under the kohen's authority and roof, or will he be redeemed by the parents for five silver shekalim in order to return to a life of complete secularism? Was there ever an occasion when a parent actually was venal enough to choose the five silver shekalim over his or her firstborn son? And yet which parent would not desire his or her child to also participate in the sacred?

The nineteenth-century sage of Frankfurt, Rabbi Samson Raphael Hirsch, provides a crucial insight into the ritual of the redemption of the firstborn as well as into fundamental Jewish theology. He maintains – in contrast to most of the other commentaries but in accordance with the chronological sequence of the Scriptures – that a ritual of redemption of the firstborn has always been a necessary act, even before they were replaced by the kohanim as the religious leaders in Israel. However, initially the redemption of the firstborn was the very antithesis of an either-or proposition (Hirsch's biblical commentary on Exodus 13:13).

Indeed, the Mishna (*Zevaḥim* 14:4) documents the permissibility and prevalence of altars of worship – mini-sanctuaries, as it were – in virtually every household in Israel, with the firstborn sons acting as the priests. These firstborns were holy – and not holy. They led the divine service, but they also worked the land (in fact, they received double the inheritance of their siblings). They were very much involved in the requirements of agriculture and the land's productivity while at the same time they also led the family in religious ritual and, presumably, in Torah study as well. Insofar as they participated in sacred ritual, they were holy; insofar as they were involved in mundane and professional activity, they had to be redeemed. There was no central Sanctuary because virtually every household had its own sanctuary; there was no professional priesthood because every family's firstborn functioned as part-time priest. God was not to be confined to one house because He was to be found in every single household; the world was not to be divided into the sacred and the secular because every aspect of life was either sacred or not-yet-sacred, with no aspect of existence empty of the divine imprint. After all, did not the firstborn "priest" and their familial altars imbue every household with the spark of the Holy, and does not our sacred scripture invest every agricultural act – from the improper plowing of ox and donkey together to the requisite tithes during the harvest to the Sabbatical year of rest even for the land – with the imprimatur of the Almighty?

The tragic sin of the Golden Calf – barely forty days after the Revelation at Sinai – radically altered this rather idyllic image of a democratically rooted and family-centered religious activity. The Almighty recognized the necessity of a central shrine of worship and inspiration, realizing – so to speak – that the Israelites were not yet ready for the conceptual and ethereal truths that "even the heaven of heavens cannot contain Thee" (I Kings 8:27) and "every place in which I shall invoke My name, I will come and bless you" (Exodus 20:21).

Consequently, a professional priestly class, totally dedicated to affairs of the spirit, had to be designated; the nation was not yet ready for the complex balancing act of a priesthood which could manage Godly and agricultural pursuits at one and the same time.

Now we can understand why the next portion, *Naso*, includes the specially designated Levite families as well as the dedication of the Sanctuary; it is because both the Tabernacle and the professional Levite clergy were the two changes wrought by the tragic worship of the Golden Calf. And this also is why the redemption of the firstborn in the post-Golden Calf period became an "either-or" proposition, although such a situation was never seen as the ideal.

Postscript: The Holy and the Not-Yet-Holy

It is recorded that the Gaon of Vilna once asked the Dubner Maggid to chastise him – and bring him to repentance. The Dubner Maggid reflected for a moment and then said: "Where is the great feat of sitting in the House of Study, completely detached from the marketplace, and emerging a great Torah scholar and pietist, a Gaon of Vilna? The trick would be to become what you are while involving yourself in the real world at the same time!"

There are two versions as to the end of the story. In one version, the Gaon of Vilna responded, "But who says I have to be a trickster?" In the other, the Gaon of Vilna sat down and wept. Rabbi Ḥayim ben

Atar (eighteenth century, Morocco), in his biblical commentary *Ohr HaḤayim* (Genesis 49:28 and Numbers 3:45), states that "in the future the divine service will return to the firstborn." He maintains that in a more perfect world which is yet to come, the professional priesthood will lose its exclusivity, the Holy Temple will be a magnet for the entire world (rather than a centralized place of worship only for Israel), and we will return to the original sanctity of the firstborn – as well as to a world which will consist not of the holy and the secular but rather of the holy and the not-yet-holy in a sacred synthesis.

When Is It Good to Take a Risk?

And with you there shall be a man of every tribe, every one head of his father's house. Of [the tribe of] Judah, Naḥshon ben Amminadav shall be the head.

NUMBERS 1:5–7

Is risk-taking positive or negative? An answer to this age-old question may be found not only in our biblical portion but in the book of Bemidbar in general.

A midrashic comment on the portion of *Bemidbar* stresses a genealogical aspect concerning Naḥshon, prince of the tribe of Judah, which rejects the idea that a conservative, risk-free existence is a genuine Torah value. Certainly such values are not to be found in the person of Naḥshon, known to us as the courageous individual who risked his life by leaping into the Reed Sea when the fleeing Israelites found themselves being chased by the charioteers of Egypt; indeed, it was only after he demonstrated his fortitude and faith that the Almighty went the next step and brought about the great miracle of the splitting of the sea.

The Midrash (also recorded in *Bava Batra* 91a) points out that this courageous Naḥshon had four sons, including Elimelekh, husband of Naomi, as well as Salmon, father of Boaz; hence Naḥshon was father of Elimelekh and the uncle of Boaz, two major personalities in the scroll of Ruth, which we read on Shavuot. Now we don't usually think of the scroll of Ruth as a book of risks, but I would like to suggest that in presenting such a genealogy, the Midrash wants to stress not only the characteristics of risk-taking which inform those descendants of Naḥshon, but also what kind of risks are favored by the Torah and what kind are not.

The fact is that courage and risk-taking – or the lack thereof – may be seen as an underlying theme of the whole book of Bemidbar. The fourth book of the Torah records the history of the Israelites' forty years of wandering the desert. When it opens we do not yet know that the people will be punished to wander for forty years, but by the time the book closes it is clear that the Jewish people have failed their first major test. When the spies return with a frightening report about the Promised Land and the ability to conquer it (Numbers 13–14), the Hebrews demonstrate a total lack of resolve, courage, and faith. They wail, they tremble, they plead not to go on with the mission. Apparently they have become too accustomed to the safe and secure desert life – manna providing a daily ration of food, a cloud by day and pillar of fire by night directing their travel plans – to take the risks into the unknown involved in the conquest and settlement of Israel.

But the Torah wants the Hebrews to act with courage, to make the first heroic and even dangerous moves which come with independence and responsibility. Naḥshon at the shore of the Reed Sea shines as the antithesis of a cowardly "desert generation." Because of his faith, and his daring, the people were saved. Indeed the Gaon of Vilna points out that the Torah first describes the Israelites as having gone "into the midst of the sea on the dry land" (Exodus 14:22), and later "on dry land in the midst of the sea" (Exodus 14:29). The initial description refers to Naḥshon and his followers, who risked their lives by jumping into the raging waters; God made a miracle for him, the waters splitting into dry land and serving as a wall (*ḥoma*) to them on the right and the left. The latter description refers to the rest of the Israelites who only entered after the dry land appeared; for them the waters became a wall – but this time written without the letter *vav*, which can also spell *ḥema*, which means anger.

Naḥshon's remarkable ability to take risks – in contrast to most of the generation of the desert – was transmitted to his son and nephew. Hence, the scroll of Ruth closes with the names of ten generations from Peretz (son of Judah) to King David, and Naḥshon appears right in the center, the pivotal figure between the age of the patriarchs and the generation of the future Messiah of the Jewish people. But while Naḥshon and Boaz are to be praised for their risk-taking, Elimelekh can only be reviled for his.

When a terrible famine descends upon Bethlehem in Judah, the home of Elimelekh, he packs up his family and decides to start a new life in the Land of Moab. Undoubtedly, this demonstrates courage on the part of Elimelekh, the ability to risk the unknown in a strange environment. But his motivation was greed; he refused to share his bounty with his starving kinsmen, and he was willing to leave his homeland and his ancestral roots for the sake of his wealth. Hence, tragedy strikes. Elimelekh dies, and his sons – to be expected – marry Moabite women. His sons die as strangers in a strange land, and even any potential progeny they may leave behind will be lost to Jewish future, to Jewish destiny. Elimelekh reaped a harvest of oblivion, from a Jewish point of view, as the fruit of his risk-taking in Moab.

In contrast, Boaz does not leave Bethlehem during the famine. And when the challenge arises to do an act of loving-kindness for Naomi and redeem Elimelekh's land – as well as to marry the stranger-convert Ruth – Boaz assumes the financial obligation and takes upon himself the social risk involved in the marriage. And the descendant from this union turns out to be none other than King David, from whom the future messianic line emerges.

Elimelekh's risk was based upon greed, and involved forsaking his land and his tradition; it ended in his death and destruction. Boaz's risk was based upon love and loving-kindness, and resulted in redemption. The Elimelekh-Boaz dialectic is a perennial theme in the Jewish world. Risk is positive, and even mandatory, from a Jewish perspective. The question we have to ask ourselves is the motivation, and that is what will determine the result.

Naso

Love Means Always Being Ready to Say You're Sorry

When a man or woman shall commit any sin that people may commit, to do a trespass against the Lord, and that person be guilty; then they shall confess their sin which they have committed....

NUMBERS 5:6–7

According to Maimonides, this verse, which obligates confession, is the basic source for the commandment of repentance; repentance is incomplete without verbal confession. Writing in his *Mishneh Torah* (*Hilkhot Teshuva* 1:1) he rules that "every commandment in the Torah... if a person violates any one of them either intentionally or accidentally, his act of repentance must be accompanied with confession before God, because it's written in the Torah 'then they shall confess their sin which they have committed.'"

Detailing the nuts and bolts of repentance, Maimonides divides the process into four pragmatic steps: recognition of sin, confession, the act of resolving never to repeat the sin, and – in order to effectuate "total" repentance – resistance from repeating the transgression when faced with a similar temptation under similar circumstances. Hence guilt, the inevitable accompaniment of sin, can be dealt with by means of repentance, which has the power to totally obliterate the act of wrongdoing.

In contrast, Freud, when he discovered the Oedipal complex, assigned mankind a guilt so profound that his message of the "haunted soul" permeates the modern sensibility, from the bleak no-exit landscapes of the Swedish director Ingmar Bergman to the comic-cosmic ones of Bergman's disciple Woody Allen. According to them, not only are we doomed to repeat the sins of our parents, but we are also limited – and even crippled – by the transgressions of our past. All of us, the theory goes, suffer from primal guilt. The past is inescapable. And inevitably, being born into a situation beyond our control, guilt is coupled with gloom. At best we learn to acknowledge our past, and make do. The past controls our present as well as our future!

But in Judaism, as we began to see from Maimonides, a violation of any of the commandments – whether it was purposeful or accidental, conscious or unconscious – may be repented for and forgiven. That and more: a sin may become the means – a sort of pogo stick – for creative betterment; a transgression may be transformed into a good deed, a black mark into a brilliant jewel – a sort of alchemy for the soul. No, Dr. Freud, not only is our present not controlled by the past, but our present has the ability to change the past. As Professor Mordechai Rotenberg of the Hebrew University establishes in his work, *Rebiographing and Deviance*, repentance is built into the theology of Judaism, allowing us not only to escape from the permanent scars of past misdeeds but through a transformative ascent, our sins become virtues – not just in the metaphoric sense, but in real psychological and interpersonal terms. Through the gift of repentance, each individual can re-biographize the events of his life, transforming transgression into a virtue.

Sources for such transformation can be found in a wide range of classic texts. For example, the Talmud (*Yoma* 86b) cites Resh Lakish, himself a repentant armed robber, as saying that "when true repentance takes place all transgressions are turned into merits," and Rabbi Abbahu (*Berakhot* 34b), who taught that "where the penitent stands is higher than that of the completely righteous individual." How is this possible? After all, "of all sad words of tongue and pen, the saddest are these: 'It might have been.'" How can we recreate, recast, the past? My rebbe and mentor, Rabbi Joseph B. Soloveitchik, discusses this issue in his classical work *Al HaTeshuva* (*On Repentance,* edited by Pinḥas Peli), and he explains it on the basis of the realization that it is usually only when one loses something – an object or a relationship – that one truly appreciates its value. Hence, tragically perhaps, only when one has lost his closeness to God and the Jewish tradition can one truly re-embrace them in depth, and then with even greater fervor and appreciation than before. As the great Psalmist King David cried out, "From the depths [of despair] do I call upon you, O God" (Psalms 130:1); it is precisely the depths of my despair that provide me with a jump-start, a push upwards to achieve a close relationship.

I would like to suggest a further insight. After all, the pen used to rewrite our lives (rebiographing) is called re*pen*tance, as we have just seen, and it itself is one of the 613 commandments in the Torah. And to repent means to turn back, to turn ourselves back to the period before we sinned, to turn the clock of our lives back as well. Even though Maimonides divides the process into four steps, confession must be particularly important to him because, in his first law in the chapter of repentance, a paragraph of eighteen lines (in my edition of *Mishneh Torah,* published by Mossad Harav Kook), the Hebrew word for confession, *vidui,* is repeated no less than thirteen times.

Perhaps by repeating "verbal confession" so often, Maimonides provides us with a clue as to the process by which Judaism turns sins into virtues.

Confessions which lead to a change of heart and personality (recognizing a sin and truly determining, and garnering the strength, never to repeat it again) differ qualitatively from confessions when lying on a psychiatrist's couch or in a dark confessional booth. Authentic confession must be expressed directly to the individual one sinned against. Such a verbal confession – when the lips utter the words to be heard – becomes not only an "at-one-ment" between two individuals who had become alienated and estranged from each other, but it also makes the individual "at-one" with himself, the self he would like to be and the self he has sadly become. It also brings together and makes "at-one-ment" between conflicting parts of a person's consciousness: heart and mind, internal feeling and external communication. It allows the individual to confront and verbally express his sin, his imperfection, his failure, to conceptualize what he has done, first to himself, and then to the other he has wronged. It enables him to reconnect with his full self as well as with others, without the mask of self-deception and without the curtain of separation. Only from such a brutal and truthful encounter with oneself as well as with other can the difficult process of change begin.

A sin (*ḥet*) is literally a missing of the mark, a disconnect, a failure to make the proper connection and reach out to the other in love. It's clear that Erich Segal's ridiculous message that love means "never having to say you're sorry" is in direct opposition to the Torah's view. Much the opposite! Saying you're sorry to another is recognition of the other, of realizing the pain of the other. Saying you're sorry in a relationship is an admission of love, a cry from one heart to another that one feels and sees the hurt that one has caused the other, that one has the courage to admit one's smallness, one's selfishness, one's self-centeredness in the presence of the other, whose love will empower the beloved to become whole, to grow, and to give again.

Words are the first tangible, external expression of a new reality; real change can only be proven by different external actions. If verbal confession cannot be spoken, if the individual cannot bring him or herself to at least face and express the crime against the other with words of sorrow and remorse, change will never be effectuated and the relationship between the two will never be repaired. Words can at least begin to create new realities, and a new reality can hopefully create a new individual and a new relationship.

Many years ago a married woman with two children came into my office, confessing that she had encouraged a relationship with a single man; they had stopped just short of adultery, her husband had found out and he now wanted to divorce her. She confronted her guilt, recognized who she had become and how much she had sacrificed for momentary lust, and spoke of how she truly loved her husband and desperately wanted to save their marriage and make amends for what had happened. After meeting with both of them, it also became clear that the husband had been neglecting his wife, that his business had taken him away from home much more often than he should have traveled, and that he too shared in her guilt – although not to the same extent. Each confessed wrongdoing to the other, each recognized the need for change, and not only did the marriage continue but it became much improved. In a very real way, the woman's transgression became transformed into a merit; it served as a spark-plug and wake-up call for two individuals to learn how to live with one another in love, consideration, and mutual commitment. Their present repentance redeemed the past and dramatically changed their future. There is no greater tribute to and confirmation of human freedom than the possibility of change, of growth, of renewal – than the mitzva of repentance.

The "Magic" of the Bitter Waters

And in the hand of the kohen shall be the bitter waters that bring about the curse.

NUMBERS 5:18

One of the strangest passages in the Bible is the law of the woman suspected of adultery which is recorded in this biblical portion. The text tells us that if a woman is suspected by her husband of having an affair with another man, and he warns her before two valid witnesses not to be alone in a secluded place with that particular individual, and nevertheless the woman is seen to have sequestered herself privately with that person, the woman becomes subject to an eerie sort of "trial" in order to establish her innocence.

The husband must bring his wife to the kohen together with an offering of barley flour. The kohen then takes sacred water mixed with earth from the floor of the Sanctuary and dissolves within this mixture a parchment scroll inscribed with the following curses which he recites to the shamed wife: "May the Lord render you as a curse and as an oath amidst your people when the Lord causes your thigh to collapse and your stomach to distend. These waters which bring about a curse shall enter your insides to cause your stomach to distend and your thigh to collapse" (Numbers 5:21–22).

The accused woman responds "Amen, amen," after which she is given the bitter waters to drink. The kohen then takes the meal offering from the hand of the woman, waves it before God, and offers it up on the altar. The woman drinks the waters. If no symptoms of the curses occur, the woman is considered innocent and the couple can resume their marital relationship in peace (Numbers 4:11–31).

What is the significance of this entire procedure? It sounds almost like voodoo, or some sort of black magic, a kind of supernatural activity of the occult which does not appear to be in consonance with biblical rationality.

To be sure, this entire "trial by bitter waters" only lasted until the end of the First Temple period (70 CE). By the time of R. Yoḥanan b. Zakkai, the Talmudic sages insisted that the test was no longer efficacious because an increasing number of men were having extramarital affairs (Yerushalmi *Sota* 1:4). Their prooftext is the closing verse of this biblical chapter (Numbers 5:31) which reads, "The man shall be innocent of iniquity, then that woman shall bear her iniquity." The sages take this to mean that it is only when the man is innocent of sexual dalliance that we can condemn the woman for her sexual immorality. But even given that limitation, the entire procedure of the bitter waters smacks of barbaric primitivism which jars modern sensibilities!

An incident occurred in Efrat about a decade ago which gave me an insight into the meaning of this ritual. Due to the positive relationships we enjoy with the local Arab villages adjoining Efrat, I am often called upon to adjudicate disputes between Palestinians and Israelis, and sometimes even between Palestinians and Palestinians. In one particular instance, two Palestinian cousins from two separate Palestinian villages were suspected of having a sexual relationship. The modesty codes are quite strict within the Muslim Palestinian community, and so the family of the young woman was incensed at the rumors of her breach of morality; her brothers even spoke of killing the young woman for dishonoring her family. The family of the young man became terrified, convinced that an "honor" killing was likely to take place (as happens not infrequently in the Middle East). The couple convinced the families to come to me for arbitration and to abide by any ruling I would hand down. I interviewed the two cousins both separately and together, listened to the testimonies of witnesses, who had seen unseemly behavior but had not seen any actual sexual activity. Based on this lack of real evidence, I ruled that there was no legitimate proof that cohabitation had taken place. I insisted however that the two get married, which they did with alacrity. I even bestowed a blessing upon their union....

The Bible emerged from the matrix of the Middle East, where jealousy is rampant and women are often considered the chattel of their husbands. A jealous husband can easily persuade himself to harm the wife whom he suspects of adultery. I therefore believe that this trial of the bitter waters provided a marvelous psychological ploy to protect the women from a husband's jealous wrath. To the best of my knowledge, there is no record in the Talmud of a woman whose thighs actually collapsed or whose stomach became distended after drinking the bitter waters; hence, the unscathed woman would generally be declared innocent and her husband would take her back. And if her fear of the consequences resulted in a confession of guilt, then the marriage deserved to be terminated with the payment of a fine, to be made by the adulterous woman. In any case, a murder by a jealous husband or on behalf of family honor would always be avoided. Hence the "trial of the bitter waters" served as marvelous protection for the woman in a society only too ready to lay the blame upon her for a suspected act of immorality.

The Symbol of (the Nazarite's) Hair

All the days of the Nazarite which he consecrated himself to God, he shall be holy. He shall let the hair of his head grow and no razor shall come upon his head.

NUMBERS 6:5

We have already investigated the special religious laws and restrictions – paralleling the privileges – pertaining to the kohanim who are from the tribe of Levi and are direct descendants of Aaron, in our commentary on Vayikra (the book of Leviticus). However, the Torah is sensitive to the need within some standard Israelites to assume an extra dimension of holiness, to the possibility that individuals from tribes other than Levi might wish to pursue a more consecrated, spiritual, and even ascetic lifestyle. In order to allow their drive to be realized in formal (halakhic) terms, our Torah reading introduces the possibility of the Nazarite. Three elements comprise the Nazarite vow, which could be assumed by any Israelite for a minimum of thirty days: the prohibition against drinking wine, the prohibition against coming into contact with the dead, and the prohibition against cutting one's hair.

It is interesting to note that two of these three prohibitions, the prohibitions against drinking wine and coming in contact with the dead, correspond to the very demands the Torah places upon the priesthood. A priest may not partake in Temple service if he has drunk wine, and he is restricted from any contact with the dead with the exception of his immediate family. (The Nazarite is not permitted exceptions, apparently because he is generally a Nazarite only for thirty days whereas the priesthood lasts throughout the priest's lifetime. Similarly, the Nazarite may not drink wine at all – not even Sabbath and festival kiddush wine, whereas the kohen is only precluded from wine before – or during – his ministering in the Sanctuary and before rendering a religio-legal ruling.)

Here the similarity ends; it is only the Nazirite who cannot cut a single hair from his head. And after the conclusion of his period of the Nazirite vow, his entire head must be shaven, and all of the hair is then burned. In the words of the Bible, the Nazirite must "shave his head in front of the Tent of Meeting, and then shall take the hair... and place it on the fire which is under the sacrifice of the peace offering" (Numbers 6:18). What strikes us about this command is that the burning of the hair seems to share the altar with the other sacrifices that the Nazirite is required to bring: burnt-offering, sin-offering, peace-offering, and meal-offering. Why dramatize in this manner the significance and centrality of the Nazirite's hair? Once the period of the vow ends, all the prohibitions against drinking wine and attending funerals are removed; there are no ceremonies for the lifting of these restrictions in any way. The sole exception is the burning of his hair under the peace offering.

Furthermore, the other restrictions – which also pertain to the kohen – are understandable. A consecrated individual must stay away from wine; it can play havoc with our emotions and desires, removing the ability to make rational decisions. And one who strives for sanctity must avoid contact with a corpse: involvement with death can often lead to depression and melancholia which prevents interpersonal activity and may even bring about alienation from God. But what is the symbolism of hair? And why let it grow long in the first place only to have it eventually burnt?

We can begin to understand the special symbolism of the hair when we take note of Rashi's comment that the reason why the laws of the Nazirite immediately follow the laws of the "suspected adulteress" (*sota*) is the psychological affinity between these two states: after someone sees the suspected adulteress in her shame, he will remove himself from wine, often the cause of transgression.

But in addition to the evil which can possibly emanate from wine, transgression can likewise come from uncontrolled hair. The Bible continues to describe the punishment of the *sota*: "And the priest shall stand the [unfaithful] woman before God and uncover her hair."

Rashi here comments that the purpose of uncovering her hair was to shame her, pointing out that a married woman whose hair is uncovered is disgraced. After all, the Mishna rules that a married woman cannot appear in public with her hair uncovered, covered hair being a time-honored symbol of the marital state (*Ketubot* 72b). Indeed, the Talmudic discussion on the Mishna deduces that a married woman is biblically commanded to cover her hair from the fact that the unfaithful wife's hair had to be uncovered. To this day, observant Jewish women who are married are expected to wear a head covering at least in public. Apparently an important and even erotic aspect of a woman's femininity is believed to be bound up in her hair and, once she is married, that hair is to be reserved for her husband.

Indeed, it is interesting to note that as halakha developed, married men were likewise expected to cover their hair; one sage even refused to see a budding Talmudic scholar because he did not cover his head of hair, a sure sign that he was still single and therefore subject to immoral urgings (see *Kiddushin* 39). The biblical story of Samson, perhaps the most difficult and problematic of the biblical Nazirites, views his hair as the source and symbol of enhanced virility, physical as well as sexual. And it may be logically assumed that in biblical times a woman seeking to commit adultery would remove her marital hair covering, allowing her hair to fall freely and loosely, when engaging in unbecoming conduct with men other than her husband.

If there exist any doubts as to the sexual symbolism of the hair, the following two citations prove this point conclusively:

The Talmud records that the High Priest Simon the Righteous

had never eaten from the guilt-offering of a Nazirite, apparently because he believed it sinful to assume unnecessary prohibitions. He made an exception, however, when he met a striking young man, beautiful of eyes, goodly of appearance, his locks arranged in curls.

> I said to him: "My son, why do you wish to destroy such beautiful hair [in becoming a Nazirite]?" He said to me: "I was a shepherd.... When I went to draw water from the well, I saw my own reflection and the evil inclination quickly threatened to overcome me and exile me from the world. I said to him [to this narcissistic impulse of self-love]: Empty-headed one, why do you assume pride in a world which is not yours, where you will eventually become worms and maggots? I swear that I will shave you off for the sake of heaven...." And Simon the Righteous kissed the young man on his head, saying "May Nazarites such as you multiply in Israel."
>
> *Nazir* 4a

Moreover, additional evidence of the sexual nature of hair and its symbolism can be found in a fascinating responsum dealing with conversion. We know that prior to a conversion there are three conditions necessary to effectuate the conversion for males: circumcision, immersion in a ritual bath (*mikveh*), and acceptance of Torah's commandments.

Circumcision, the excision of the penile foreskin, symbolizes the relinquishing of a gentile past prior to entering the covenant of Abraham; immersion in the *mikveh* symbolizes the *rebirth* of a new being into the *nationality* of Israel; and the acceptance of the commandments is the commitment to a *new lifestyle* and *ideological religious* framework.

Obviously, for women, there are only two necessary steps to the conversion process, ritual immersion and acceptance of commandments. But then how do women express their rejection of a formerly "no-holds-barred" gentile lifestyle? Professor Mordechai Friedman, in his work on the Cairo Genizah, *Jewish Polygamy in the Middle Ages*, cites a responsum from approximately a thousand years ago, discussing the petition of two sisters to convert to Judaism. They are instructed to remove (shave off) their hair and ritually immerse themselves after accepting the commandments. At least according to this view, the removal or shaving of the hair for women parallels removal of the foreskin for males; both connote sexual eroticism.

It would therefore seem that from very ancient times hair for men and women has been a symbol of physicality and of the sexual impulse. This is perhaps because of the beauty attributed to the hair and/or because hair, if allowed to grow unchecked, becomes unkempt and wild, similar to the evil impulse.

The very possibility of "Nazirite-by-choice" confirms the biblical acceptance of "different strokes for different folks" in the religious realm, although the Nazirite state is not really encouraged. Most individuals are urged not to become Nazirites; those who take the vow must bring a sin-offering at the end of the period of their vow, presumably because they have denied themselves permissible enjoyments. Apparently, only in extreme instances of narcissism can this "extra ascetic religiosity" be tolerated. And Nazirut is usually limited to thirty days. And, at the end of the day, the Nazirite must not use his heightened religiosity as a means of incurring positions of leadership for himself, as a badge of religious one-upmanship. He must take the hair and place it under the peace offering, as a sacrifice to God. In effect, he is taking his virility and sexual libido and dedicating it, sublimating it, into a higher service to God.

The Priestly Benediction: The Source of All Blessings

> *And God spoke unto Moses telling him to speak to Aaron and to his sons, saying: "This is how you must bless the children of Israel. Say to them: 'May God bless you and keep watch over you. May God make His face give light towards you, and be gracious unto you. May God lift up His face to you, and give you peace.' [The priests] shall place My name upon the Israelites and I shall bless them."*
>
> NUMBERS 6:22–27

It is most understandable that these majestic words be oft-repeated by rabbis from the pulpit, be invoked by parents in their blessings to their children during the Friday evening Sabbath meal, and of course be chanted by the priests each morning as part of the *Amida* (or, in the Diaspora, by the cantor, who stands in place of the kohen).

But is it not strange that it is precisely those words of the Priestly Benediction that each and every Israelite recites after making the requisite blessings over Torah study as part and parcel of the daily morning prayers? If indeed it was deemed necessary to recite actual biblical verses after thanking God for having given us the Torah, why do our sages choose specifically these verses which seemingly should belong exclusively to the kohen?

One answer may be suggested by the divine charge to Moses just before the Revelation at Sinai, "And you shall be unto Me a kingdom of priests [*mamlekhet kohanim*] and a holy nation" (Exodus 19:7). Apparently the mission of Israel is to be an entire nation of priests, every man a kohen (see Sforno, ad loc.). Hence every morning every Israelite, in his or her daily prayers, makes reference to the ultimate vocation – in preparation for the messianic age – as a priest.

Another answer is to be found in a magnificent insight offered by Rabbi Aharon Kotler (1892–1962), the founding dean of the famed Lakewood Yeshiva kollel, concerning the festival of Shavuot.

We know that the Jewish year consists of three major festivals: Pesaḥ, Sukkot, and Shavuot. The major thrust of the first two festivals is not merely to commemorate the historic event which took place on those dates but is rather for us to reexperience a seminal moment in Jewish history and to make it a part of our existential present. Hence, we actually taste the bitters and salt tears of the Egyptian slavery as well as the matzot and wine of exhilarating freedom during the Pesaḥ Seder and we actually build for ourselves and dwell for seven days (eight days in the Diaspora) in the protective booths which symbolize the divine grace and compassion with which we were ensconced during our difficult desert experience. It is through practicing these rituals and reliving these events that all Jews gets to see themselves as if they actually left Egypt and personally felt divine redemption and protection.

But if ritual refashions a moment in time into a moment for all times, why then, asks Rabbi Kotler, did the Torah not imbue Shavuot with any specific ritual commandments? Was it not necessary to facilitate the recreation of the Shavuot experience of the revelation of Torah for the Jewish people over the centuries? Compared to Pesaḥ and Sukkot, Shavuot is a naked branch on a naked tree, a single day instead of a complete seven, devoid of biblically mandated special foods, or symbols, which would enable us to reexperience Sinai.

Rabbi Kotler emphasizes that a primary purpose of the Festivals of Pesaḥ and Sukkot is to instill within the Jews of every generation a profound faith in God, the redeemer and protector of His people. This is especially important because, in the tragedy of our exile, there would be many periods in Jewish history subsequent to the Exodus when the Israelites would not be free, when the descendants of the generation of the desert would not feel the divine protection encompassing them; hence the necessity for the Torah to freeze, as it were, the moment of our redemption from Egypt and the desert booths which served as rays of divine protection and glory, and would prevent the Jews from despairing of God's love.

This however is not the case regarding Shavuot. On this holiday, there is no need for rituals to preserve and eternalize something that happened in the past. What God gave us then, we have now: our holy Torah. The content of the Revelation at Sinai is still with us in the form of a Book of Books. *Targum* teaches that the great sound of the Revelation has never ceased (Deut. 5:19). The author of the Psalms makes this clear when he writes, "The skies recount the glory of the Almighty, and the firmament proclaims His handiwork," a description of nature that leads right into a meditation on the Torah, "The Torah of God is perfect, restoring the soul, the testimony of God is trustworthy.... The precepts of God are upright.... The commandment of God is lucid.... The fear of God is pure.... The judgments of God are true" (Psalms 19:2–10). What is the connection between nature revealing the glory of God and the Torah revealing the glory of God? Just as the former testifies to God's having created the world by its very existence in the here-and-now, so does the latter testify to His revelation by directing our lives in every generation in accordance with its laws and ideals.

Indeed, when we make the blessings over the Torah each morning, although we begin by thanking the Almighty "who has chosen us from among all other nations" in the past tense, we conclude the blessing in the present tense: "who gives us Torah." The Revelation did not merely happen in the past so that we must be taught ritual ways to eternalize it into our present. The Revelation remains with us today and every day – just as it was then!

From this perspective, I understand very well why the verses from the Torah which are chosen to be recited after thanking God for having revealed the Torah are specifically the priestly blessings. God keeps watch over us, illuminates us with His presence, and grants us divine peace through the words and the teachings of His Torah. By studying the Torah and living by its precepts we bring the divine gifts of protection, light, and peace into every day of our lives. Indeed, the divine name is placed within and upon us through our adherence to the divine commands. As the holy Zohar explains, the Torah is the name of the Holy One, blessed be He; He gave it to us and planted it within us. At the Sinaitic Revelation, God declared that He has given us Himself, as it were, His blessing, His light and His peace, His name, within the words of the Torah.

I believe that this understanding gives yet another level of interpretation: if we attempt to image, to "pictorialize" in a very literal way, the words of the Priestly Benediction, the first verse describes God, as it were, looking down upon us, "keeping watch over us" from His lofty abode above us; the second verse suggests that God and Israel are on the same level, since God descended to the earth to give us His Torah and direct our lives, and that He "makes His face give light *towards*" us; the third verse pictures Israel standing higher than the Divine, as He, as it were, "lifts up His face" to us. How can we understand God having to lift up His face to us, mere flesh-and-blood mortals?

I believe the answer is that God has provided us with the book, the divine soul with the formula for perfecting the world, but we must open it and study it, we must interpret it properly and apply it to our needs and our society, in accordance with His will. "It is no longer in heaven," declare our sages. The Torah was given to us, and it becomes our task to understand its lessons, to unlock its secrets, to utilize its blueprint for a perfected world that is the Oral Law, much of which is given over to Jewish religious leadership in every generation to apply and interpret. Once the Almighty has entrusted His "soul" to us, He becomes dependent upon us, as it were, to utilize His pledge in wisdom, sensitivity, and sanctity.

Postscript

There is one more aspect of the Priestly Benediction deserving of comment. When the kohanim rise to invoke God's blessing upon the congregation, they first recite their own blessing, as is customary that an individual does before fulfilling a commandment: "Blessed are Thou O Lord our God Sovereign of the universe, who has sanctified us with the sanctity of Aaron, and has commanded us to bless His nation Israel with love." Why must the kohen discharge his obligation "with love"? And if he should feel embittered that particular day, if he just had a falling out with his wife or his neighbor, or his child, would that invalidate his benediction? Is there any other precedent for the necessity of performing a specific commandment "with love"?

My first response would be that the phrase "with love" serves to intensify the priestly task of teacher, the priestly mission to "teach Your laws to Jacob and Your Torah to Israel" (Deut. 33:10). The God of love who gave a Torah of love would expect His emissaries to teach that Torah to His children with love.

Secondly, when the Land of Israel was divided amongst the tribes, the kohanim had no portion of land in Israel; they lived in the cities of refuge in order to teach and influence those "imprisoned" there, they were not responsible to work the land because they ministered in the Temple. Each received sustenance by means of the "tithes"; "God was his portion." In the business world, I want my fellow humans and even competitors to "make a living," but in no way do I want them to do better than I do! Hence no businessman can truly bless another with a full heart; "Do well but not as well as I do. Just make sure that I remain top banana, the head 'honcho.'" Hence, we never really bless each other with a full heart, in total love. With the kohen, however, it was different. He lived off the largesse of the people, getting a portion of their produce as his "take-home pay": 1/40, 1/50, or 1/60, depending on the farmer's generosity. Hence it was to the kohen's financial benefit that those he was blessing have ultimate financial success; the greater the yield of the fields, the greater the percentage of gift-offerings that he would receive. He truly could bless the Israelites with all his heart!

And finally, perhaps the word "love" (*ahava*) in the Priestly Benediction is not a description of the kohen's emotional state of being as he blesses his congregation, but is rather the basic content of the blessing itself; the kohen is blessing his people first and foremost with love for every Israelite, because if the Jewish people will truly be united in love for one another no external force will be able to destroy us as a nation or deter us from realizing our goal of world peace.

The Greatest Blessing: To Dream a Great Dream

Master of the universe, I am Yours and my dreams are Yours.... So may You transform all of my dreams for myself and for all of Israel into good dreams; may You guard over me, be gracious to me, and accept me.

PRAYER FOR AN UNINTERPRETABLE DREAM (RECITED IN THE PRIESTLY BENEDICTION)

Few passages in the Bible are as well known as the Priestly Benediction. In Israel the kohanim rise to bless the congregation every single morning, while in the Diaspora Ashkenazi Jews are permitted to include this special benediction only on the festivals. Additionally, there are many life-cycle celebrations, such as circumcisions, redemption of the firstborn, bar and bat mitzvas, and even weddings which are punctuated by this priestly blessing. In effect, the kohen stands as God's representative, as the "agent of the Compassionate One," as the spiritual leader and as the Torah teacher, and in this function as teacher and guide he calls upon God to bless the congregation. As Moses declares in his final blessing to the Israelites, "[the Priests and Levites] shall guard Your covenant, shall teach Your laws to Jacob and Your Torah to Israel" (Deut. 33:9–10).

Both the Talmud (the ninth chapter of *Berakhot*) and our prayer liturgy declare: "At the time of the priestly blessings, the congregation responds, 'Master of the Universe I am Yours and my dreams are Yours.'" Apparently our sages saw a profound connection between the dreams of the Congregation of Israel and the function of their priests and leaders. Now what exactly is the nature of this connection?

I would suggest that, first and foremost, true leaders and educators must inspire their students, congregants, and/or nation with a lofty vision, with an exalted dream. The Psalmist and sweet singer of Israel, King David, declares in the Psalm which we recite each Sabbath and festival before the reciting of the Grace after Meals, "When the Lord returned with the restoration of Zion we were as dreamers" (Psalms 126); after all, if the Jews had not dreamt of the return to Israel throughout their long exiles, we never would have returned to our homeland.

We recognize the same idea – but from an opposite vantage point – when we understand the cause behind the great tragedy of our book of Numbers. In the fourth book of the Bible, the Jewish people descended from the great heights of the Revelation at Sinai to the disastrous depths of the sin of the scouts, the rebellion of Koraḥ, the sin of Moses, and the demise of that entire generation in the desert. What caused such a mighty fall? The Bible itself begins its account of the descent with the words, "And it was that the people were as murmerers [*mitonenim*] an evil thing" (Numbers 11:1). Rabbi Yaakov Mecklenberg, in his nineteenth-century biblical commentary *HaKtav VeHaKabbala*, explains the difficult Hebrew word *mitonenim* as meaning "wandering hither and thither" aimlessly and without purpose or direction, from the Hebrew *ana* (literally "where to"). Simply put, this great Torah leader was saying that the Israelites had lost the dream and the vision which they felt at Sinai when they cried out "We shall do and we shall internalize," accepting upon themselves the divine mission of being a "kingdom of priests and a holy nation." They descended into acts of self-destruction because they lost the dream of Israel, because they no longer were committed to climbing the ladder uniting heaven and earth, because they stopped believing that they could unite heaven and earth.

The Hebrew word for dream is *ḥalom,* and – with a simple switch of letters – it spells *ḥamal,* which means love and compassion. The priest who inspires with his dream must first and foremost love his nation; only if he loves the Israelites will they believe themselves worthy of being loved, will they believe in their ability to realize the dream and achieve the vision. Great leaders such as Franklin Delano Roosevelt, Winston Churchill, and David Ben-Gurion lifted their respective nations to unheard of heights because they helped make them believe in themselves.

The same Hebrew word *ḥalom,* with another switch of letters spells *loḥem,* which means fighting, battling – if need be – to achieve the necessary goals. A great measure of imparting a dream is to impart idealistic sacrifice on behalf of that dream.

The word *ḥalom* can also spell *leḥem* or bread; a dream must be nourished with the material necessities of programs, tactics, and strategy necessary to accomplish the dream.

The letters of the word *ḥalom* also spell *melaḥ,* or salt. Salt symbolizes tears – the tears of sacrifice and commitment – as well as our eternal covenant, since salt never putrefies. Salt must therefore accompany our sacrificial offerings and our Sabbath and festival *ḥallot* – a symbol of our covenant with God, the covenant which guarantees Jewish eternity and ultimate redemption, with the fulfillment of our mission. At that time we will all be the priests and teachers to the world.

And finally, *ḥalom* is linguistically tied to *ḥalon,* a window, a light to the outside world. The dream with which the kohen must inspire the Israelites is a dream which encompasses the entire world, the dream of "Through you shall be blessed all the families of the earth," the dream of "They shall beat their swords into ploughshares and their spears into pruning hooks."

The Priestly Benediction expresses the fruition of our dream, the period of peace for which we all yearn. To achieve it we must dream the great dream, the dream of God Himself, when "God will be one and His name will be One," when "Knowledge of the Lord will cover the earth as the waters cover the seas." Yes, the Jewish people – as well as its leaders – must be dreamers. And perhaps it is only those who believe in a God who is invisible who will dare to dream the impossible, and it is only those who dream the impossible who will ever achieve the incredible.

Beha'alotekha

The Anatomy of Leadership: What Must the Leader Ignite?

When you kindle the Menora...
NUMBERS 8:2

Our Torah portion recounts the watershed experience of the Israelites in the desert: the beginning of the end, the devastating denouement which unravels into the demise of an entire generation locked out of the Promised Land. What caused the miracles of the Exodus, the inspiration of the Sinai Revelation, the desert constellation of proud, flag-raising tribes surrounding the Sanctuary of God to so pitifully degenerate into the faithless, fearful, rebellious, and reactionary squabbles which characterize the succeeding chapters of the book of Numbers?

Our sages signal the beginning of the change by dramatically suggesting that chapter eleven of the book of Numbers begins a new and separate biblical book: the verse opens, *vayehi,* literally "and it was," but onomatopoeically suggesting trouble, *vay,* woe and distress (*vayehi ha'am k'mitonenim*). It is a small but tragic book within a book which we are now about to read, a tale of self-destruction. How did it happen? In order to attempt to answer the initial question, let us review this Torah reading of *Beha'alotekha* from its very beginning – which is Numbers, chapter eight – and we shall find that in addition to our query concerning the genesis of the national disaster, many smaller questions abound.

First of all, our biblical portion appears to be recording a collection of disparate incidents which seem to lack any cohesive connection. The portion of *Beha'alotekha* begins with the kindling of the Menora by Aaron – a Sanctuary accoutrement and divine service which would have been far more appropriately placed in the portion of *Tetzaveh,* which initially discusses the construction of the Sanctuary and the role of Aaron and his descendants therein (Exodus 25–30). Indeed our most classic commentary, Rashi, is disturbed by this apparent misplacement, from the book of Exodus to the book of Numbers, and he therefore connects the opening of *Beha'alotekha* to the description of the gifts of the princes of the tribes at the dedication ceremony of the Sanctuary (which we read at the conclusion of the previous biblical portion of *Naso*). Rashi cites a midrash in which Aaron is upset that the kohanim had been overlooked at the dedication ceremonies, and so, in effect, God tells Moses to appease Aaron: "Your task, [Aaron], is greater than theirs [the princes of the tribes)], because you will prepare and kindle the Menora" (Rashi, ad loc.).

But Rashi's comments seem to raise more questions than they answer. First of all, if Rashi is correct, then the Menora kindling should have concluded the portion of *Naso* instead of opening the portion of *Beha'alotekha*. Secondly, why would Aaron be satisfied for not having been given a public role in an auspicious ceremony with the consolation prize of the onerous task of cleaning and kindling the Menora early every morning before a non-existent audience?! It's almost like telling the invited guest speaker at a fancy public dinner whom the hosts forgot to introduce that he ought not be concerned, since he will be honored with clearing the tables and cleaning the dishes early the next morning.

What then follows in the biblical text is a myriad of disparate incidents: the Levites are chosen over the firstborn for religious leadership, the second-chance opportunity of bringing the Paschal lamb sacrifice is provided for those who were ritually impure or a distance away from the Sanctuary on the fourteenth of Nisan, a cloud by day and a fire by night is directing the camp of Israel, the trumpet call which summons the nation to war and inaugurates the festivals is described, the heads of the army of each tribe are named, Yitro's return to Midian is recorded, and the Ark of God is praised for its power to scatter the enemies of Israel. What conceptual scheme can possibly unite these various and disconnected commands and occurrences?

And then begins chapter eleven, the "new book" of the Bible:

> And it was ["*vay*," "woe"] that the people were *k'mitonenim* [as murmurers] an evil thing in the ears of God; and when God heard it, His anger was kindled, and the fire of God raged a fire among them, which devoured them until the outermost part of the camp.
>
> Numbers 11:1

Here the questions are even more disturbing. What does the term *mitonen* mean? As we saw in our last commentary, this is the only time the word appears in the Bible – and the commentaries are all perplexed. It sounds close to *mitlonen*, which means "to complain," and therefore most translations render "murmerers," following the Rashbam. But what were they murmuring against? The Bible does not record any reason for their murmurings, but does insist that it was considered evil by God, who expressed His apparent anger by dispatching a devouring fire.

And then, given the correlation between the fire and the murmuring, one would expect the Israelites to push all future complaints onto the "back burner." But, then, seemingly out of nowhere, the Israelites cry out for meat (Numbers 11:4). This is the last thing we expect to hear, not only because it flies in the face of the punishment they just received but also because they seem to be complaining for no reason. After the splitting of the Reed Sea they had complained of hunger, and the Almighty solved the problem with the miraculous heaven-sent manna, a type of coriander seed; and long before Marx and Engels, each family received a sufficient portion for each family member – each in accordance with his or her need. Moreover, according to the Midrash, they certainly had no cause for complaint, since the taste of the individual portion of manna was determined by the culinary desires of the individual, when he or she made the blessing before tasting the "seed." If one could think beef-wellington and receive that exact flavor from the manna – and without calories and cholesterol – who would need any other kind of food?

And then the most disturbing problem of all: when Moses bitterly complains to God about his difficulties in leading such an ungrateful, querulous, and impatient nation which is now desirous of meat, the Almighty responds, "Gather for Me seventy men from amongst the wise elders of Israel" in order to appoint rabbinical and judicial leaders to assist Moses in his duties of leadership. The people cry for meat – and God gives them rabbinical judges. How does the divine solution answer the problem?! (Although I am certainly aware of the fact that many congregations "devour" their rabbis, I hardly believe that God was thinking in such terms!)

I would like to begin my response to all of these questions by suggesting that – surprisingly and tragically – it is often when an individual has "everything," and should be most grateful and satisfied, that he or she feels most at a loss. Witness the biblical testimony, "But now our souls are dried up, with nothing but the manna before our eyes" (Numbers 11:6). Why should their souls be dry? They ought to be fertile and blessed, energized with limitless possibilities! Why should newly-freed individuals, divinely protected against any onslaught from the elements, sound like inhabitants of T.S. Eliot's *The Waste Land*? They should see the desert as their gateway to freedom! And why should manna affect their *souls*? It is the *body* which requires the nutrients, and it is the *body* which responds to delectable flavors and exotic tastes!

The great psychologist and founder of logotherapy, Victor Frankel, in his wise and thought-provoking book *Man's Search for Meaning*, maintains that the most profound existential human desire is not the search for pleasure (as Freud thought), nor is it the search for power (as Jung and Adler thought), but is rather a search for meaning and significance! He argues that the concentration camp victim with the obsessive goal of saving the life of his child lived each day with more zest than the retired American millionaire who is bereft of plans, purpose, goals. "Pity the person who has realized his every dream" – because the true excitement of life is a byproduct of the striving, is the adrenalin produced in the heat of the chase to capture the prize.

The Bible introduced the downward slide of the Israelites with the Hebrew word *k'mitonenim*, translated as "like murmurers." But the Hebrew *mitlonen* means murmur or complaint; *mitonen* is comprised of two Hebrew words, suggests Rabbi S.R. Hirsch – *met*, a corpse, and *onen*, a mourner found in the initial stage of mourning between the period of the death and burial of the deceased. This strange and compound word reflects a sense of impotence, malaise – the sadness, frustration, and emptiness which comes from a feeling that there is nothing left for the individual to do, there is no purpose to any of his actions at this point. The mourner is overwhelmed with feelings of frustration, purposelessness, emptiness. Ponder the fact that tiredness rarely comes from hard and satisfying work; the retired, bored businessman is the one who yawns the most.

When God freed the Israelites from Egyptian slavery and provided them with all their needs in the desert, they lost the dreams and ideals which had sparked their lives and ignited their energies while they were still slaves in Egypt. Now they want "meat," which may just be a way of saying that they want something to bite their teeth into! Enough with living the "life of Riley" in a divinely supported desert kollel!

Enough with the imagination creating the perfect menu. Fish is better, even those salty, smelly sardines which the Nile spit up together with its frothy film, because although they tasted putrid, while we ate them we could still dream of better times to come – and work to bring those dreams to fruition. Yes, we crave "cucumbers and watermelons and onions and leeks"! What these vegetables have in common is that they have to be planted, nurtured, and harvested. They require sun, water, care, patience, and, most important of all, work. No overnight onions, no express melons. The language of "dry souls" tells us that although God provided everything necessary for the body, the Israelite soul was bereft of purpose, significance, meaningful dedication to an ideal. We have seen that the author of *HaKtav VeHaKabbala*, Rabbi Yaakov Mecklenberg, interprets *mitonenim* as coming from the Hebrew *ana*, whither, where. The Israelites were wandering hither and thither, here, there, and everywhere in search of a goal and direction, desperately seeking a compass to point towards a clear vision and goal, a program of action that would give meaning and purpose to their lives. They had it all – and therefore they lacked what everyone needs most: a purpose to their lives, a reason for being, a program of action to give meaningful direction to their days.

I believe that both interpretations of *mitonenim* are saying the same thing. The nation which had been so certain of its mission when it came out of Egypt – the freed slaves who had felt in every fiber of their being that they were "a holy nation and kingdom of priests"; the Israelite who had sung at the Reed Sea, "You shall bring us and plant us in the mountain of Your inheritance.... Your hands, O God shall prepare a Sanctuary" (Exodus 15:16–17) – had lost their focus, had forgotten their ideal.

The Israelites did not know what they wanted because they did not understand what they needed – like a baby who is *kvetching* for something, and will continue to *kvetch* and reject whatever he is given because he doesn't understand that he is teething and that is what is causing his discomfort. The Israelites thought it was the meat, or the fish, or the watermelon that they wanted – but each *kvetch* led to another *kvetch*, since what they really needed was a goal, a significant purpose.

And the truly tragic truth is that the Israelites lost their spiritual compass because they felt removed – even alienated – from Moses, that fiery leader who had initially inspired the Egyptian slaves with a vision of freedom in order to serve their God of compassion, morality, and peace in Israel, in order to spearhead a universal movement to enthrone God as King of the Universe (Exodus 15:18). But Moses couldn't maintain the excitement, couldn't sustain the vision, could no longer nourish the dream. Why not?

Perhaps it was because he had become too close to God, too involved in constant divine communication in order to receive the Torah, that he lacked the requisite time, energy, and patience to slowly and incrementally pastor and educate a stubborn and complaining people. Gersonides (also known as the Ralbag) goes so far as to interpret in this way the biblical words "they [the nation] would not listen to Moses because of his [Moses'] impatience," his inability to inspire the Hebrews with their mission to bring about world redemption (Exodus 6:9, Gersonides ad loc.). Perhaps Moses simply became too tired... the *kvetching* nation could wear down even a Moses!

I believe this understanding will lead us to the glue which binds together the various segments of our Torah portion *Beha'alotekha*: the search for leaders who will reignite the fire and reinspire the dream, a cadre of visionaries who will help Moses direct the people to begin working again towards their covenantal goal. Hence, after appointing Aaron as the custodian over the kindling of the Menora, our biblical portion explains that the firstborns lost their initial position of leadership to the kohanim because they worshipped the Golden Calf, because they followed false gods of materialistic and hedonistic excess. Our portion goes on to teach that if there are those who are ritually defiled and cannot participate in the national-religious ritual of the Paschal lamb at its appointed time they must be given another chance at another date (Pesaḥ *Sheni*); and this second chance even extends to those who were away from the place of sacrifice at the appointed time, and even to those who may have been there geographically but were distant psychologically, emotionally, religiously – even to those who may have been at the doorsteps of the Holy Temple, but lacked the will, the spiritual desire, to participate in the national sacrifice (Numbers 9:9, Rashi ad loc.). Leadership must reach out to the alienated, to the spiritually distant.

Religious inspirers must imbue the nation with the realization that they are being directed by God – in the guise of a cloud by day and a fire by night – and must instill within them the courage to go to war if need be to protect their nation, their mission, their future destiny. Leadership must point the people towards the idea of Torah, a morality and a lifestyle which expresses its goals by means of sacred-time celebrations, and which has the power – when adhered to – to scatter our enemies to the wind. Yitro, who originally counseled Moses concerning the necessity of additional rabbinic-judicial leadership, leaves the desert for Midian; perhaps he returned to his home because he had foreseen the crisis but was not listened to in time to have prevented it from coming.

Finally, why does our portion begin with the Menora? The Menora, or candelabrum, symbolizes the Israelite nation, light unto the nations of the world. The single most important task of leadership is to foster the fuel, to kindle the spark, to fan the flame, to ignite the imagination, to provide the illumination. This is what Rashi has God say to the kohanim, biologically destined to lead as teachers of Torah, in his opening commentary to *Beha'alotekha*: "Your task is greater than theirs [the princes of the other tribes]: you kindle and prepare the Menora." You must imbue the Menora, Israel entire (*Klal Yisrael*) the light of all the nations, with the vision and the mission to enter the Land of Israel and redeem the world.

Hence the truest task of a leader: to supply the vision and the volition, the dream and the desire. Moses did that most effectively for the Hebrews in Egypt, for fleeing freedmen at the shores of the Reed Sea, and he did it for all future generations of Jews through the divine words he left as his legacy for eternity. Perhaps it was precisely his second focus which made it impossible for him to truly lead the desert generation with the day-to-day, minute-to-minute concern that that congregation, as well as every congregation, require; perhaps it is truly "mission impossible" to be involved with the eternal generations as well as with one's own temporal generation at one and the same time. But the angst of the desert generation calls out to leaders of every single generation to the end of time: give us meaning or you give us death; inspire our lives with significance, or we will dry up and die. Ignite our souls with a passionate ideal, and we will follow you to the ends of the earth.

A Hasidic Postscript

A Hasidic rebbe once told his disciples that every modern invention contains an important message from God. "What can we learn from the telephone?" they asked. "That what you say at one end of the world can be heard at the other end; two people can keep a secret – but only if one of them is dead." "What can we learn from a telegram?" "That every word must be counted, and that every letter costs money." "What can we learn from a train?" "That if you come one minute late, you can lose the entire trip. But most importantly, you can learn from a train that one fiery engine can move along thousands of people – but there must be fire in its belly!"

The Ram's Horn and the Trumpet: The Secret of Jewish Music

Make yourself two silver trumpets. Make them out of beaten metal. They shall be used by you to assemble the community and for causing the camps to break camp for their journeys.

NUMBERS 10:2

Although the beginning of the book of Genesis records that Yuval was the inventor of the lyre and the pipe, when it comes to the performance of the commandments in the Torah, the only instruments which play any role are the *shofar* (ram's horn) and the *ḥatzotzrot* (silver trumpets). So in a sense (at least from the Torah's point of view), it is these latter two which are uniquely Jewish instruments, each with their specific, symbolic significance; the lyre and pipe are part of the heritage of humanity at large.

The *shofar,* as we know from *Parashat Emor* in Leviticus, is virtually synonymous with *Rosh HaShana,* resonating the creation of the world and intoning our dream of ultimate perfection of the world in the Kingship of God. The *shofar* next appears in *Behar*, the portion right after *Emor*, where we are commanded to sanctify the fiftieth year as a jubilee. With the completion of the forty-nine-year period of seven sabbatical cycles, the *shofar* proclaims the freedom of all slaves, and the return of the original owners to their ancestral homes and lands – the redemption of the land. And it was the *shofar* that was heard emanating from Mount Sinai during the divine revelation of the Torah (Exodus 19:19). Hence the *shofar* symbolizes creation, revelation, and redemption, the perfection of the world and humanity through the Torah's commandments.

Indeed, the very word itself, *shofar*, literally means beauty – the majesty expressed in the horn that crowns the ram's regal bearing, the beauty of the ram. Perhaps it's no coincidence that one of the two Jewish midwives who defied Pharaoh's edict to kill all male Jews at birth – in effect the first redeemers of the Jewish people – was named Shifra, from the same root as *shofar*. It is no surprise, then, that the instrument marking such important occasions as the giving of the Torah, the Kingship of God on the birthday of the creation of the world, as well as the redemption of the Land of Israel, are all served by an instrument whose essence is majestic beauty.

But what about the *ḥatzotzra*, the silver trumpet? Its name connotes the very antithesis of beauty: tz-a-r means pain, narrow straits, the same root from which we derive *Mitzrayim* (Egypt), the land which caused pain and oppression to the Jews. In fact, the Torah alludes to this idea when it uses the words *hatzar hatzorer*, "the adversary who oppresses you" (Numbers 10:9) in the next to last verse in the segment dealing with these "silver trumpets."

The tenth chapter of Numbers in *Beha'alotekha* opens with God commanding Moses to make two silver trumpets, *ḥatzotzrot*, and then, for ten verses, the Torah gives us the various occasions and requirements for the sounding of these "silver trumpets," when the Israelites set out on their wanderings and when they had to assemble for war.

At this point, the *ḥatzotzrot* are very much in line with their name, expressing pain and angst, wanderings and war.

But is it all pain and angst? The same biblical section of silver trumpets also commands us to use this instrument to herald the festivals and new months, genuine occasions for joy. "And in the day of your gladness, and in your appointed seasons, and in your new moons, you shall blow with the trumpets over your burnt offerings" (Numbers 10:10). Undoubtedly, even within a world of suffering, there are moments of victory and happiness. Moreover, we must also remember that our festivals and new months also reflect angst as well as exaltation, fear as well as freedom. After all, on Pesaḥ we recall the matza, which is "bread of affliction," the food we ate as slaves in Egypt, as well as the "bread of faith" we took with us to the desert. And the *Sukka* recalls our wandering in an alien, dry desert as well as divine rays of protective splendor; similarly Rosh Ḥodesh reminds us that the essence of the moon lies both in its waxing as well as its waning nature, which expresses incompletion and imperfection at the same time that it holds out hope for ultimate wholeness and redemption. Might not the real lesson of the *ḥatzotzra* be that it is in the challenge of the angst and the pain, in our ability to overcome the limitations and rise above the evils of servitude and exile, that the highest joys of human accomplishment and success are found?

And indeed, it is important to note that the Torah, in the *ḥatzotzrot* segment, categorizes two kinds of occasions, and two kinds of sounds. One is perhaps the expected *terua* sound, a broken sigh-sob (*ra'o'a,* broken): "And when you go to war in your land against the adversary that oppresses you, then you shall sound an alarm [*terua*] with the trumpets." *Terua* is also sounded when the Jewish people must break camp, embarking on a long journey, wandering from place to place, the forty years in the desert being a prophetic foretaste of the thousands of years of exile and wandering the Jews would have to endure.

But in addition to the *terua* sound, the Torah also commands the *ḥatzotzrot* to blow a *tekiya,* a straight, exultant, expansive sound, demonstrating that even within this world of imperfection, and perhaps emanating from our empowerment to rise above and overcome that pain and suffering, the very *ḥatzotzra* can be employed to express a *tekiya* sound of joy and well-being, of eventual perfection and redemption. The dual nature of the festivals, the very dual nature of life in the world wherein the sweet may emerge from the bitter, the honey a by-product of the bee's sting, is expressed by the two interconnected sounds of the *ḥatzotzra,* the *terua* and *tekiya* which emanate from the silver trumpet: witness Naomi

Shemer's song, "Concerning the honey and the sting, concerning the bitter and the sweet, concerning all these things, please guard them for me, my good God." Both are necessary, the bitter as well as the sweet, for the true challenge in this world is to turn the matza of slavery into the matza of freedom, to make sweet lemonade out of bitter lemons.

With this understanding, let us revisit the Rosh HaShana *shofar*. The Bible calls the first day of the New Year "the day of the *terua* sound shall it be unto you" (Numbers 21:1), the day of the staccato, broken sound. Why a broken *terua* emanating from the beautiful majestic *shofar*, and on the day of our celebration of the creation of the world, no less?! The answer ought to be indubitably, if not painfully, clear. God created an imperfect, incomplete world – with evil as well as good, with chaos as well as order, with darkness as well as light (Isaiah 45:7). Our task is to complete it, to perfect and repair it, to mend it and make it whole. We must turn a broken *terua* into an exultant *tekiya*!

Timely and Timeless Torah

And it came to pass, when the Ark traveled forward, that Moses said, "Rise up O God, and scatter Your enemies; and let them that hate You flee before You." And when it rested he said, "Return O God, unto the myriads [literally ten thousands] of the families of Israel."

NUMBERS 10:35–36

I would like to invite you to join me in a fascinating detective search, an intellectual journey whose destination is the understanding of a strange typographical biblical insertion in this portion of *Beha'alotekha,* which gives rise to an even stranger rabbinical assertion. Tradition ordains that the two stirring verses quoted above be bracketed, as it were, by two inverted *nuns,* the fourteenth letter of the Hebrew alphabet. So strong is this scribal tradition that even the printed Bible texts set these verses off with the two inverted *nuns.* The Talmud raises the issue of this curious typography, explaining – in the name of Rebbe, primary transmitter of the Mishna – that "in the Torah parchment this section is preceded and followed by a reversed *nun*...because it ranks as a biblical book by itself" (*Shabbat* 116).

I would suggest that our sages are granting these verses the status of a separate book because they encapsulate the true potency of our Torah; indeed, these verses are teaching us that the true source of our strength, endurance, and eternity as a nation is our Torah, and our Torah alone!

Lest we make the mistake that might makes right, and that physical prowess ensures survival, we must be mindful of the fact that the Egyptian pyramids, Babylonian ziggurats, Olympian idols, Roman coliseums, Nazi swastikas, and Bolshevik hammer and sickles have indeed been scattered by the winds of history, while the pages of our Torah parchment – which can be overturned by a strong wind – have nevertheless enabled our beleaguered and often powerless nation (at least for two thousand years of exile) to emerge strong and influential; indeed, it is because of that Torah that we have succeeded in rising from the ashes of Auschwitz, returning as a sovereign nation to our homeland, and effecting an ingathering of exiles from Ethiopia, India, Bosnia, and Russia.

But why utilize the Hebrew letter *nun* to express the truth of the power of our book? In *Berakhot* (4b) we are taught that the *Ashrei* prayer, comprised primarily of the 145th Psalm, which we are enjoined to say thrice daily, follows the pattern of the letters of the Hebrew alphabet by having each of its verses begin with another letter of the alphabet in proper order from *aleph* to *taf*. However, one letter is conspicuous by its absence: "Why is there no *nun* in *Ashrei*? Because the fall of Israel begins with it, as it is written: 'Fallen, [*nifla*], she shall not again rise, O virgin of Israel [Amos 5:2].'" This Talmudic passage states that *nun* is the last letter we would expect to find encompassing a "book" attesting to Israel's eternity. However, we must remember that the *nuns* which surround our verses are inverted!

If we turn to Nahmanides's explanation concerning the rainbow which God placed in the sky as an expression of His covenant with Noaḥ, we find that, for this great sage, the symbolism of the rainbow is that of an inverted bow [as in bow and arrow]:

> He [God] has not made the rainbow with its feet bent upward because it might have appeared that arrows were being shot from heaven.... Instead He made it the opposite of this in order to show that they are not shooting at the earth from the heavens. It is indeed the way of warriors to invert the instruments of war which they hold in their hands when calling for peace.
>
> Nahmanides on Genesis 9:13

If the *inverted* bow, or rainbow, of the covenant with Noaḥ symbolizes the very antithesis of war, the inversion expressing not war but peace, then it is logical to assert that the inverted *nun* of this portion symbolizes the ascent of Israel rather than her demise. Indeed, the Talmudic passage we cited previously goes on to reinterpret the verse from Psalms by merely changing the punctuation: "The fallen [daughter of Israel], she shall never [fall] again; Rise, O Virgin of Israel" (Amos 5:2). In effect, our two reversed *nuns* are a silent covenant between God and the Jewish people that the Torah, eternal source of strength of our nation, has the power to scatter all our enemies as long as we, the People of Israel, always move together with the Ark! In effect, ours is a portable Torah which we must always take with us.

Permit me to develop this idea one step further – and attempt to elucidate the deepest meaning of the words of these verses. "When the Ark traveled forward" alerts us to the significance of the necessity of the Ark, and the Torah it encompasses, to travel together with the nation, albeit a little bit ahead – but never so far ahead that it leaves the people behind. Perhaps this is the real significance of Rashi's comment: "Since the Ark was three days ahead of where the Jews were when they were traveling, therefore Moses said, 'Stand and wait for us; don't go further away'" (Rashi on Numbers 10:35). Rashi is teaching us that Moses was scrupulous about making sure that the Ark was never more than three days ahead. Remember the well-known adage of folk-wisdom: If you're one step ahead of the generation, you're a genius. If you're two steps ahead, you're a crackpot! Obviously we require the proper religious leadership to ensure that the people are in step with the Torah – but the Torah must be in step with the people as well. Hence our sages are forbidden from legislating a decree that the majority of committed Israel cannot abide by.

Furthermore, the latter portion reads: "And when it rested he said 'Return O God unto the myriads [literally ten thousands] of the families of Israel.'" The root of the word "when it rested," *nuḥo,* derives from the same root as sweetness, gentleness (*noaḥ* in Hebrew), expressing the idea that our Torah must be sweet and gently accepting and inclusive. Seen in this light, the verse enjoins us not only to endeavor to make Torah relevant, but also to see to it that it be an embracing and accepting Torah, a Torah of love and inclusiveness. After all, does not the Talmud teach:

> For three years the schools of Hillel and Shammai debated the law, until a heavenly voice declared…"These and those are the words of the living God, and the law is like Beit Hillel." If so [if both views emanate from God], then why is the law decided in accord with the school of Hillel? Because they are pleasant and accepting [*noḥin*], always teaching their view together with the view of the school of Shammai and even citing the position of Shammai before citing their own position.
>
> *Eruvin* 13b

If our Torah is a law of accepting love and not of fanatic hatred, of warming light rather than of destructive fire, then the myriads of families of Israel shall truly return to the welcoming words of God.

A Personal Postscript

I'd like to share a personal story. Some readers may already know from my writings in the past that I was not born into an observant family. Because the yeshiva in my neighborhood was considered far more academically challenging than the local public school, my parents consented to my grandmother's urging that I receive a day school education. But living in a non-observant home required certain balancing skills. On Friday nights I would join my grandmother for the Shabbat meal, and every Shabbat lunch I was invited to the home of the principal of our yeshiva, Rabbi Menahem Manes Mandel, who was a major religious influence in my life.

After returning to my neighborhood of Bedford-Stuyvesant, I would spend a quiet hour with my mother, a kind of quality time when we would both talk about what was closest to us. At that time my mother smoked three cigarettes a day, and on Saturdays she would save her afternoon cigarette for her relaxed talk with me. The latter part of the afternoon I would spend with Saul Berman, the son of a prominent community rabbi and my special "Shabbos" friend.

But one particular Shabbat, while my mother and I were busy talking, there was a knock on the front door. When my mother opened the door and saw it was my Shabbos friend, she was clearly a bit discombobulated; she hid the cigarette she was holding behind her back – and I jumped to explain that I would meet him at his home in about thirty minutes.

When my mother came back into the living room, still holding the cigarette, she looked at me and said rather sadly, "I think God made a mistake by putting you and me together. You're religious, and every day becoming even more religious. I'm afraid that despite my best efforts, you'll end up an Orthodox rabbi. Why should God have given me a son like you? He should have put you with my religious parents instead of with me!"

But then my clever mother made an about-face. "On second thought," she said, "I think I understand why God did what He did. Perhaps He made me your mother so that you would learn to love everyone, even people who aren't necessarily observant." In retrospect, that attitude more than any other – which I truly learned from my mother – has been a guiding principle of my life.

Complaining vs. Kvetching: What Is the Difference?

Woe, the nation was kvetching *evilly in the ears of the Lord, and the Lord heard, and His anger inflamed.*

NUMBERS 11:1

This biblical portion, with the "nagging complaints" of the Israelites, arouses a fiery anger emanating from God which destroys the edge of the camp and eventually leads to an "extremely severe plague," in which the complaining, craving Israelites are buried in what Moses calls "the graves of craving" (*kivrot hata'ava*; Numbers 11:31–35).

What is difficult to understand is the marked difference between God's reaction to the complaining Israelites here in the book of Numbers and His reaction to their complaints in the book of Exodus. After all, the Israelites were never "easy customers," not even after their having experienced the great wonders of the ten plagues, not even after the stunning Revelation at Sinai, not even after the mind-blowing miracle of the splitting of the Reed Sea. Then, only three days after the splitting of the sea, they only find "bitter" waters to drink, and "the people complained against Moses" (Exodus 15:24). God immediately – and without comment – provides Moses with the bark of a special tree which sweetens the waters.

And then again, only thirty days after the Exodus, upon their arrival at the Tzin desert, they complain bitterly because they have no food: "If only we had died by God's hand in Egypt.... You had to bring us out to this desert, to kill the entire community by starvation!" (Exodus 16:1–3). God immediately – and without comment – provides the manna. And finally, when they leave the Tzin desert and encamp in Rephidim, they again quarrel with Moses over their lack of water and God tells Moses to strike a large boulder at Ḥorev with the same staff he had previously used to strike the Nile River and turn it into blood; this time water would (and did) come out of the rock (Exodus 17:1–7)! And although Moses names this place "Testing and Strife" (*Masa Umeriva*), what immediately follows is the successful war against Amalek, won for the Israelites by the divine response to Moses' hands upraised in prayer to God.

How different is God's reaction to the similar complaints only one year later (see Numbers 1:1), when a fire consumes the edge of the camp and a plague results in mass graves. Why the change?

Rabbi Moshe Lichtenstein, in his illuminating study *Moses: Envoy of God, Envoy of His People* (in Hebrew, *Tzir VeTzon*), suggests that the requests and complaints in Exodus were for the basic necessities of life, water, and bread. Although the Israelites should have had greater faith, one can hardly fault them for desiring their existential needs.

In our biblical portion of *Beha'alotekha*, however, they are not complaining about the scarcity of water; they are complaining about the lack of variety in the menu! The text even introduces the subject by stating that the nation was *kvetching* (in Hebrew, the strange word *mitonenim*, rather than the usual *mitlonenim* for complaining) evilly in the ears of God – without even mentioning what they were complaining about (Numbers 11:1). And for this unspecified complaint, God's fire flares. After this punishment, the nation cries out, "Who will give us meat to eat?" and then continues with, "We remember the fish we ate for free in Egypt, and the cucumbers and the melons, and the leeks, and the onions, and the garlic; our spirits are dried up with nothing but manna before our eyes" (Numbers 11:4–6). What do they want – meat, or fish, or melons, or garlic?!

God's response is also strange; He tells Moses to appoint seventy elders (Numbers 11:16), and sends the Israelites quails to eat. They ask for meat and God first gives them rabbis! And while they are eating the quail, they are smitten by the severe plague. Why are they complaining, and why is God so angry? And if, indeed, He is disappointed, even upset, by their finicky desires, why give in to their cravings and why send them rabbis?

Herein lies the essential difference between the complaints in Exodus and the complaints in Numbers. In Exodus the nation had a clear goal; they were committed to the mission of becoming a kingdom of priests and a sacred nation, and were anxiously anticipating the content of that mission, a God-given doctrine of compassionate righteousness and moral justice which they must impart to the world. In order to receive and fulfill their mission they had to live, and so they (legitimately) requested water and bread, survival food. If they did not survive, they would certainly not be able to redeem.

One year later, in Numbers, they had already received the Torah. And, since their necessities were provided for, they were complaining, *kvetching,* without having specific complaints. And they were craving – all sorts of gourmet cravings – from meat to garlic. God understood that had they still been inspired by their mission, had they remained grateful for their freedom and the opportunity it would afford them to forge a committed and idealistic nation, they would not be in need of watermelons and leeks, they would not be craving something that they themselves had never tasted. Tragically, having achieved and received their anticipated goal of Torah, the once sought-after object of ultimate sanctity had lost its glamour, its appeal, its allure. In its stead were nonsense empty cravings, with the fancy menus in the non-kosher French and Italian fancy restaurants. The Israelites turned in their former idealistic goals for a fancy variety of gourmet dishes, for the proverbial "mess of pottage." No wonder God was disappointed and angry. And so he sent them the quails, knowing that once they received the "meat," they would cease craving for it, hoping that perhaps seventy more rabbis would be able to restore their lost idealism!

God, Moses, and Tzipora: Can the Three Commune Together?

And Miriam and Aaron spoke against Moses because of the Ethiopian woman whom he had taken [to wife]; for he had taken an Ethiopian woman [as his wife].

NUMBERS 12:1

Apparently, the criticism of Miriam and Aaron against Moses had something to do with his marital relationship. The traditional commentaries, *Targum Onkelos* and Rashi, both agree that they were referring to his Midianite wife Tzipora, who was beautiful (*Kushit* in Hebrew also has the connotation of beautiful, since "black is beautiful"), and whom he had divorced (which is why, they would argue, the biblical text repeats twice that he had married her in past tense). And the heart of their critique comes in the very next verse: "And they said, 'Was it only with Moses that God spoke; did He not also speak with us!' And God heard" (12:2). Apparently they were carping against a brother who was considered to be holier than they were – and yet he had divorced his wife. Slanderous gossip! Does this not seem like picayune, small-town family jealousy, hardly worthy of great biblical personages like Miriam and Aaron?!

Further, what are we to learn from this last phrase, "And God heard"? God hears everything! Hence, the verb "heard" in this context probably means "acquiesced," or agreed (as in Leviticus 10:20). But God did not agree with their critique. Immediately following this conversation, the Almighty gave a thundering acclamation of the uniqueness of Moses, his humility, and the very special relationship he enjoyed with God, who spoke to him "mouth to mouth" and not through any intermediary dream or vision; and of course God expressed His anger at the slandering siblings and punished Miriam (Numbers 12:5–9). What is the story behind the gossip? And did God agree or disagree with the charge of Moses' siblings against him?

Maimonides gives us a unique glimpse into his philosophy of prophecy in the interpretation he provides for these verses; and if Maimonides is correct, he helps us to understand both the greatness and weakness of Moses at the same time. Indeed, paradoxically, Moses' strongest asset may emerge as the source of his most tragic flaw.

In Moses' farewell speech and charge to his nation, he recounts the awe-inspiring and miraculous Revelation at Sinai, when – in the midst of fire, clouds, and heavy mist – they all heard a "great voice which did not cease" (Deut. 5:19, *Targum* ad loc.), a divine voice which is continuously audible. And so the Bible declares:

> When Moses would enter the Tent of Meeting [of the Sanctuary] to speak with [God], he would hear the voice [which emanated from Sinai, interprets Rashi] speaking [to itself, and calling out] to him…from atop the Ark-cover…from between the two cherubs.
>
> Numbers 7:29

Maimonides (*Mishneh Torah, Hilkhot Yesodei HaTorah* 6 and *Guide for the Perplexed* Part II) explains that the Almighty is constantly emitting divine messages, much like electric waves (*galei teder*) constantly in the atmosphere; the challenge for the individual is to develop his or her mind, heart, and soul to reach the point of becoming "satellite dishes," so that they may have the capacity to hear, internalize, and transmit these divine communications to others.

A prophet is an individual who has developed himself intellectually, spiritually, and emotionally to such an extent that he becomes a "receiver" of divine messages. In most instances of prophecy, the prophet experiences only rare moments of these revelations after which he "leaves" (or is left by) the intense Divine Presence, as it were, and rejoins the rest of humanity to carry on with his day-to-day affairs.

And that was precisely what happened to the entire congregation of Israel on the sixth day of Sivan, seven weeks after their exodus from Egyptian slavery, when they stood at Mount Sinai. Everyone heard the divine voice – each in accordance with his individual capacity as a receiver – after which we read, "Go, tell them to return to their tents" (Deut. 5:26), to rejoin their wives, their families, and the rest of human civilization.

Moses, however, was in a unique category. His intellectual-spiritual capacity was so finely honed, so exalted and sublime, that he remained constantly in a state of receiving the divine communications. In the language of Maimonides, Moses' active intellect was in constant contact with the divine active intellect. And so after God told the rest of Israel to return to their tents, He told Moses, "But you remain standing here with Me so that I may [continue to] tell you all the commandments, statutes, and laws which you must teach them" (Deut. 5:27).

Moses understood this to mean that he must never return to his familial tent, that his constant and intense contact with God obviated regular human contact, made normal human relationships impossible. And indeed, Moses was a "man of God" rather than a man of the people. Since he spoke to God "mouth to mouth," he was "heavy mouthed," of heavy speech, "a *kvad peh*" – not necessarily one who stuttered but rather one who eschewed "small talk," who had no patience with the all-too-often paltry and petty concerns of average individuals. As Gersonides explains it, "the people stopped listening to him – especially later on when it came to conquering the Land of Israel – because of his [Moses'] impatience with them and heavy-duty divine service with God [Moses' *kotzer ruaḥ* and *avoda kasha*]" (Exodus 6:9).

Miriam and Aaron didn't understand why Moses had not returned to his wife and family after the Revelation, why he'd divorced Tzipora. They assumed that just as they had been told by God to return to their tents, so had Moses been told the same. And the truth may well have been that although God had in fact informed Moses to remain with Him on a more steady basis, had recognized the more unique spiritual sensitivity within Moses, He had not meant for Moses to exclude his family. The Almighty believed that intensive commitment to God should lead to more intensive commitment to people, not the rejection of people. After all, since every human emanates from the womb of the *Shekhina*, closeness to God ought to naturally lead to closeness to the God found inside of every human being created in the divine image.

Indeed, Moses' closeness to God had forced him to develop a strategy of "distance" leadership – either from the lofty heights of Mount Sinai or the inner sanctum and splendid supernal isolation of the Tent of Communion, far removed from the encampment (Exodus 33:7–11). It was Eldad and Medad, the new generation of prophets, who prophesied from within the encampment itself, in the midst of the people (Numbers 11:26). Moses recognized his failing; to his everlasting credit, when his son Gershom (according to Rashi) ran to tell his father that Eldad and Medad were prophesying *in* the encampment, were competing with him, and Joshua wanted them killed, Moses responded, "Would that the entire nation of the Lord would be prophets" (Numbers 11:25–29). Moses just couldn't orchestrate devoting himself to his God and the individuals of his nation at the same time.

Perhaps on the familial level God tried to communicate the necessity of interpersonal relationships by communicating to Moses from between the two cherubs, objects of the Ark-cover in the form of a young man and a young woman. The biblical scroll known as the Song of Songs has been interpreted as a metaphor, comparing the human love between husband and wife to the divine love between God and Israel, a concept which led Rabbi Akiva to describe it as the Holy of Holies. The very comparison between human and divine love exalts love between a man and a woman to a lofty level. And God commanded the Israelites to "love your friend like yourself, I am the Lord," suggesting that the very foundation of human love lies in the fact that each of us has a part of the divine within him- or herself so that each of us is inextricably united, essentially bound up, with the "other" as well as with God in a sacred triangle (Leviticus 19:18, Ibn Ezra ad loc.). This is certainly true of husband, wife, and God, as the Talmud attests when it interprets the "friend" in "You shall love your *friend* like yourself, I am the Lord" as referring to one's spouse (*Kiddushin* 42, in the name of Rabbi Yehuda amar Rav, states that the marital couple under the nuptial canopy are liturgically referred to as "*re'im ahuvim*," loving and beloved friends, on this basis).

At the same time, God, as it were, also realized that it was precisely Moses' closeness to the divine that caused him to be impatient with his people, that the prophet's involvement with the eternal ideas and ideals made it exceedingly difficult for him to graciously orchestrate the exalted realm of the divine with the more mundane considerations on earth, to listen to the lofty words of God and the lowly complaints of Israel at the same time. Hence God might have been sympathetic to Miriam and Aaron's critique, but at the same time He had to chastise them for their slander, emphasizing the uniqueness of Moses' relationship to God and the necessity of not judging another until one stands in his or her place. Since they were on a lower prophetic level than he was, they ought not judge him negatively.

In the final analysis, however, it was precisely Moses' exalted spiritual state which, while it enabled him to communicate an eternal Torah for all generations, was likewise responsible for his inability to persuade his own generation to conquer Israel, and hence the necessity of his own burial outside of the Promised Land. Moses' greatest gift – his very profound communication with the Divine which permitted him to convey the word of God to the generations – was at the same time his tragic flaw, which prevented him from influencing his generation to conquer the Land of Israel, settle it, and begin the process of redemption. Moses' very closeness to God and eternity prevented him from being the necessary shepherd of his people in the desert generation, a shepherding without which they could not be persuaded to follow God's will. Hence Israel's entry into the Promised Land would have to await a new leader, one who might be less a man of God but more a man of the people.

Shelaḥ

Why Send Scouts in the First Place?

And God spoke unto Moses saying, "Send out men for yourself to spy out the Land of Canaan, which I give unto the children of Israel; of every tribe of their fathers shall you send a man, every one a prince among them."

NUMBERS 13:2

As the portion of *Shelaḥ* opens, we read how God commands the Israelites to send ahead men to spy out and explore the Land of Israel.

And we know the tragic results of this "spy" mission. The report, which emerged from ten out of twelve, was a negative and discouraging one, which only served to divert the Israelites from their God-given mission of the conquest of the land of Israel. Hence the agonizing question which this portion evokes is: Why did God command the sending of scouts in the first place? Why risk a rebellion in the ranks by requesting a committee report which may well go against the divine will to conquer and settle Israel?

A totally different perspective, not only as to why God commanded Moses to send out the scouts but much more profoundly as to how God operates in the world and why, is to be found in a remarkable interpretation given by Rabbenu Tzadok HaKohen of Lublin (1823–1900), a great Hasidic master, in his commentary on the Torah, called *Pri Tzaddik*. He points out a striking analogy between the incident of the scouts and the gift of the second tablets which came as a result of the sin of the Golden Calf, both conceptually as well as textually: in both cases the Almighty saw the necessity of involving – even to the extent of establishing a partnership with – the people, the nation of Israel.

In what way were the second tablets an improvement on the first tablets which Moses smashed, and which God congratulated him for smashing (Exodus 34:1, *Yevamot* 62a)? What was "built into" the second tablets which would be more likely to prevent a fiasco of the proportion of the sin of the Golden Calf, which occurred only forty days after the gift of the first tablets? The fact that the first tablets had been "written with the finger of God" (Exodus 31:18), and were in actuality the very "script of the divine," whereas the second tablets were "hewn out" by Moses (Exodus 34:1) and thereby were created as a result of human involvement, suggests the difference: the first tablets were the product of divine creativity alone; the second tablets involved human cooperation, setting the stage for rabbinical interpretation, decrees, and enactments which are such a major portion of what we call the "Oral Law." The Oral Law not only accepts but requires the direct participation of rabbinical leadership, and even the involvement of the masses of committed Jews (*Pri Tzaddik* on Exodus, *Ki Tissa* 3, and on Numbers, *Shelaḥ* 2).

Of course, we believe that the major principles and salient laws of the Oral Torah were also given by God. However, the sages of each generation must actively interpret the Torah and often plumb from its depths great innovative concepts necessary for the needs of that generation. Indeed, in a stunning Talmudic passage, the rules of rabbinical exegesis can even cause the Almighty Himself to accept a decision of the majority of the sages, causing Him (as it were) to cry out "My children have conquered Me" (*Bava Metzia* 59b). The very words with which God commands Moses to "hew out" the second tablets, "*psal lekha*" (Exodus 34:1), also contain a nuance: you, Moses, have the authority and the obligation to determine whether an activity or object is *pasul* (improper and invalid). The sages are given the power to add decrees and enactments (*gezerot* and *takkanot*) to the body of the Torah, many of which – such as lighting candles on the eve of the Sabbath and festivals, the kindling of the Ḥanukka menora, and the reading of the Purim Megilla – have become major expressions of our Torah commitment and lifestyle (Deut. 17:8–11). Moreover, no such decrees or enactments can become part and parcel of the Torah of Israel without the endorsement of the majority of the committed people who have the right of acceptance or rejection. The masses of committed people, the hoi polloi or *hamon ha'am,* have also initiated customs throughout the generations which assume the status of Torah law (*minhag Yisrael din hu,* the customs of Israel are law).

All of this suggests a Torah which is not the product of ossified paternalism – as divinely perfect as such a Torah might be – but is rather the result of a living partnership between God and His people. Apparently, the Almighty believed – after the tragic trauma of the Golden Calf – that only a Torah which would involve the active participation of the Israelites could survive the seductive pitfalls of idolatry and immorality.

Fascinatingly enough the phrase "*psal lekha*" (Exodus 34:1) parallels the words God uses to command the scouts, "*shelaḥ lekha,*" send out for yourselves, in the beginning of our portion. God apparently understood that a mission as important as the conquest of Israel could not take place without the enthusiastic approbation and active participation of the people.

Of course opening up the process – be it Torah interpretation or the appointment of a reconnaissance committee – is fraught with danger. But it was a chance that God understood had to be taken if He desired His nation to be more than marching robots. He didn't want us to receive a Torah on a silver platter or to be brought into the Promised Land on eagles' wings; He realized that despite the inherent risk which came from involving the people, excluding them would be a more likely prescription for disaster. Just as a wise parent and a sagacious educator understand that children/students must be "involved in the process" so that hopefully they will continue the path even after they achieve independence, the Almighty set the stage for our continuous devotion to Torah and our third return to Israel – despite our many setbacks – by insisting on the participation of His people!

One might also argue that in the words of Rabbenu Tzadok lies the pivotal reason for the ten scouts' rejection of Moses' goal as well as for God's higher plan for his people in history. Throughout the Egyptian and desert experience, God had acted in a thoroughly paternalistic manner, as it were, bringing about miracle after miracle and providing food, shelter, and protection for the desert wanderers. In effect, the Israelites were in a "Kollel for the masses," with the divine Rosh Yeshiva providing manna (they didn't even have to go to the bank to cash the Kollel checks), housing, and directions as to their comings and goings, with a cloud by day and a fire by night. They didn't have to work and they were spared the major battles against the Seven Nations. Is it any wonder that the majority of the tribal princes wished to prolong this rarefied, ethereal Kollel-desert experience and rejected the responsibility-ridden decision-inducing war-perpetrating entrance into Israel?!

God, on the other hand, expected the Israelites to enter a new phase in their development, to begin to become engaged in directing their own destiny, in accepting the challenges and confrontations involved in conquering a land, irrigating the swamps, fertilizing a desert, forging a society. And God also saw that the response He received after all His steady support and committed care was *kvetching* and complaining, carping and criticizing – no real appreciation, and certainly no mature acceptance of responsibility. And so God commanded the reconnaissance mission as the next stage of Israel's development, the stage in which the members of this covenantal people must begin to stand on their own feet, make their own decisions, take responsibility for their failures, and – with the divine guidance to be found in the Torah and the divine guarantee that not only will they never be destroyed but also that they will eventually prevail – direct their own destiny.

Rabbenu Tzadok goes on to teach that when the scouts were initially commanded to "be of good courage, and bring of the fruit of the land" (Numbers 13:20), this was an allusion to the initial fruit which brought disaster upon humanity, the fruit of knowledge of good and evil. The problem with the Garden of Eden was that everything had been provided by the Almighty; had we remained in Eden, there would have been no risks, no challenges, and no real involvement. The repair (*tikkun*) for this primordial transgression – a transgression which was really inevitable given the paternalistic reality of the situation – is the human production of fruit in partnership with God in the Land of Israel. We can only return to the Garden of Eden if we ourselves remake the world into an Eden with our own blood, sweat, and tears, with humanity assuming the risks and overcoming the obstacles.

The scouts were not yet ready for the challenge. Are we? What can greatly help us in our decision-making is the knowledge that God believes in us and has faith that we can and eventually will do it! And the first step is for Jews of the Diaspora to come home – to the only Jewish homeland. As for those of us living in Israel, we must especially strengthen ourselves, and take from the fruits of the Torah of Zion with an open and cupped hand, always ready to give out what we have; hence we must truly become a kingdom of priests who will export God's ways and God's will to all corners of the earth. What Rabbenu Tzadok is teaching is that we dare not wait for the Messiah; the Messiah is indeed waiting for us!

And You Shall Love Israel Your Land

And they shall seek out [vayaturu] *the Land of Canaan which I am giving to the children of Israel.*

NUMBERS 13:2

Of all the sins the children of Israel commit in the Bible, the most serious sin of all takes place in the portion of *Shelaḥ*. The scouts' severe report is the direct cause of the death of the desert generation.

However, as we discussed in the last commentary, what is difficult to understand is that the suggestion to establish such an ill-fated reconnaissance team came directly from the Almighty Himself. We have considered the necessity of involving the nation in the decision to conquer the land; now we shall attempt to understand what God wanted the scouts to actually report.

Rabbi Elchanan Samet, in his excellent study of the weekly Torah portions, suggests an insight which at the same time provides a textual underpinning for a magnificent homiletic interpretation given by Rabbi Joseph B. Soloveitchik. The secret to understanding lies in the verb form used in the charge given by the Almighty. "Send for yourselves men who will seek out [*vayaturu*] the land," the verb *tur* appearing no less than twelve times in this very sequence, the very number of the members of the delegation itself. In fact, when Moses himself retells the story in his farewell address (Deut. 1:22, 24), he has the Israelites all coming to him and saying, "Let us send men before us that they may check out [*vayaḥperu*] the land… and spy [*vayeraglu*] it out," using two verb forms very different from the *vayaturu* used by God in our portion.

A careful search reveals that in other biblical contexts the verb form *tur* is used similarly to the way it is used in our biblical portion, as in, "the Lord God who walks before you, He will do battle for you… to seek out [*latur*] for you a place in which you may settle your encampment" (Deut. 1:23). Even the prophet Ezekiel (20:6) declares that "on that day I shall raise my hand for them to bring them out of the Land of Egypt to the land which I have sought out [*tarti*] for them. A land flowing with milk and honey, a most precious land for them among all the other lands."

The power of the specific verb form *tur* used by God is even more clearly expressed in the very conclusion of this Torah reading, where we encounter that same verb form in a totally different but most revealing context.

Almost inexplicably, this Torah portion, which mainly deals with the scouts, concludes with the commandment to wear ritual fringes on the corners of our four-cornered garments: "and [the blue and white threads] shall be for you for a fringe so that you may look upon it and remember all the commandments of the Lord and do them; and so that you not seek out or lust [*taturu*] after your heart and after your eyes which lead you to commit acts of harlotry [*zonim*] after them" (Numbers 15:39). And when punishing the Israelites, God once again makes reference to the sin of the scouts as having been an act of harlotry (*znut*), "and your children shall be shepherds in the desert for forty years, thereby bearing [the sin] of your harlotry [*znutekhem*]" (Numbers 14:33).

The picture is becoming very clear. The Almighty was not at all interested in a reconnaissance mission to scout out the land or even in an intelligence delegation to assess the military practicability of engaging in an act of conquest. Perhaps that was what the Israelites had in mind when they asked Moses to send men before them to check out the land, which probably meant to see by which roads it would be best to enter and which cities ought to be attacked first (Deut. 1:22–23). The Almighty had a very different design in mind. God wanted to impress them with the uniqueness, the chosenness of the land which He Himself had picked for them, the land that would be their ultimate resting place, the land which was good and not bad, which produced luscious fruits and full-bodied animals, the land whose produce developed strong and capable men; God wanted them to conquer the land with great anticipation and desire (Numbers 13:1–2, Nahmanides ad loc.).

Rabbi Soloveitchik goes one step further. In the Bible, the Torah of Israel and the Land of Israel are both called *morasha,* which means heritage (Exodus 6:8; Deut. 33:4), but which our sages linked to *me'orasa,* which means betrothed and beloved. God understands that the conquest of the Torah of Israel as well as of the Land of Israel by the People of Israel will require strong feelings of love for each of these grand enterprises. And just as the rabbis of the Talmud command us not to marry a woman unless we first see her and know that we love her (*Kiddushin* 41a), so did God ask Moses to send a group who would give the kind of visual description of the Land of Israel to the People of Israel which would inspire them to love the land and even lust after the land. God understood that such an emotional attachment was absolutely crucial if the Israelites were to overcome all of the obstacles involved in conquering the land, settling it, and forging within it a holy nation and kingdom of priests.

Alas, the people – especially the scouts – did not understand the divine command. Their sin was in misunderstanding the purpose of their journey; they took it to be a scouting enterprise rather than an inspirational foretaste of what waited in store for them after their conquest, a reconnaissance mission rather than an observer's picture of a beautiful and luscious patrimony worthy of their love and sacrifice.

Our generation – so similar to the Israelites who went from the darkness of Egypt to the light of freedom and stood at the entrance to the Promised Land – must do whatever is necessary to recapture and strengthen the love of Israel if we are to succeed in properly settling it.

The Downfall of the Scouts May Have Been a Fallout of Jewish Democracy

Send out men… to explore the Canaanite territory… each one the representative of the tribe of his fathers, each one of them a [tribal] prince… all of them were leaders of the children of Israel.

NUMBERS 13:2–3

The great and grave transgression of the desert generation was the sin of the scouts, the refusal of all but Joshua and Caleb to attempt the conquest and settlement of the Land of Israel, the desired goal of the Exodus from Egypt. And despite the divine guarantee of success (Exodus 6:6–8), despite the miraculous plagues against Egyptian society and the splitting of the Reed Sea, despite Moses' clear endorsement of the conquest – the ten princes of tribes won the day and convinced the Israelites to remain in the desert.

At this point in Jewish history, the failure of leadership is impossible to comprehend. After all, God's track record on behalf of the newly-freed slave-nation had been impeccably successful! What could possibly have made these tribal princes stop short of achieving the whole point of the Exodus, their arrival upon the sacred soil of their final resting place and the land of their inheritance (*menuḥa venaḥala*)?

I believe that the beginning of the possible reason for the negativism of the ten scouts lies in the manner in which significant appointments were made in early Israelite history. The Talmudic sages pick up on what appears to be a superfluous verb utilized in the account of the appointment of Betzalel as chief architect of the Sanctuary – a verb which is slightly changed between the two almost identical recordings of Betzalel's appointment. Initially the biblical text records (Exodus 31:1–5): "And the Lord spoke to Moses, saying, 'Behold [or see (singular), *re'eh*], I have called by name Betzalel.'" And then, in reviewing the appointment four chapters later, the Bible states (Exodus 35:30–35): "And Moses said to the children of Israel, 'Behold [or see (plural), *reu*], the Lord has called by name Betzalel.'" The verb "behold" is not really necessary, and the switch from singular to plural from the first account to the second seems to require some explanation.

The Talmud provides a fascinating – and very modern – interpretation (*Berakhot* 55a). R. Yitzḥak, making use of the verb "behold" or "see," takes it to mean the request of consent or approval. From this perspective R. Yitzḥak derives from this word that "it is improper to appoint a leader over a congregation unless it is with the consent of the congregation." Hence, God first said "behold," or "see" (*re'eh*) to Moses, an individual, to obtain his consent to the divine appointment of Betzalel as chief architect of the Sanctuary; Moses then sought the approval of the entire congregation for Betzalel's appointment, using the plural *reu*. In effect, therefore, biblical appointments require the democratic consent of the people in order for them to be effective.

Fascinatingly enough, as Judaism developed, the democratic method of electing a leader became more and more accepted. The judges who ruled after Joshua were charismatic individuals who were fundamentally chosen by public assent; even the manner in which a king was appointed seemed to depend upon the *vox populi*: "When you shall come to the land which the Lord God is giving you and [if] you shall say, 'Place over us a king like all the nations round about,' then you shall surely place upon yourself a king" (Deut. 17:14–15; see the Netziv's commentary emphasizing that "you shall say" means only on the basis of public approval). Maimonides rules that in the absence of a prophet or a *Sanhedrin,* the king was to be elected by the majority of Israelites (commentaries on Mishna *Keritot* 1:1), and Jewish communities throughout the Middle Ages were governed by seven good representatives, a city council, who were publicly elected (*Ḥoshen Mishpat*).

Taking all of this into account, it seems logical to assume that these twelve scouts, each an important personage representing his tribe as its president or prince (*nasi*), had each been elected by his tribespeople; if the chief architect required public assent, most certainly the president or prince of each tribe required the approbation of the majority of the tribe in order to hold the office of *nasi.* And it also stands to reason that were the Israelites to conquer and settle the Promised Land, dividing their patrimony in accordance with sectarian tribal needs, the new reality would occasion new elections.

I would suggest that everything I have written so far was understood as well – and even better – by the scouts, princes of their respective tribes. They were certainly honorable men, who – on the conscious level – would deny being influenced by the possibility of their losing office in a situation of new elections. But the subconscious desire to retain a position of honor and power works in insidious and devious ways. The sacred Zohar maintains that it was the (subconscious) fear of new elections which prompted the ten princes to lobby in favor of the status quo of the desert rather than the risks involved in the reality of conquering and settling the Promised Land.

It's the Last Word That Counts

> *But* [efes] *the nation that dwells in the land is mighty and the cities are very large and fortified.*
> NUMBERS 13:28

Long before President Franklin Delano Roosevelt coined the phrase, the Midrash spoke of the one day that would forever live in infamy; but that day is the ninth of Av, linked to the loss of both Temples, the Jewish expulsion from Spain, and the Nuremberg decrees of the Nazis. According to our tradition, the source of this black, bleak day was when the twelve scouts returned from a mission to scout the land. Recorded in this portion, *Shelaḥ,* Moses fulfilled God's command to send forth men to gather information.

> Are the people... strong or weak, few or many? Is the inhabited area good or bad?... the soil rich or weak?... trees or not? Strengthen yourselves and bring back... the land's fruits.
> Numbers 13:18–20

Forty days later the men returned with their report. Yes, the land flows with milk and honey,

> as you can see from its fruit. But the nation… is mighty… the cities are very large and fortified… the giants' descendants we saw there…. The land… consumes its inhabitants. All the men we saw were huge…. We were like grasshoppers in our [own] eyes.
>
> Numbers 13:27–33

Two of the scouts, Joshua and Caleb, tried to ease the fear of the people, but their words failed to assuage the panicking and weeping nation. "We wish we had died in Egypt," cried the Israelites (Numbers 14:2). Chaos reigned. God told Moses that he wanted to bring a plague and put an end to this nation, with its short memory. Moses convinced God that He could never completely abandon the Jews. Still, they had to be punished; the ten spies died in a plague and the rest of the nation was condemned to wander forty years in the desert – they would never reach the Promised Land alive. And the ninth day of Av is forever after a day of Jewish tragedy.

However, let us be fair: why should the messenger be destroyed because of the message he brings? Twelve good men, leaders, go on a mission. Do they know what they will encounter, and when they do, should they not share their fears? Is the Torah suggesting their report is rife with lies, misinformation? On the contrary, the facts are an accurate response to each of Moses' questions. So how are we to understand the nature of their sin, the ominous character of the day?

I would suggest that they did sin in the content of the report – but it was not in what they said, but rather in the order in which they said it.

Moses was well aware of the inherent dangers in setting up such a reconnaissance committee. He asked the necessary questions, and since he realized that the results might frighten more than they fortified, he concluded his list about the nature of the cities and the strength of the people with an admonition: "Strengthen yourselves, and bring fruit from the land" (Numbers 13:20). Princes of the tribes of Israel as they were should have been true to the common-sense advice of the Mishna in *Avot*, which teaches that a wise person always responds in the order he's questioned, first things first. The scene that Moses envisioned unfolding upon the scouts' return is one in which they first respond to the questions about the land's inhabitants – which may be a bit fearful – then to his queries about the land itself – which is truly beautiful and fruitful, a land flowing with milk and honey – and finally display the incredibly abundant fruits of the land. And by the time they goggle over the fruit – the luscious, wine-producing grapes with which they returned – their audience will have forgotten about the strong inhabitants. The essence of Moses' instructions is *vehit'ḥazaktem* (and you shall strengthen yourselves): become strengthened yourselves and strengthen your anxiously awaiting kinsmen by showing them the marvelous produce of this amazing land. Moses wanted the bottom line of the scouts to be the astonishing and inspiring grapes!

But Moses' instructions were reversed. First, the spies responded to the beauty of the land and the lusciousness of the fruits – and then quickly got that information out of the way and out of the minds and hearts of their audience. Yes, the land flows with milk and honey, look at these fruits, but.... And their words turned grim and frightening. The final "but" – the Hebrew word "*efes*" – actually means "naught," literally turns to naught all of their previous praise of the beautiful and tantalizing quality of the land's produce. In reversing Moses' order, the spies turned what should have been a great moment into an infamous one.

And it's the one who writes up the minutes of the meeting – and how he ends the report – which determines the outcome of the vote!

Why Leaders Are Rejected

Caleb silenced the nation toward Moses and he said, "We shall surely ascend and conquer it."

NUMBERS 15:30

The worst sin of the Bible is the sin of the scouts. Ten of the scouts returned from their reconnaissance mission to Israel with a negative report: they urged against the attempt to conquer and settle the Promised Land. But why did the Israelites listen to these ten scouts – and not to Moses, and not to Aaron, and not to Joshua, who were each presumably in favor of the conquest of Israel? And what about the ten princes of tribes? Where did they go wrong? What happened to true Jewish leadership?

When the negative report was announced to the Israelites, Moses fell on his face before the entire congregation. "Then Moses and Aaron fell on their faces before all the assembly of the congregation of the children of Israel" (Numbers 14:5). Apparently he realized that to a certain extent the fault lay with him. After all, it was he who sent the scouts on their mission in the first place, and every leader knows that one dare not establish a commission of enquiry unless one is ready to accept its recommendations. Moreover, Moses never even screened the report before it was given in order to mitigate or modify the content. The people might logically have concluded that Moses was ready to accept whatever decision the scouts came to.

We have already seen that Gersonides explains Moses' strange behavior by suggesting that this master of prophets was so close to God that he had become removed from the mentality of his people, that he was incapable of conceiving of the possibility that the people could come to a decision which went counter to the divine will. Moses lacked the desire – and perhaps even the ability – to do outreach, to convince a wayward nation. He had no patience for transgressors, much like the exalted *tzaddik* who no longer has the empathy which will enable him to find the right words to reach the transgressor – the *tzaddik* is in another world!

Aaron was apparently opposed to remaining in the desert or returning to Egypt. He fell on his face together with Moses; both brothers comprised a united front in favor of entering the Promised Land. However, his words were not taken that seriously. After all, in the song of the sea Moses chanted "Your hands will prepare the sanctuary of God" (Exodus 15:17). The priestly class obviously had an axe to grind, would be naturally desirous of a permanent Holy Temple in the Land of Israel.

The ten princes of the tribes who voted against the conquest of Israel might very well have done so in order to secure their political positions. The holy Zohar suggests that they were at least subconsciously aware of the very real possibility that upon entering the Promised Land there would be new elections, and that perhaps they would not be reelected. It was to their advantage therefore to remain in the desert where their power was assured.

Most interesting was the role of Joshua who was, after all, slated to be Moses' successor. He himself opposed the negative decision of the scouts but apparently did not succeed in convincing the nation. Why not? The sages of the Talmud suggest that he did open his mouth to attempt to marginalize the negative report; however he was soon quieted "when the masses cried out, 'shall a broken head [*rosh ketiya*] speak out?'" (*Sota* 35a).

What is the meaning of this strange term of dismissal, "broken head," which the Israelite mob used for Joshua? The Netziv, in his biblical commentary *HaAmek Davar,* gives a fascinating insight: "The people suspected that Joshua wanted to bring the Israelites into the Land of Israel in order that he could be the 'head of the entire generation,' as they had been informed would occur. As long as they remained in the desert – with Moses as a leader – Joshua would only be a small-time leader, a broken head, rather than a great head [a *rosh katan* rather than a *rosh gadol*]."

I believe that all of these various commentaries reflect a very important message for us today. None of the recognized leaders of the people were able to influence this most critical decision because each was suspected of having personal or partisan interests in the outcome. Only that individual who is seen as being above personal and selfish desires has a real chance of moving the masses at a critical juncture. This explains why the Bible insists that there be a fundamental distinction between the executive arm of government and the priesthood; religion must be above politics and neither priest nor prophet may aspire to political office. Moral direction can only come from one who is purely objective and devoid of any personal motivation.

Are We Israelis or Are We Jews?

We are not able to go against those people, for they are stronger than we.

NUMBERS 13:31

Ever since the Exodus from Egypt, setbacks plagued the nation – disillusionments, complaints, rebellions – but the reconnaissance mission in our portion of *Shelaḥ* was the straw that broke the camel's back: the egregious sin of the spies. The tragedy of the evil report of ten out of twelve "princes" of Israel on that fateful ninth day of Av – subsequently the memorial day of both destroyed Temples – reverberates throughout Jewish history, and for good reason! How can a people whose entire raison d'être was to enter the Land of Israel to unfold their destiny as a holy nation suddenly turn around and subvert this goal because of an intelligence report! How can the grandchildren of Abraham, whose first command from God was "Get thee forth from thy land, thy birthplace, thy father's house to the land [of Israel] which I shall show thee," cast aside the greatest goal of the patriarchs and matriarchs, of Joseph, Moses, and Aaron, and decide to choose the desert over the land? How can the generation which witnessed the stupendous miracles of the Egyptian plagues and the splitting of the Reed Sea throw out the entire book of Genesis, whose closing verses, although framed in Egypt, leave no doubt in anyone's mind as to the ultimate direction of the Jewish people?

> And Joseph said unto his brethren: "I die, but God will surely remember you, and bring you up out of this land unto the land which He swore to Abraham, to Isaac, and to Jacob." And Joseph took an oath of the children of Israel saying, "God will surely remember you and you shall carry up my bones from here [to be buried in the Land of Israel]."
>
> Genesis 50:24–25

How then is it possible for the Israelites to suddenly abandon their destiny just because conquering the land is not risk-free?

To understand what's going on we have to consider the figure who, together with Joshua, resisted the trampling of the defectors, and assumed the task of spokesman for the side of the angels: Caleb ben Yefuneh.

When the report of the scouts was finally presented to the nation, the wondrous fruits of a land of milk and honey took a back seat and were even rendered meaningless when contrasted with the fear-inducing detailed deception of the dangerous types that inhabited the terrain, the giant Ḥittites, Jebusites, and Amorites (Numbers 13:28). Alone among the spies, Caleb stepped forward and " stilled the people toward Moses and said, 'We should go up at once and possess it [the land] for we are well able to overcome it'" (Numbers 13:30). Take note that while the basic report emphasized "them," the huge inhabitants, Caleb emphasized "it," the land, totally ignoring the daunting gentile nations. From his perspective, "it" is our only homeland; we are well able to overcome all obstacles – because we must! The masses responded by switching the subject away from the land and back to the strength of its inhabitants: "We are not able to go against *those people,* for they are stronger than we" (Numbers 13:31).

Why was the people's attention turned towards the inimical local population, and why did they seem apathetic about the drama and destiny hidden behind every slab of stone and scintilla of sand in the Holy Land of Israel? How is it possible that the princes of the tribes could have so easily forgotten the goals of Genesis, the vision of our forebears, the patrimony of our patriarchs?

"What happened to our forebears prefigures the experiences of their children," teaches Nahmanides, as the central principle of his biblical commentary. And in the instance of the fundamental question we are asking, the answer is clearly written on the faces and in the deeds of present-day Israeli leadership. Just as there were two radically different ways of viewing Israel then, close to thirty-five hundred years ago, within the group of the twelve scouts, so there are two radically different ways of viewing Israel today, in the most modern halls of debate.

Apparently, the traumatic events in Egypt, the 210 years of slavery culminating in an unexpected, miraculous escape, were so overwhelming that the vast majority of the people began to look upon the Exodus as the beginning of their newfound existence! Indeed, the very first of their newly received and enthusiastically accepted divine commandments was, "This month shall be unto you the beginning of months" (Exodus 12:2); a new era was at hand, the first day of the rest of their lives, and the first of the months of the year would henceforth be Nisan, the anniversary of the Exodus.

The new nation had little time for the memories of those remote grandparents Abraham, Isaac, and Jacob. At best they remained relics of an irrelevant past, their staffs and robes, coins and shards, featured in special exhibits of the Lower East Nile museum. The Israelites saw themselves as proud Exodus Jews, relegating the book of Genesis to a primary source for scholars of ancient history. But the land so lovingly described and so hauntingly yearned for in the book of Genesis had no practical application for most of the survivors of the Egyptian enslavement, for the majority of the heroes of the Exodus. Their immediate logistical question was whether or not the Israelites had a military advantage, the charms and traditions of a particular land notwithstanding. If there was no clear military edge, then there was no point to continuing. Besides, they might very well make do in the desert, or even return to the exile of Egypt!

But not Caleb. It's not that he rejected the report as an exaggeration. On the contrary, he was there, and could vouch for every word. But he carried another spirit within the essence of his being, the spirit of the land of his ancestors, the pull of the God-given destiny of his nation.

Initially when Moses directed the tribal leaders to embark on their "spy" mission, every reference was in the plural, as it should be, since the text deals with the twelve scouts. But at one point, in mid-verse, we find the following switch: "And they went up into the south, but he came (*vayavo*) unto Ḥebron" (Numbers 13:22). Rashi, the greatest and most popularly studied of our commentaries, explains, "Caleb alone went there, and prostrated himself on the graves of the ancestors."

Clearly our sage interpreter is attempting to explain the source for the unique position of Caleb, and suggests that he understood that the Exodus could only have emerged from the matrix which was Genesis, that the source of the strength of the heroes who jumped into the Reed Sea was the teachings of Abraham, Isaac, and Jacob. Caleb's nation was not born in Egypt; it was born in Ḥebron, Israel! Hence, in the very next chapter, when God punished the entire generation because of the sin of the spies – "Surely they shall not see the land which I swore unto their fathers" – He made one notable exception: "But my servant Caleb, because he had another spirit... him will I bring into the land" (Numbers 14:23–24). What kind of spirit? I would submit the spirit of the love of the land and fealty to the vision of the patriarchs of Israel!

In effect, the ideological struggle today in Israel can be seen as a great divide between the Jews whose sense of history goes back to Abraham, and to Ḥebron, with a deep historical and cultural attachment to the land of Jerusalem and to our Bible, and those who call themselves Israelis, for whom the year 1948 represents a new beginning and a new culture, whose epicenter is Tel Aviv and whose national literature is Amos Oz and Shulamit Har Even.

If indeed, our history only begins in 1948, the Palestinians fit into the landscape of the Muslim Middle East much better than we do, and perhaps we ought to resurrect Uganda in order to realize our national aspirations, God forbid. Only if we recognize our four-thousand-year-old roots in this land do we deserve to have finally come home – and no nation willingly gives up its homeland, especially after experiencing the cruel vulnerability of a homelessness whose most cruel expression was the Holocaust. The ten scouts were Exodus Israelis; Caleb and Joshua were also Genesis Jews. Caleb looked back to Abraham; we need Israeli-Jewish leadership which will look back to Caleb!

A Moslem Postscript – And a Dire Warning to Israel

Salah Ta'amri is a most articulate and well-educated Palestinian leader, a former member of the Palestinian National Council in charge of the Arab villages in Judea in the days of Yasser Arafat. He takes a moderate position on Middle Eastern affairs, even suggesting a two-state solution. He was captured by the Israelis soon after the outbreak of the First Lebanon War, and during his brief prison term he taped many dialogues with the Israeli columnist Aharon Barnea; from these taped discussions emerged a book, *My Enemy, My Friend*.

He was released from prison. Unfortunately, as the member of the Palestinian National Commission in the 1990s responsible for the Arab villages bordering on Efrat, he did everything he could to foil the people-to-people expressions of friendship, sport-meets, and business associations which had begun to take place between the Palestinian villagers and the residents of Efrat. In 1995, after having partnered with the mukhtar of Vadi Nis to send a young, bright Palestinian to medical school, I received an initial gift of $250,000 to begin an emergency clinic in Vadi Nis, with the newly-minted doctor as resident physician. The Palestinians I was dealing with were summarily imprisoned; the medical supplies I obtained for them were "returned to sender." After innumerable telephone calls – and a meeting with Yasser Arafat – Ta'amri set up a meeting with me in his Bethlehem office. "You're an ugly Israeli," he growled at me. "You want to help the Palestinians? First leave Efrat; then get out of Jerusalem; then exit from Tel Aviv." "What about your book, your two-state solution?" I asked. That was when he believed that Israel could win militarily, he explained; now he was convinced that Israel would lose. Why? Two days before his release from the Israeli prison, he told me, he was exercising in the prison courtyard and he saw the Israeli prison guard eating a pita and falafel. "How dare you eat a pita today?" he asked. "I'm still the guard, you're still the prisoner," answered the Israeli. "I tell you what to eat; you don't tell me what to eat!" "But it's the fourth day of the Festival of Passover," said Salah Ta'amri. "The Bible forbids Jews from eating bread on Pesaḥ for seven full days." Responded the prison guard: "I don't give a damn about what a book written four thousand years ago has to say about what I can and cannot eat." Salah Ta'amri then looked at me with blazing eyes, and what follows is my recollection of his words, which seared through my soul: "At that moment, I experienced an epiphany; I knew the Israelis would lose the war to the Palestinians. If the Israelis don't care about what the Bible says about Passover, they won't care about what the Bible says about Israel either – and you Israelis will need a lot of motivation to fight for Israel. You're in a tough neighborhood where you're not wanted. Without the biblical motivation, you don't stand a chance."

Seeing Is Not Believing: It Is Believing Which Determines What, and How, One Sees

We were like grasshoppers in our [own] eyes, so that was how we appeared in their eyes.

NUMBERS 13:33

How could the scouts have so unfairly undermined their own prowess and the prowess of the Israelite nation? Remember that these same scouts, who were princes of their respective tribes, had once been part of a bedraggled, besmirched, and beaten-down collection of slave laborers who stood up to the mighty empire of Egypt – and emerged victorious! The leaders of this newly formed and emergent nation had just seen with their own eyes the divine might unleashed against the Egyptian totalitarian despot and his immoral, slavery-based society, a host of miracles starting with the Nile River turning into blood with its climax their successful escape, the splitting of the Reed Sea that resulted in the drowning of the entire Egyptian cavalry. After such unrivalled military successes, how could they have concluded that it would not be possible to conquer the land? If they didn't believe in their own strength, surely they should have believed in the strength they would derive from God?

Furthermore, God Himself had told them – back when He first promised to extricate them from Egypt – that "I shall bring you to the land which I lifted My hand in oath to give to Abraham, to Isaac, to Jacob, and which I shall give to you as an everlasting inheritance for your descendants" (Exodus 6:5). At the very least, the Egyptian experience should have taught them that even the weakest of peoples derives unimaginable strength when its chief commander is the Almighty Himself! To be alone with God is always to be with a majority of One!

The Bible's unique usage of specific verb forms to create ideational connections provides what I believe to be the solution to our problem regarding the scouts of nearly four thousand years ago, as well as to our national problem today. The verb form "*ure'item*," you (plural) shall see or look upon, appears three times in the Pentateuch, and two of those times are in our biblical portion of *Shelaḥ*. The first is in the instructions Moses gives the scouts, "You shall see [or look upon] the land, as to which qualities it contains" (Numbers 13:18), and the second is found in the passage of the ritual fringes, "You shall see [look upon] the fringes and remember all the commandments of the Lord" (Numbers 15:39).

Once again, in addition to the verb "*tur*," which appears with regard to both the land and the ritual fringes, we see a fascinating linguistic parallel between the incident of the sin of the scouts and the commandment of ritual fringes. Obviously there must be a connection between these two passages, but what is it?

Both passages deal with the sense of sight, whose subtext grapples with the underlying question as to whether seeing is merely an ocular and therefore an objective exercise – as in "seeing is believing" – or whether one's subjective attitudes and preferences color those objects or events which we perceive and significantly influence our perception of them, which is "believing will color your seeing." You shall look upon the land – and you shall see the promised and desired land of your forefathers, of your patrimony, of your divine mission; you shall look upon the ritual fringes of the garment covering one's body – and you shall see not the physical and erotic aspects of the physicality beneath, but rather the blue-white of the heavens, the throne of divine glory, the 613 commandments of divine Torah. (The Hebrew word *tzitzit* is numerically six hundred, with the five knots and eight strings on each garment corner adding up to 613.)

And here the case in point is the nature of the inhabitants of Canaan whom the scouts were now observing. Who and what did they see? The Bible records: "And all of the people whom we saw on it [the land] were people of great dimensions.... We saw there the giants" (Numbers 13:32–33). And then later on we read, "And so one individual [scout] said to the other, 'Let us make a [new] leader and return to Egypt'" (Numbers 14:4).

However only one generation later, when Joshua, Moses' successor, conquered the Land of Canaan with the Israelites, he also sent out scouts who were guarded and hidden by Raḥab, and who saw the very same people:

> And she [Raḥab] said to the men, "I know that the Lord is giving this land to you and that fear of you has fallen upon us; all of the inhabitants of the land are melting before you."
>
> Joshua 2:9

The Israelites even declared in Moses' song at the Reed Sea, shortly before the scouts were dispatched: "A trembling fear grasped the inhabitants of Philistine" (Exodus 15:14). Will the real nature of the inhabitants of Canaan express itself?

The truth is that just as "beauty is in the eye of the beholder," that is, in the subjective sight of the individual, so is everything else. Our Torah portion actually explains what lay behind the exaggerated report of the scouts concerning the physical prowess of the Canaanites. It was a result of the Israelites having compared themselves to grasshoppers. The real sin of the scouts was that they stopped believing in themselves, in their mission, in their covenant with God. Bereft of their relationship with God, they saw themselves as grasshoppers; as a consequence the Canaanites saw them as they saw themselves, and the "grasshoppers" saw the Canaanites as giants.

There is a well-known Mishna in *Avot* (*Ethics of the Fathers* 5:25) which says it all:

> Turn [the Bible] over and over again, for everything is in it. And by means [of Torah] shall you look....

So did Rabbi Shraga Feivel Mendelovitz, the headmaster of the Torah Vadaat Academy, translate the passage: One must look out at the world with Torah eyeglasses, and view every person and phenomenon with a Torah outlook. It is incorrect to say that "seeing is believing"; it is more correct to say that "believing is seeing," since our beliefs profoundly affect our visual perceptions. Did the Reed Sea split, or was the low tide of the "strong easterly wind" responsible for the safe crossing of the Israelites? Was the Six-Day War a divinely wrought miracle or was it rather a function of the dismally poor military capacity of the Arab world? Are we Israelis occupying someone else's land *by right of our strength,* or are we inhabiting areas which have been ours for the past four thousand years and were guaranteed to us in the Covenant of the League of Nations and contained in the Treaty of Versailles *by the strength of our historic rights*? It all depends upon how we view history, how we view ourselves, and how we view the divine covenant!

When Does God Reject Repentance?

Do not go up because the Lord is not within you.
NUMBERS 14:42

The ten scouts who returned with an evil report were killed in a plague, and the bitter announcement that the Israelites would wander for forty years in the desert, where that generation would die out without entering the Promised Land, had been heard by all. And then came a startling turnaround, at least on the part of some of the nation.

Upon hearing what God had in store for them, the people had a change of heart, and seemingly attempted real repentance by changing course:

> And they rose early in the morning, and began climbing toward the top of the mountain, declaring, "We are here, and we will go up unto the place that God promises, for we have sinned."
> Numbers 14:40

But instead of their change of heart being greeted with joy, Moses warned them not to go up to the mountain. He uttered a series of distinct warnings: "Why are you going *against* God's word?… Do *not* proceed. God is *not* with you…. *Do not* be killed by your enemies…. You have gone away from God, and now God will *not* be with you" (Numbers 14:41–43).

Ordinarily one warning should have been enough, but Moses kept driving home the message that their decision was dangerous. But the Israelites did not listen, and their sudden enthusiasm turned into disaster as they ended up being attacked and destroyed by the Amalakites and Canaanites who swooped down upon them.

From the perspective of repentance being the admission of one's transgression, and complete repentance being correcting one's misdeed in actual practice, it's difficult to understand Moses' rejection of the people's "remorse." Isn't it paradoxical that when at least some of the Israelites finally decided that Moses was right all along and they were wrong, and were willing to make amends by going up to the Promised Land, they were chastised by Moses and killed by the Amalakites and Canaanites? And the very difficult word describing their manner of going up (*vaya'apilu*; Numbers 14:44) is translated by Onkelos to mean "evilly" and by Rashi to mean "insolently, impudently"; Rashi further cites the *Midrash Tanḥuma* which bases the Hebrew word on *ofel*, which means "darkness," because they acted on their own without divine permission. And we can readily understand how *Neturei Karta* and Satmar Hasidim will use this against modern Zionists, who came up to the Land of Israel without God's having sent His Messiah to bring them up; they call us Zionists *ma'apilim*, and they maintain that a terrible punishment yet awaits us.

Can it be that they are right? After all, why doesn't the Almighty accept the repentance of the *ma'apilim*?

The Sforno clarifies matters. Commenting on the word *vaya'apilu* (Numbers 14:44), he writes that the *ma'apilim* were prevented from achieving true repentance, just as Pharaoh was prevented from achieving true repentance: "Their hearts were hardened just as the heart of Pharaoh was hardened, and he [Pharaoh] did not listen to [Moses and Aaron]" (Sforno ad loc.).

Let us attempt to understand why Pharaoh's heart was hardened and he was thus barred from the possibility of repentance and forgiveness. Remember that Pharaoh hardened his own heart during the first five plagues – refusing to free the Israelite slaves no matter what. He relented after the fifth plague – but not because he understood that the Lord of the universe created every human being in His image and so abhors slavery. Pharaoh had neither changed his mind nor his idolatrous outlook; he was merely frightened of the plagues and felt that he and his Egyptian nation had suffered enough. God is always ready to accept the true penitent – but he is not ready to accept the die-hard, bigoted autocrat who has run scared! And so God hardened Pharaoh's heart and did not allow his fear to change the policy of slavery in which he still believed.

This is very similar to the case of the *ma'apilim*. God wanted the Israelites to conquer the land because they loved the land; because the initial vision of the Covenant between the Pieces, which obligated them to teach ethical monotheism to the world, was inextricably bound up with the land; because their patriarchs and matriarchs lived and died in the land; because only one nation-state, facing the challenges of a nation-state, can influence other nation-states; and because the land was their origin as well as their guidepost, their destination as well as their destiny. But these *ma'apilim* did not attempt to go up to the land because of these reasons; they hardened their hearts, which remained impervious to the beauty and history of the land. They merely feared the plague and they were terrified of dying in the desert. Hence God could not accept their "going up," which is merely an expression of their fear of divine punishment but is not at all a testimony either of their faith in God's command or of their true desire to live in the Promised Land. At least the Zionists who rallied around Theodor Herzl were certainly enamored of the land, of its biblical history, and of its historic promise.

There is also a second way of looking at Sforno's analogy. God hardened Pharaoh's heart because He had an educational master-plan which needed to be taught and learned. God wanted to teach the Israelites and the world for all generations that He – and only He – was the God of the earth (the Nile, and whatever comes forth from the earth, and the waters on earth), the atmosphere (animals, locusts, darkness, etc.), and the only arbiter over life and death. This educational message could only take place by means of the ten plagues; were the Israelites to be allowed to leave before the killing of the firstborn, for example, the climax of the lesson would have been missed!

This sheds a totally new perspective on the incidents in our Torah reading. It must be noted that initially, when Moses dispatched the scouts, there were two possibilities: either the Jews would attempt to conquer the Land of Israel (which was Moses' goal) or they would return to Egypt (as Datan and Aviram wanted). And so the evil report declared that their preference was to return to Egypt: "let us make a leader, and let us return to Egypt" (Numbers 14:2–4).

At this point God realized, as it were, that if the Israelites could still prefer the certainty of slavery over the challenge of freedom, then they were still ruled by an immature mentality which pushed them to "escape from freedom"; they lacked the necessary independence to undertake the challenge of conquering and settling a land, of taking their own destiny into their hands. Obviously, then, they were not yet ready for freedom.

This was the purpose of the third alternative provided by God and Moses: the forty-year sojourn in the desert. Wandering in the desert, camping from place to place, still protected by God but nevertheless within a difficult climate of uncertainty, was not so much a punishment as an educational experience. The desert was to wean the Israelites away from Pharaoh, to teach them to begin to order their own lives without military battles, and so to prepare them for independence.

This divine alternative frightened the Israelites even more. They would have neither the dream of Israel nor the security of Egypt. Hence they decided to go up to the land anyway, not realizing that it was too late, that the rules of the game had changed. God had decided they were not yet ready for Israel; the necessary prerequisite to national sovereignty had to be a forty-year course in living in this desert. Indeed, God did forgive the Jews – and he wasn't punishing them. He was merely teaching them, just as the plagues had taught them. He realized that they were not yet ready for the challenge of independence in Israel.

Koraḥ

Good and Bad Controversies

And Koraḥ took…
NUMBERS 16:1

Is controversy a positive or a negative phenomenon? Since the ideal of peace is so fundamental to the Jewish ideal – to such an extent that we even greet and bid farewell to each other with the Hebrew word *shalom*, peace – I would expect that controversy would be universally condemned by our classical sources. But apparently there is a way to argue and a way not to argue. The Mishna in *Avot* (*Ethics of the Fathers* 5:20) distinguishes between two types of controversy: "A controversy which is for the sake of heaven, like that of Hillel and Shammai, will ultimately continue to exist; a controversy which is not for the sake of heaven, like that of Koraḥ and his cohorts, will not continue to exist."

In addition to the problematic issue of the positive description of a "controversy for the sake of heaven," it is difficult to understand why the Mishna refers to one type of controversy as that of Hillel and Shammai, the two antagonists, and the other as that of Koraḥ and his cohorts, rather than Koraḥ and Moses, which we would have expected.

I believe that the answer to our questions lies in the two legitimate definitions of the Hebrew word for controversy, *maḥloket*: Does it mean to divide (*leḥalek*) or to distinguish (*la'asot ḥiluk*), to make a separation or a distinction? The former suggests an unbridgeable chasm, a great divide which separates out, nullifies the view of the other, whereas the latter suggests an analysis of each side in order to give a greater understanding of each view and perhaps even in order to eventually arrive at a synthesis or a dialectic, a resolution of both positions!

With this understanding, the initial comment of Rashi on the opening words of this Torah portion, "And Koraḥ took," becomes indubitably clear. "He took himself to the other side to become separated out from the midst of the congregation." Since Koraḥ made a great divide between himself and Moses, the Mishna in *Avot* defines his controversy as that of Koraḥ and his cohorts; he was interested in nullifying rather than in attempting to understand the side of Moses. On the other hand, when the Talmud describes the disputes between Hillel and Shammai, it decides that:

> These and those [both schools] are the words of the living God. If so, then why is the law decided in accord with the school of Hillel? Because they are pleasant and accepting, always teaching their view together with the view of the school of Shammai and even citing the position of Shammai before citing their own position.
>
> *Eruvin* 13b

According to this view, "these and those [conflicting opinions] are the words of the living God," the Almighty initially and purposefully left many issues of the Oral Tradition open-ended in order to allow for different opinions, each of which may well be correct when viewed from the perspective of the divine. Indeed the Mishna in *Eduyot* teaches that the reason our Oral Tradition records the minority as well as the majority opinion is because a later *Sanhedrin* (Jewish supreme court) can overrule the decision of an earlier *Sanhedrin*, even though it is not greater than the earlier one in wisdom or in number, as long as there is a minority view recorded on which the later *Sanhedrin* may rely for its reversal of the earlier decision; and most halakhic decisions rely on a minority decision in cases of stress and emergency (Mishna *Eduyot* 1:5, Maimonides and Ra'avad ad loc.). In the world of halakha, minority dissenting views are never nullified; these opinions are also part of the religio-legal landscape, and can become the normative law of the majority at another period in time or for a different and difficult individual situation within the same period.

The Talmud likewise powerfully and poignantly confirms the importance of dissenting views in order to challenge and help clarify the alternate opinion. R. Yoḥanan and Resh Lakish were brothers-in-law and study partners who debated their conflicting opinions on almost every branch of Talmudic law. When Resh Lakish died, R. Yoḥanan was left distraught and bereft. R. Elazar b. Pedat, a great scholar, tried to comfort R. Yoḥanan by substituting for Resh Lakish as his learning companion.

> Every opinion that R. Yoḥanan would offer, R. Elazar would confirm with a Tannaitic source. R. Yoḥanan lashed out, "Are you like the son of Lakish? Not at all! Previously, whenever I would give an opinion, the son of Lakish would ask twenty-four questions and I would answer him with twenty-four responses; in such a fashion, the legal discussion became enlarged and enhanced. But you only provide me with supporting proofs. Don't I know that my opinions have merit?" R. Yoḥanan walked aimlessly, tore his garments and wept without cease. He cried out, "Where are you, son of Lakish, where are you, son of Lakish," until he lost his mind. The other sages requested divine mercy, and R. Yoḥanan died.
>
> *Bava Metzia* 84a

This fundamental respect for the challenge of alternative opinions – so basic to the Talmudic mind – is rooted in another Mishna (*Sanhedrin* 37a), which sees the greatness of God in the differences among individuals and the pluralism of ideas. "Unlike an individual who mints coins from one model and every coin is exactly alike, the Holy One blessed be He has fashioned every human being in the likeness of Adam, and yet no human being is exactly like his fellow! … And just as the appearances of human beings are not alike, so are the ideas of human beings not alike." It is precisely in everyone's uniqueness that we see the greatness of the Creator.

This great truth was one of the teachings of Rabbi Avraham Yitzḥak HaKohen Kook, who claimed that multiplicity of ideas is actually the key to understanding God's truth:

> "Scholars increase peace in the world." A multiplicity of peace means that all sides and all views must be considered; then it will be clarified how each one of them has its place, each one in accordance with its value, its place, and its specific issue…. Only through a collection of all parts and all details, all of those ideals which appear to be different, and all disparate professional opinions, only be means of these will the light of truth and righteousness be revealed, and the wisdom of the Lord, and His love, and the light of true Torah.
>
> *Ein Ayah*, end of *Berakhot*

Holiness Must Be Achieved

The entire congregation is holy.
NUMBERS 16:3

Koraḥ stages a rebellion against Moses; hence he is the adversary and antithesis to Moses, pictured by the subsequent sages and commentaries as the personification of a unique evil in the world. But unlike the serpent in the Garden of Eden, Koraḥ stands tall not only with two legs, but with a powerful and convincing argument as well: a position which echoes throughout history.

Koraḥ says to Moses and Aaron, "You have gone too far. The entire congregation is holy, and has God in their midst. Why are you setting yourselves above God's congregation?" (Numbers 16:3). After all, on the surface his argument appears to be both logical and just.

Indeed, did not Moses himself command the nation, "You shall become holy" (Leviticus 19:2)? And the Koraḥ Defense Committee would maintain that if, in fact, everyone is equally holy, leadership becomes a mere function of opportunity; affirmative action must become the order of the day. The era of the old guard rule (Moses' family) must come to an end; Koraḥ's family must be given its chance to express its inherent holiness!

True, God revealed Himself to Moses at the Burning Bush, and spoke directly only to him; but perhaps, if Koraḥ had been raised in the palace of the pharaohs, and if he had had the opportunity as a free man of princely background to slay the Egyptian task-masters, undoubtedly God would be speaking to him as well. After all, we are all holy! It's just that some have received more special opportunities than others!

On the surface, Koraḥ's words contain a glib truth.

In reality, however, Koraḥ and Moses represent two different ways of looking at the world, two different philosophies of life. When Moses brought down the Torah on Sinai, God did not declare everyone to be holy; after all, He created a world in which Cain had killed Abel and Pharaoh had enslaved an entire nation. What God did do was to place into the world the possibility of achieving holiness. "You shall become holy," he commanded – in future tense, in potential, and only by means of arduous commitment to a lifestyle of 613 commandments. "All families of the earth shall be blessed by you" – but only if you live by My word and become a light unto the nations! "The formation of the heart of humanity is evil from its inception" – but since humanity is also created in the image of God, the evil can be overcome and holiness can reign supreme. However, this depends on how you live and how you act. "I have set before you this day life and death, good and evil. Choose life." Your deeds become the cardinal factor determining whether or not you've achieved holiness; meritocracy, not affirmative action, rules the day!

Now when Koraḥ argued that everyone was holy, that he too could have achieved what Moses achieved had he only had the proper opportunity, was he defending holiness or uprooting holiness? After all, if everyone and everything is holy, then the word "holy" loses its meaning. By arguing for holiness in the way that he did – holiness now – Koraḥ was really arguing against holiness. We need not work for it, or strive to achieve it. We already are!

And perhaps this is why the Midrash pictures Koraḥ as taunting Moses on the commandments of tzitzit (ritual fringes) and mezuza, the two commandments dealing with the most basic human needs and expressions: clothing and shelter. Does a garment which is wholly *tekhelet* still require a thread of *tekhelet* in its ritual fringes? Does a house filled with Torah scrolls still require a mezuza (which has only a small portion of a Torah scroll) on its doorpost? And when Moses replied in the affirmative, Koraḥ laughed at the lack of logic in Moses' teaching!

But Koraḥ missed the point. Moses was teaching that the human being must constantly strive to improve, to become more holy than he was before; humans must never dare rest on their laurels, because evil is always lying in wait to ensnare, even at the mouth of the grave. Hence even a house filled with Torah scrolls still requires a mezuza at the front door, and even a garment which is wholly *tekhelet* still requires ritual fringes. Never be complacent, always remain on guard and strive to add another dose of sanctity.

The twentieth century had more than its share of "we are holy" philosophies, letting it all hang out, sanctifying every instinct and thought. It doesn't matter if it was Norman O. Brown or Herbert Marcuse of the Living Theater, the rage in the Western world has been to free the id from the prison of the superego, and if the id is holy, then everything must be holy. But behind such views of an "anything-goes" holiness, nothing goes. If everything is special, nothing is special.

Fundamentally, Koraḥ was saying that "as is" is holy – because nothing can change, grow, or develop. And that is the meaning of Koraḥ's name. The Hebrew root K-R-Ḥ can either mean bald – and no hair grows on a bald head – or ice, and no vegetation developed during the Ice Age. "As is his name, so is he." Koraḥ rejected the command to become holy, the command of meritocracy, because he was cynically scornful of one's ability to grow and develop and change and inspire.

But Moses' (and God's) approach is different.

When Moses announced to the rebels the means by which God would determine who was holy to Him, he had Koraḥ and his men bring fire in the fire pans and offer incense. Fire symbolizes the possibility of change, but only after a specific process takes place: by means of heat, the hardest materials can be made to bend and melt, can be transformed from solid to liquid and to many states in between. Incense changes the environment; its sweet-smelling fragrance can remove the rancid odor of death and decay, can transform the slaughtered carcasses of the animal sacrifices into an experience of commitment to God which can perfect – and perfume – the world. Moses' vision was one of optimistic faith, the rising flames which bring out the fragrance of the incense and soar heavenward to the divine. Material objects, humanity, the very world can be changed, elevated, sanctified – but it depends on merit, on commitment, on achievement!

Koraḥ's punishment and death fit his crime and philosophy. Koraḥ and his cohorts were swallowed alive by the earth. From the perspective of the earth and the grave, all who enter its bowels are equal. The earth makes no distinctions, remains oblivious to titles or accomplishments. The earth is the ultimate "equal-opportunity employer." After one is buried underground, there is no longer any possibility of change or growth.

The *parasha*'s final proof that Aaron was the one chosen by God – and the symbolism which serves as the crowning proof of our thesis – involves the command to write the names of each of the tribes' leaders on twelve staffs, to be placed in the Tent of Communion before the Ark of Testimony. The next day Aaron's staff, representing the house of Levi, had blossomed, giving forth leaves and almonds, as if it were a tree. And a tree is the most basic symbol of that which grows and develops. After this, God said to Moses that no one should ever again deny the authority of Aaron's priesthood.

Koraḥ, Our "Holy Grandfather": Is "Holiness Achieved" a Desirable End-Game?

> *And they assembled themselves together against Moses and Aaron, and said unto them: "You take too much upon you, for the entire congregation is holy..."*
>
> NUMBERS 16:3

Koraḥ, the arch-rebel against Moses and the Aaronic priestly leadership, is usually regarded as an evil, if brilliant, scoundrel, who received the just desserts of his mutiny when he and his followers were swallowed up by the earth. But there is an alternate, almost radical view of Koraḥ which also exists, specifically in the Hasidic tradition. The famed Kotzker Rebbe used to refer to him as "our holy grandfather," "*unzer heilige zeide.*" What could this sage possibly have had in mind? Will the real Koraḥ please stand up? From the usual, more traditional perspective, the very first word in our Torah portion establishes Koraḥ's true character: "*Vayikaḥ Koraḥ ben Yitzhar ben Kehat ben Levi veDatan veAviram bnei Eliav,"* "and Koraḥ the son of Yitzhar, the son of Kehat, the son of Levi, with Datan and Aviram, the sons of Eliav… took" (Numbers 38:1). The Torah doesn't spell out exactly what it was that he "took," since no object for the verb in question appears in the text. This leads Rashi to quote the *Midrash Tanḥuma*: "And Koraḥ took: he took himself to one side with the intention of separating himself from the community so that he might raise a protest regarding the [validity of the authority of the] priesthood." But there may also be a more general interpretation to this opening verse. Despite the fact that Koraḥ uses noble and inspiring language by invoking the democracy of sanctity – "all the congregation are holy, every one of them, and God is among them; why then do you lift yourselves above the assembly of the Lord?" (Numbers 16:3) – he was merely couching self-serving ambition in idealistic words. If that which sums up all of Koraḥ's true motivations is the verb "and he took" – minus the objective case – then Koraḥ was a "taker"; his real desire was to *take* the leadership away from Moses and Aaron, to *take* the leadership for himself!

But if that is the case, how can we understand the appellation which the Kotzker Rebbe bestowed upon Koraḥ, "our holy grandfather"?

In his work *Pri Tzaddik,* Rabbenu Tzadok HaKohen of Lublin studies this alternative view of Koraḥ, revealing what the Kotzker Rebbe might have had in mind when he called Koraḥ holy, *"unzer heilige zaide."*

In his explanation, the *Pri Tzaddik* alerts us to a concept of creation found in the teachings of the Ari HaKadosh. The Ari speaks of two ways of looking at human communities; linear (*yashar*) or circular (*igulim*). In a circle, everyone is equally distributed, the distance between the center and the edges is always the same, and everyone is equally important; there is neither head nor tail. But a linear format expresses something quite different: there are those who progress more rapidly, those who progress less rapidly, and those who hardly progress at all.

How does this relate to Koraḥ? The *Pri Tzaddik* cites a Talmudic passage at the conclusion of *Ta'anit* (31a): "In the days to come, God will hold a circle for the righteous. He will sit in their midst in the Garden of Eden, and everyone will point with his finger towards Him." Apparently the Talmud is teaching us that at some point in the future, "when all the wicked of the earth will be turned to You [God] and everyone will accept upon themselves the yoke of Your kingship" (the *Aleinu* prayer), at the time of universal repentance and redemption, then all of humanity will sit in a circle in which everyone will be equidistant from or rather equi-near to God, with no need for a head table and a rear guard. The Divine Presence will rest upon every individual equally.

Although the Talmud speaks of this stage of "circularity" as being reserved for the World to Come, the period of the culmination of history, Koraḥ apparently maintained that the thunder, lightning, and divine Revelation at Sinai were indeed the signposts of that new era – the exodus of a lineal society and the entrance of a new circular (or *igul*) reality. With Sinai, Koraḥ believed that humans had become transformed into angels, everyone had been equally infused with the divine spirit, from serving-maid to prophet, and that equality was the order of the "new day."

This is what the Midrash means when it has Koraḥ mock Moses for insisting that a prayer-shawl completely made of *tekhelet* (purple-blue dye) still requires a thread of purple-blue in its fringes and that a house filled with Torah scrolls still requires the Torah portion of the mezuza on its doorposts. The Jews post-Sinai, argued Koraḥ, are to be compared to a garment which is wholly *tekhelet* (purple-blue), to a house filled with Torah scrolls. In the light of such all-encompassing spirituality, a single ritual fringe or a lone parchment scroll hardly seems necessary or salutary; indeed, the commandments – whose purpose was, after all, to bring us close to God – are superfluous, and no longer mandatory.

In this reading, Koraḥ represents a pattern that would constantly repeat itself in Jewish history; various "religious" figures and their representatives would claim that the millennium is at hand, the circular model is about to be enacted and therefore the ritual commandments could be seen as unnecessary and might be abrogated. Christianity adopted this philosophy, insisting that divine grace equalized humanity and rendered halakhic fealty – commitment to religio-legal details – anachronistic; this was the position of Shabbetai Tzvi, who himself claimed to be the Messiah, as well as of Reform Judaism from a certain perspective, which taught that the Enlightenment together with nationalism predicated upon universal human rights had rendered ritualistic religion obsolete. The *Pri Tzaddik* – and the Kotzker Rebbe – would argue that Koraḥ must have felt this way because he himself had become so inspired and infused with sanctity as a result of the Revelation at Sinai that he had truly emerged as the holy grandfather. Unfortunately, however, he misread the status of the Israelite nation in general. The people at large was not yet ready, had not yet left the linear reality for the circular millennium; indeed the Israelites were yet to serve the Golden Calf and refuse to conquer the Land of Israel.

The Jewish people were still in the desert, surrounded by a linear reality replete with successes and failures, progress and retrogress, leaders and followers, righteous religionists and hypocritical charlatans. The all-purple-blue prayer shawl still requires the one thread of purple-blue *tekhelet*; even the house filled with Torah scrolls still requires the single mezuza parchment. After all, such shawls and such houses are the exception rather than the rule. The commandment is "you shall become holy." Yes, we are a people of *becoming*, not yet (perhaps never yet) of *being*; perhaps the most important commandment is the very striving, the striving which spurs us on to ever greater heights. Moses understood; Koraḥ did not.

Two Different and Distinct Rebellions against Moses

> *The earth opened its mouth and swallowed them.... A flame came forth from the Lord and consumed the 250 bearers of incense.*
>
> NUMBERS 16:32

Rebellion against Moses! The situation in the desert goes from bad to worse in this Torah portion, descending from a rebellion against God's will and Moses' religio-political objective by the refusal of the Israelites to conquer Israel (the sin of the scouts) to an actual mutiny against Moses the leader. Fear of a powerful enemy which can even overwhelm – and subvert – the anticipated goal of entering the Promised Land might be understandable; but why would so many Israelites be willing to push aside the many miracles of the Exodus from Egypt and display such ingratitude to a leader who was Mandela magnified a hundredfold? After all, Moses took an oppressed and enslaved people, and at enormous personal sacrifice forged them into a God-enthused, human-being-sensitized, responsible, and independent nation! Why rebel against Moses?

To deepen our enquiry, it would appear that there were two rebellions, not one; and two different causes for rebellion, at that. The key to understanding what really caused the desert mutinies emanates from an insight expressed by the medieval biblical commentator, Ibn Ezra, who picks up on the fact that there were two different punishments meted out to the rebels: "the earth opened its mouth and swallowed up" one group (Numbers 16:32), and "a flame came forth from the Lord and consumed the 250 bearers of incense," the other group (Numbers 16:35). And there is even a difference of opinion as to with which group to include Koraḥ! Writes Ibn Ezra:

> There are those who say that Koraḥ was amongst those swallowed up by the earth ... and there are those who say that he was burnt to death.... It is my opinion that only Datan and Aviram were swallowed up by the earth and Koraḥ [was burnt together with] the incense bearers.
>
> Ibn Ezra on Numbers 16:35

Let us revisit the biblical text and attempt to reconstruct what actually occurred – as well as the characters' motivations. Koraḥ may have couched his words in the palatable and persuasive tones of democracy, but he was more a demagogue than a democrat. What he was really after was the priesthood, his frustration stemming from the fact that the brothers Moses and Aaron had assumed for themselves both the kingship and priesthood respectively. "You take too much upon you," he ranted, "for the entire congregation is holy and God is in their midst; why do you raise yourselves up above the assembly of the Lord?" (Numbers 16:3).

But let us look carefully at Moses' response. Moses sees Koraḥ's mellifluous, crowd-seeking words and understands precisely what Koraḥ is really after. Koraḥ's major rebellion is against Aaron; he wants to be the High Priest! Therefore, Moses challenges Koraḥ to offer up censers with incense as a sacrifice to God, an act which is ordinarily a priestly responsibility. And therefore Moses literally charges the rebel with "seeking also the priesthood" and casting aspersions against Aaron (Numbers 16:5–11)!

This will also explain why the famed Kotzker Rebbe refers to Koraḥ as the "holy grandfather." After all, even if Koraḥ could be charged as guilty of grasping ambition, he was ambitious for a closer relationship to God, a more central role in the divine service. He, like Nadav and Avihu (the sons of Aaron) before him, wished only to bring an offering to the Lord – even if he hadn't been commanded to do so. He aspired for sanctity – but refused to accept the fact that there were divine limits upon the sacred, that one must be deemed worthy to come close to the divine, that overly zealous and fanatic individuals can perform despicable acts in God's name if they are not controlled. And so Koraḥ and his band of followers are consumed by a fire sent by God – the very punishment meted out to Nadav and Avihu, and for a very similar reason (Leviticus 10:1–3, Rashi ad loc.).

But then there was a second rebellion, which for the sake of convenience, joined up with the first. Datan and Aviram, although they banded together with Koraḥ, had an entirely different agenda. They (at least according to the Midrash – which I believe stems from this interpretation) were long-time opposers of Moses' authority as well of his religo-political agenda; they had never wanted to leave Egypt, and now they saw their opportunity to bring the Hebrews back to Egypt, to turn back the clock of Jewish history. According to the Midrash, they were the two fighting Israelites encountered by Moses at the very beginning of his career as a Hebrew, when he called out to them: "Wicked one, why do you strike your brother?" (Exodus 2:13). They refused to accept his chastisement, responding: "Who appointed you as a ruler [*sar*] and judge over us? Do you wish to slay us as you slayed the Egyptian?" (Exodus 2:14). They resented Moses having taken command, and they were perfectly content to remain in Egypt and "cooperate" with Pharaoh's policies. They had no interest in the challenges of a Jewish state in Israel. They did not see their roots as emanating from Ḥebron or their destiny as linked to Jerusalem. They wished to live in the most comfortable place – and the fleshpots of Egypt won out. They were ready to assimilate, to become true Egyptians, and were certain that after a short period, their servitude in Egypt would be over.

Moses recognized the fact that Datan and Aviram had an agenda different from that of Koraḥ; they were rebelling against him, his rule, his plan to lead the Jews to Israel – not against Aaron. He therefore asked to meet them separately (Numbers 16:12). They refused to come, saying: "Was it not enough that you took us out of the land flowing with milk and honey [sic; Egypt for them is the land flowing with milk and honey] to die in the desert that you also wish to rule over us, yes to rule!" (Numbers 16:13). And these words resonate with the challenges directed at Moses much earlier by the two Hebrew fighters, "Who appointed you ruler [*sar*] over us?" (Exodus 2:14). And when the punishment of the opening of the earth to devour the sinners was being executed, the Bible emphasizes the fact that Moses and the elders came to Datan and Aviram (Numbers 16:25); they may have lived in the dwelling place of Koraḥ, but they were not identified with him in that biblical context other than with regard to where they lived. And it was they and their families who were swallowed up by the earth (Numbers 16:26–35), even the men of Koraḥ along with them (Numbers 16:32) – *but not* Koraḥ himself! Datan and Aviram together with their cohorts certainly received their just punishment of disappearing into the earth – since it was the fruitfulness of the Land of Egypt and the materialism of the earthly existence which led to their rebellion against a prophet of God, who may have lived on earth, but who gave to his people an eternal bond with the heavenly spheres of the divine, which they did not begin to appreciate.

Koraḥ's Agenda Revisited: A Heavenly Kollel in the Desert Sands

You [Koraḥ] seek also the priesthood?
NUMBERS 16:10

What was the real attraction of Koraḥ's rebellion to all of the Hebrews, the political agenda behind the stated words of the rebels? There must have been more to Koraḥ's argument than mere personal gain, since not a single member of the congregation took a stand on behalf of Moses.

Allow me to make the following suggestion. By this time, the scouts had pretty much squelched the dream of conquering Israel – so the question that remained was where to go. There were Israelites represented by Datan and Aviram who probably never wanted to leave Egypt in the first place and now yearned to return there. They joined the chorus of the ten scouts: "It is better for us to return to Egypt…. Let us appoint a new leader and return to Egypt" (Numbers 14:4–5).

But this was clearly not Koraḥ's argument; he was coming from an altogether different place: "for the entire congregation is holy and has God in their midst. Why must you lift yourselves above the assembly of the Lord?" (Numbers 16:3). Moses charged Koraḥ with wanting to be a holy kohen (Numbers 16:10), and therefore tested Koraḥ and his group with the censers of incense.

I believe, however, that Koraḥ was going further than that; he wanted all of the Hebrews to become kohanim. After all, "the entire congregation is holy and has God in their midst" – both literally in terms of being created in God's image and figuratively in terms of their relationship to the Sanctuary and the *Shekhina*. Did not everyone hear God's voice at Sinai, and did not Moses charge the whole assembly of Israel with being a "kingdom of priests" (Exodus 19:6)? And so Koraḥ logically maintained that the best way for all the Israelites to carry out their priestly function as divine agents was to stay where they were – in the desert! Koraḥ was not rebelling against Aaron; he was rebelling against Moses, against dirtying the hands of the Israelites with the mud, the plows, the armaments, and the politics involved in forming and maintaining a nation-state.

The desert experience provided a magnificent opportunity for all Israelites to devote themselves to divine service and to the study of Torah without distractions. No one had private land to till, everyone received their portion of manna delivered to the door and their shelter in the desert booths or – even better – the clouds of glory which protected them. There was even a divinely sent cloud by day and pillar of fire by night to direct their travels. They were living in a perennial Kollel, with all their needs taken care of. What could be better than the Almighty Himself as the Kollel's dean, providing for every necessity and making every travel decision? Why leave a "sandy, serene, sacred tower" for the challenges of war, politics, and economic disparities which plague every nation-state?

So why was Koraḥ reviled and punished? I believe that it is because he didn't understand the function and purpose of a Jewish state, or the function and purpose of Torah. God doesn't only desire an exalted, "holy" nation that lives in sacred, sandy isolation. God chose Abraham to become a blessing for the world (Genesis 12:3) and revealed His Law to us so that we could teach it to all of humanity as a light unto the nations.

The true function of a kohen is to teach, and the kingdom of kohanim exists to teach the world (Exodus 19:6, Sforno ad loc.). But we can only teach others if we demonstrate that we can solve our own national, existential, and ethical problems of peace and war, capitalism and socialism ourselves, by means of the divinely bestowed wisdom of Torah.

God did not choose us to warm ourselves alone with a fur coat (a "*tzaddik in peltz*"); He chose us, rather, to light a fire which will bring the warmth of peace and security to all of humanity. This is to be done from a land where we can imbue every aspect of our agricultural, industrial, sociological, and political lives with the compassionate righteousness and moral justice of His Torah. We dare not stay in the desert; we must go up to Israel, become a nation-state, and join history! Torah is not meant to live in splendid, sandy isolation from the world and its challenges; Torah is meant to sanctify the world, the land, the army, and the economy. Torah must perfect the world, not escape from it.

And this, too, was the egregious error of Datan and Aviram. Perhaps they, too, were "religious" Hebrews who felt that the best way to influence the world would be to live in Thebes, Cairo, or New York and teach from there; hence their desire to return to Egypt. However, you cannot truly influence a nation unless you are in charge of its government, setting the foundations and limits of its societal structures. Otherwise, you become influenced and compromised by that nation which "allows" you in, and "suffers" your presence.

This is the profound lesson we must learn from Joseph, Grand Vizier of Egypt. He rose to unique, perhaps unprecedented, greatness. He even succeeded in teaching Pharaoh about *Elokim,* Creator of heaven and earth (Genesis 41:38). But when he had to discharge the economic policies of Egypt, he enslaved all of the Egyptians, making the Egyptian monarch a totalitarian despot who "owned" all of his Egyptian subjects (Genesis 47:13–27). In his service to another nation and its ruler, Joseph was forced to compromise the cardinal message of creation: that every human being, created in God's image, must be free and inviolate. The authentic and uniquely Jewish message can only be delivered from our own homeland, as a nation-state performing as a significant actor on the stage of history, with our lines expressing the eternal words of the universal God of morality and peace.

It Is the Attitude of the Dissenter Which Counts

There shall never be a dispute like that of Koraḥ and his cohorts.

NUMBERS 17:5

When is dissension and argument positive, healthy debate which is the glory of our Talmud and a healthy expression of "these and those are the words of the Living God" (*Eruvin* 13b), and when is dispute negative, a venomous cancer which can destroy the very underpinning of our nation? Apparently Koraḥ's rebellious dissent is negative, as the Talmud maintains:

> Rav said: "He who is unyielding in a dispute violates a negative command, as it is written, 'There shall never be a dispute like that of Koraḥ and his cohorts.'"
>
> *Sanhedrin* 110a, Numbers 17:5

But can we glean from this statement operative guidelines as to when it is right and when it is wrong to argue?

Rabbi Isaac Bernstein of London, in a masterful lecture, cited the Ḥatam Sofer, who claims that it is the attitude of the dissenter – and not the subject of his dissent – which makes the difference. This sage bemoans the fact that all too often, when two people argue, one (or both) of the parties involved will claim that only he or she has a direct pipeline to God; consequently he or she has the only right opinion, and the other must be delegitimized. These individuals, claiming that they are arguing "in the name of God and Torah," maintain that they can never be compared to Koraḥ, since they are defending the faith, and Koraḥ was denying the faith. However, Koraḥ also felt that he was defending God and the sanctity of every Israelite against Moses and Aaron's elitism. Moreover, the Ḥatam Sofer refers to R. Eliezer in the Talmud – who actually did have a pipeline to God (*Bava Metzia* 59b) – but was nevertheless bested in debate by the sages.

The Talmud records how R. Eliezer disagreed with his contemporaries on the status of a particular oven. He was absolutely convinced that he was right, and to prove his claim, he asked for a series of signs from heaven demonstrating the accuracy of his halakhic opinion. And the signs came from heaven, confirming R. Eliezer's position. Nevertheless, since his was a minority view in the face of a majority ruling, the *Sanhedrin* ruled against R. Eliezer (despite his signs), and his refusal to relent led to his excommunication. The case of R. Eliezer is brought to teach that even if you are certain that God is on your side, you dare not read the other view out of the realm of legitimacy.

Supporting his view, the Ḥatam Sofer reads the verse, "Do not be like Koraḥ, and his company, [who argued that] God spoke by the hand of Moses [only] to him," to Koraḥ, claiming that only Koraḥ understood God's words properly (Numbers 17:5). Those who maintain that God speaks only to them, that only they knows the truth, and that their opponent has no possibility of truth are guilty of Koraḥ's sin! Hence an illegitimate and therefore improper debate is one which seeks to delegitimize the other side, declaring that only one side possesses the whole truth!

Rabbi Bernstein further directs us to two other fascinating sources. We have a Mishna in *Sukka* with the following law:

> If a man's head and the greater part of his body were within the *Sukka* and his table was within the house, Beit Shammai declared it invalid and Beit Hillel declared it valid.... Beit Hillel says to Beit Shammai: "Was not the incident thus, that the elders of Beit Shammai and elders of Beit Hillel went to visit R. Yoḥanan the son of the Ḥorani, and they found him sitting in a *sukka* with his head and the greater part of his body within [the *sukka*], and the table inside the house and outside of the *Sukka*, and they did not make any comment about it, implying that the Academy of Shammai had acquiesced in this case to the Academy of Hillel!?" Beit Shammai said to them: "Here [specifically] is the proof [to our position]." [The elders of Beit Shammai] did say to him [R. Yoḥanan]: "If it is in such a way that you always perform [the mitzva of *sukka*], then you never [successfully] performed the commandment in your lifetime."
>
> Mishna *Sukka* 2:7

How are we to understand the Mishna? Does there not seem to be an inner contradiction within the Mishna as to whether or not the elders of Shammai did or did not comment to R. Yoḥanan about his performance of the commandment of *sukka,* or lack thereof?

This issue is addressed in the work of Rabbi Naftali of Vermaiser, the author of the commentary *Maleh Ratzon,* that deals with seemingly contradictory statements in the Talmud. He explains the Mishna as follows: the elders of Beit Shammai and the elders of Beit Hillel had indeed been present together at the *sukka* of R. Yoḥanan, and they all saw that their host conducted himself in accordance with the law of Beit Hillel. Beit Shammai, although of a different opinion than Beit Hillel, said nothing – because of their respect for Beit Hillel and because they understood the validity of a dissenting opinion different from their own. Only after the elders of Beit Hillel left the *sukka* did the elders of Beit Shammai clarify their alternative position by presenting another viewpoint. This sensitivity displayed by the representatives of the two major and opposing academies in Mishnaic times emphasizes the fundamental pluralism in the Talmud: two views may be at loggerheads, but each side must respect and learn from – rather than revile and delegitimize – their opponents without giving up their insistence upon their dissenting opinion for themselves! And two opposing sides in a debate can and must socialize with each other!

The second source that Rabbi Bernstein cites is the Lehmann Haggada, composed in the nineteenth century. Commenting on the Four Questions, Rabbi Marcus Lehmann cites Rabbi Ephraim of Lunschitz who interprets the question of "why is this night different from all other nights" in terms of "why is this exile [night is synonymous with exile and suffering] longer than any other exile." His answer is because this is the night of "matza," or dissension (see Exodus 21:22)!

Rabbi Lehmann continues:

> There has been no lack of pious and holy men and women in the many centuries of the present exile, but salvation could not appear because of the innumerable conflicts dividing the people. Sects and parties have continuously disturbed the peace of the exile.

And then he discusses the petty and trifling affairs that divided and affected the people. Even when the community reached illustrious heights there was bitter fractionalization within the structure:

> For about two hundred years the study of Talmud blossomed amongst German Jewry as never before.... Yeshivot were found in every city in which Jews dwelled, Prague, Furth, Frankfurt-am-Main, Mainz, Worms, Mannheim, Karlsruhe, Berlin, Breslau, Frankfort-am-Oder, Halberstadt, etc.... Then there arose an unholy dispute which was directed particularly against the great Rabbi Yonatan Eybeschutz. The damage caused by this dispute, and the extent to which it contributed towards dissuading young people from studying the Torah and demoralizing the ranks of the God-fearing cannot be adequately described.

Rabbi Lehmann is writing about an event that took place in the early part of the eighteenth century. But in the early twenty-first century, can we say that we have adequately absorbed the lessons of the dangers of dispute and dissension? Have Koraḥ and Koraḥ-ism truly been swallowed up by the earth, never to be heard from again? Would that it were so!

Ḥukkat

From Jerusalem to Ashes to Life Eternal

This is the statute of the law which God commanded, saying, "Speak unto the children of Israel, that they bring you a red heifer."

NUMBERS 19:1–2

One of the most profound mysteries of the Bible is the rite of the red heifer, called a *ḥok* (statute) because it belongs to the group of divine decrees which human logic cannot penetrate.

Detailed in the first twenty-two verses of our Torah reading, the ceremony certainly sounds strange to the modern ear: a heifer, which is completely red, without blemish, and upon which no yoke has been brought, shall be slaughtered outside of the encampment of Israel; cedar wood, hyssop, and a scarlet thread shall be cast into the burning pyre of ashes, and a "personage of purity" (*ish tahor*) shall gather the ashes in a sacred place, mix them with spring water (*mayim ḥayim*, waters of life) and use the mixture to purify those who have been contaminated by contact with a corpse. What can we possibly make of such a primitive-sounding ritual?

We must be mindful of the fact that all other impurities other than a death impurity find their purification by the defiled individual's immersing himself or herself in a *mikveh*, a gathering of freshly running spring water or specially collected life-giving rainwater; in effect, in all these instances, the defiled individual actually purifies him- or herself! Only in this rite of the red heifer does the kohen, representing God Himself, effectuate the purification. It is as though the Bible is teaching us that we can save ourselves from many of our weaknesses, we can rise above many of our temptations, but only God can ultimately redeem us from death.

And from this perspective, the symbolism of the red heifer ritual begins to make sense. A heifer is the consummate symbol of life, the cow's mother-milk serving as the universal expression of maternal nurturing of her young; red is likewise the color of blood, and blood is the life-force, the very *nefesh* of the living organism. However, although human beings come in various shapes, sizes, personalities, and powers – they can be as tall and proud as the cedar tree and as mean and humble as the hyssop plant – the angel of death ultimately conquers them all, because the scarlet thread of human sin condemns each of us to the common destiny of mortality.

Following the sacrifice, the personage of purity gathers the ashes of the remains, mixes them with the life-giving waters of the divine and, born-again, purified life emerges even from the surrealistic specter of death itself. Inherent in this symbolism is that historic Israel – mother nurturer of the continuity of humanity by means of the Abrahamic "compassionate rightness and moral justice" which Israel taught and must continue to teach – is destined to be slaughtered, but will always rise again to life and to the fulfillment of her mission and destiny.

This symbolism of the red heifer assumed new significance for me after a trip to Frankfurt and Berlin I took just a few years ago. Ohr Torah Stone's Joseph Straus Rabbinical Seminary has sent close to three hundred rabbis and their families to communities throughout the world, from Caesarea to Curacao to Guatemala City to Johannesburg to Lincoln Center – with eight of our graduates presently in Germany. While in Berlin, I made it my concern to visit their newly completed Holocaust Memorial at the very center of the city, not far from the last bunker from which the "mad Führer" (may his name be blotted out) committed suicide.

The open-air memorial consists of 2,711 stones, monuments of various shapes and sizes. Walking amongst the narrow, massive slabs of stone, one becomes lost within a giant cemetery, feeling helplessly and hopelessly minute and insignificant within a maze of monuments whose eerie, death-imbedded caskets seem to have overtaken world and life; I even felt a panic attack, was almost ready to scream out loud in fear and anxiety, when I saw the sight of blessed steps of exit from this mass and massive tomb. One then descends into a netherworld of hell, where pictures and stories of Holocaust victims evoke their life experiences and all of their future potential that was snuffed out, inexplicably and cruelly torn asunder from the tree of life by monstrous and subhuman hands. How many medical and scientific advances were simply burned to ashes in the death factory called Auschwitz! How many Nobel Prize winners, how many giants of humanity!

I stumbled away from the experience feeling as though I had just awakened from a horrific nightmare. The symbolism of the monuments continued to haunt me months after I returned to Efrat; after all, those who lost loved ones in the Holocaust don't even have graveside monuments to weep over. Each empty stone screams out with any name, with every name, with my name, and with my children's names, because a part of each human being was killed in those death camps whose perpetrators attempted to destroy every last vestige of humaneness.

But I also came away from the experience feeling cheated by the memorial. Something was missing, the essence was missing, the victorious ending was missing. Because, you see, the Jewish people won the war which Hitler tried to wage against us. Yes, he succeeded in destroying six million of us, but as he records in *Mein Kampf*, he wasn't waging a war against six million Jews. He was waging a war against the last Jew, against Judaism, against what he called a slave morality of compassionate righteousness and moral justice, of sensitive concern for the weaker vessels, of a God of ultimate power who insists upon human protection of the powerless. And in that war, Hitler failed!

Yes, we won that war. Alas, the brilliantly alive "red heifer," a metaphor for the Jewish people, a people who nurture the world with the milk of morality of the Ten Commandments and the milk of human kindness of "You shall love the stranger" and "You shall love your neighbor like yourself" was, to a large extent, tragically and inexplicably slaughtered beyond the "human encampment" in Auschwitz and Treblinka. But the Almighty God, the "Personage of Purity" Himself, gathered the ashes, Himself mixed them with living waters of rebirth, and Himself transformed those ashes into the fertile soil of the recreated sovereign State of Israel. And the "Personage of Purity" Himself mixed the ashes with the life-giving wellsprings of Torah, our tree of eternal life, and in addition to our national physical being, likewise revived our spiritual being, Torah centers, and *Daf Yomi* Talmud study groups to an unprecedented and unparalleled degree all over the world. In the immediate aftermath of the Holocaust, who could have predicted the rise of the State of Israel; who could have foreseen hundreds of thousands of Jews studying *Daf Yomi* every day?

Indeed, it boggles the mind to think that Judaism is reawakening even in the failed Führer's own capital city of Berlin, where three new yeshivot have been dedicated over the past several years. Imagine the historical irony of the fact that the only two growing Jewish communities in the world today are in Israel and in Germany!

And take note: there are 2,711 monument stones in the memorial, and when the artist Peter Eisenman was asked as to the significance of that number, he said there was no significance, it was purely arbitrary. However, if you check Google, you will find that there are 2,711 folio pages in the Babylonian Talmud studied in *Daf Yomi*! And this is more than coincidence. Adolf Hitler is now mercifully long dead. Curiously enough, one of his personal effects within his self-inflicted suicide bunker was the tractate *Pesaḥim*, a Gemara of the Vilna *Shas* (six orders of the Talmud) which tells of the Pesaḥ festival of Jewish freedom and redemption. The American State Department decided to give this sacred text to Rabbi Herzog, then chief rabbi of Israel, whose wife showed it to me in the early 1970s. Apparently the devil incarnate, who was obsessed with Judaism, had hoped to bury the last Talmud tome in existence. Instead the Talmud tome buried him! Indeed, 2,711 pages of the Talmud have literally walked out of the 2,711 monument stones, and have granted to the Jewish victims the eternal life of Jewish victors, who will yet teach the world the message of universal freedom and redemption which is the vision of the Pesaḥ Seder.

A Biblical and Historical Postscript

We learn from the rite of the red heifer that only God, the Personage of Purity, can redeem from death; and in our post-Holocaust generation, He has certainly done so. There ought to be a final glorious exhibit in the Berlin Holocaust Memorial which features pulsating present-day religious Jewish life in Germany, as well as a magnificent tribute to the reborn State of Israel.

> Thus says the Lord your God ... I will open your graves and cause you to come up out of your graves and bring you into the Land of Israel.... And I shall put My spirit in you and you shall live and I shall place you in your land.
>
> Ezekiel 37:13–14

The Leader Must Take Responsibility for His People

> *Speak unto the children of Israel, that they bring a red heifer, faultless, wherein there is no blemish, and upon which there never came a yoke.... And the one who gathers the ashes of the heifer must immerse his clothes; he remains ritually impure until evening.*
>
> NUMBERS 19:2–10

One of the most profound mysteries of the Torah is the law of the red heifer, a ritual by which an individual who has become ritually defiled by contact with a corpse is purified by a kohen, who sprinkles him with a mixture of burnt ashes of a completely red heifer with water, into which must be thrust a piece of cedar wood, branches of hyssop, and a scarlet thread of wool (Numbers 19:1–6).

Not only are the various ingredients of this ritual difficult to fathom, appearing to be some kind of voodoo applied by Indian medicine men (God forbid!); perhaps the strangest aspect of all is the fact that while the impure person upon whom the ashes mixture is sprinkled emerges purified, those kohanim involved in the carrying, the burning, and the thrusting of the cedar wood all become defiled. How can the very same object be a purifying agent and a defiling instrument at one and the same time? It is no wonder that our Talmudic sages applied the words of King Solomon, wisest of all mortals, "I attempted to be wise, but it only moved further away from my understanding" (Ecclesiastes 7:23), to the mystery of the red heifer.

Moreover, why does the Torah record this particular ritual here, at the conclusion of the desert sojourn of the Israelites? Rabbi Abraham ibn Ezra explains that these laws were also given at Sinai, but were included in this context because the ritual must be prepared and performed by the kohanim, within the context of *Koraḥ-Ḥukkat* which teaches about the gifts to be given to the kohanim by the Israelites once they enter Israel. But the rules of the kohanim belong much more to the books of Exodus (the portions of *Teruma, Tetzaveh, Vayak'hel,* and *Pekudei*) and Leviticus (the Holy Temple sacrificial cult) than to these stories of desert dissatisfaction, rebellion, and intrigue in the book of Numbers. Why is the ritual of the red heifer sandwiched between the sins of the scouts and of Koraḥ in the two previous portions and the transgression of Moses in the segment immediately following?

Rabbi Joseph B. Soloveitchik masterfully answers a significant part of our first query, insisting that the ritual of the red heifer can be understood rationally! To what may the ritual of the red heifer and the purifying kohanim be compared? To a hapless individual who finds himself drowning in quicksand. Certainly he must be rescued but the rescuer, who must lift the victim up from the quagmire, will of necessity become soiled in the process. Hence, those who prepare the mixture of purification are themselves defiled by it! Their very contact with those who have been defiled will perforce cause some defilement to transfer to them!

My revered teacher went one step further. Is it then fair, he asked, that those who attempt to purify become themselves impure in this process? Yes, he explained, once we understand that it is the religious leadership which has the responsibility of purifying society. Had the kohanim uplifted humanity to higher spiritual and ethical attainments, people would not have become contaminated by impurity in the first place. Hence it is only right that this same religious leadership assume the obligation of becoming defiled when so many Jews have been alienated from Torah and sanctity on its watch. The leaders must leave the ivory tower of the *beit midrash* (study hall) and reach out to the masses of Jews wherever and in whatever state they may be, even if it means that these very leaders will be removed from the environment of pure sanctity. As God tells Moses, spiritually ensconced in the ethereal realms of the heaven receiving the Oral Law, "Go down, descend from your supernal heights, because your nation is acting perversely with the Golden Calf; I only bestowed greatness upon you for the sake of the nation; if your nation is sinning what do I need you for?!" (*Berakhot* 32a). Leave this exalted Kollel, reach out to your errant congregants, and attempt to lift them up to a higher spiritual level. This is your responsibility, since every Jew, and especially a Jewish leader, is a co-signer for every other Jew and must take responsibility for their transgressions!

The timeless message of the kohanim, who come to purify with the ashes of the red heifer, is a powerful one to the leaders of every future generation: you must assume the risks of responsibility!

Even Moses had to suffer the fate of his generation since he did not prevent the Israelites from the transgression of listening to the scouts. Even the Jewish nation – also symbolized by the red heifer, as we have seen – must be taken out of the encampment to be slaughtered, albeit to be brought back to life by the *ish tahor* (personage of purity), for not teaching the world "compassionate righteousness and moral justice." Such is the heavy price – and fateful destiny – of leadership.

A Hasidic Postscript

The third day of Tammuz marks the eleventh anniversary of the passing of the Lubavitcher Rebbe. In my eyes as well as in the eyes of countless others – even many who, like myself, never became real Lubavitcher Hasidim – he was truly the leader of this past generation. From the time that I made the decision to become the rabbi of Lincoln Square Synagogue at age twenty-four until and including my *aliya* to Efrat and the establishment of the Ohr Torah Stone Institutions, I never made a significant move without seeking his sage advice. The one word which most characterizes his phenomenal style of leadership was his assumption of responsibility: he took responsibility for Jews all over the world, from Melbourne, Australia, to Johannesburg, South Africa, to Auckland, New Zealand, to Bangkok, Thailand, to Kiryat Malakhi, Israel. He inspired hundreds if not thousands of his disciples to become his emissaries in communities throughout the world, each one assuming a small share of the enormously heavy burden carried with such grace and faith by their revered Rebbe.

The Rebbe provided a magnificent addendum to the interpretation Rabbi Soloveitchik gave to the ritual of the Red Heifer. Yes, those who prepare the mixture of purification – the one who burns the heifer to make the ashes; the one who thrusts into the mixture the cedar wood, the hyssop, and the scarlet thread; the one who gathers the various ingredients together; and the one who carries them – all of these become defiled in their pursuit of purifying those who are impure. However, the one who actually sprinkles the mixture upon the individual defiled and thereby effectuates the actual purification remains pure (Numbers 19:21, Rashi ad loc.). Hence the Rebbe made a promise to each of his *shliḥim* (emissaries) all over the world – to those individuals who did the actual purifying themselves, the junior partners of the Rebbe who took responsibility to perform God's work of purification: these actual purifiers were guaranteed, they and their families, to remain pure, no matter how isolated they may be. It is through these emissaries that the Rebbe's legacy lives on.

The Leader Must Love His People to the Point of Sacrifice

And he [Moses] said to them: "Listen now rebels" ... and he struck the rock twice.
NUMBERS 20:10

Rabbi Nahman of Bratslav tells a tale of a king who was beside himself because his only son was behaving like a rooster: he divested himself of all of his clothes, romped about under the table, ate corn and fodder, and would only emit sounds of "cock-a-doodle-doo." When all of his trusted doctors failed to find a cure, he sought in desperation the advice of a rabbi. The first thing the rabbi did was disrobe, get under the table, and introduce himself to the hapless prince as a fellow rooster. After several days of cock-a-doodle-dooing together, the rabbi began to eat real food. "You can be a rooster and still enjoy a scrambled egg and vegetables," said the sage – and the prince joined him in the meal. And so, stage by stage, the rabbi brought the prince out from under the table and into the world of human discourse and relationships. But in order to effectuate the cure, the rabbi himself had to enter the quasi-animal world of the diseased prince.

But then why leave the hallowed halls of the *beit midrash* in the first place? Why attempt to purify those who are defiled if you run the risk of becoming defiled yourself? The answer is indubitably clear: that's what love of Israel is all about! The kohen, the Jewish leader, must love his people to such an extent that he is willing to sacrifice a portion of his own spirituality in order to bring those who have wandered far away closer to their religious roots. Rabbi Yisroel Salanter so defined *mesirat nefesh*, the commitment of one's soul for Torah: it cannot mean giving up material opportunities for the sake of Torah, for that would be *mesirat haguf* (the commitment of one's body); it must mean giving up a little bit of my portion in the World to Come so that my fellow Jew can have a portion as well.

And perhaps that is the responsibility of leadership as well. After all, it can be justifiably argued that if the religious leader had done a proper job, no Jew would ever become defiled!

What has this to do with the punishment of Moses? God told him to speak to the rock, and he struck the rock; he expressed displaced anger at a thirsty and complaining Jewish people. He even lashed out at them, referring to them as "rebels," criticizing not only their negative actions by ungratefully and unfaithfully *kvetching* for water but also denigrating their very personalities by classifying them as "rebels." He had lost the ability to empathize with them, to "get under the table with them" and feel their discomfort – as he had done so effectively when they were slaves in Egypt and first began their desert experience. We cannot blame him for having lost patience – after all the ingratitude and rebellions he had suffered. But the irreversible fact is that in striking the rock to extract the water he demonstrated that he no longer had the requisite love for his people which is the primary requirement for Jewish leadership.

The kohen, on the other hand, scion of Aaron who "loves all creatures and brings them close to Torah," takes the life-giving water of eternal Torah and transforms the dead ashes of the red heifer into the life-giving purity of the religious ritual; the kohen, representative of God, affirms the eternity of Israel and the ability of every Jew to be purified from death to eternal life within the continuity of the traditions of his people. And his love for Israel is so great that he is willing to defile himself in order to bring redeeming purity to his fellow Jews who have become impure.

The Leader Must Respect His People: Kehal *vs.* Edah

And Moses and Aaron assembled the assemblage [kehal] *before the rock; and he* [*Moses*] *said to them, "Listen now, rebels, from this rock shall we* [*be able*] *to extract water for you?" And Moses lifted his hand, struck the rock twice with his rod, and much water emerged to give drink to the witness community and their cattle.*

NUMBERS 20:10–11

Moses entered the stage of Jewish history by striking (the Egyptian), and exited from the stage of Jewish history by striking (the rock). His first act of striking out against the Egyptian taskmaster was out of love for his people and outreach to his real brethren, an act of courage and self-sacrifice which forced him to leave the house of Pharaoh; his second act of striking out against the rock, but really against the Hebrews – whom he called "rebels" right before he struck the rock –

was an act of displaced anger, deep frustration with a nation which had defied his teachings and allowed rebellion after rebellion to undermine his and God's authority.

Rabbi Jacob Harlap (1883–1951), close disciple and confidante of Rabbi A.Y.H. Kook, in his multi-volume *Mei Marom,* describes the change in Moses' mindset towards the Hebrews by distinguishing between two descriptive nouns for the Israelite crowd which are usually taken for synonyms: "*kehal*" and "*edah,*" assemblage and community. An assemblage consists of the many individuals who assemble together, the separate and disparate persons who make up a crowd; a community is guided by a specific purpose, which serves to unite (com-unity), and connotes individuals united by their commitment to historic continuity from generation to generation. Indeed, *edah* really means witness, and the continued survival of the nation of Israel despite exile and persecution in accordance with the divine covenant serves as eloquent testimony to the reality and truth of God's presence and of Israel's mission: humanity perfected in a world redeemed.

With this introduction, let us take a fresh look at our biblical reading. Immediately following Miriam's death, the desert wells dried up and the Israelites assembled as a crowd of disparate rabble (*vayikahalu*) in complaint against Moses and Aaron. In response, God addressed Moses,

> Take the staff, and you and Aaron assemble the witness *community* [*hak'hel et ha'edah*]. Speak to the rock in their presence and it will give forth its water. You will thus bring forth water from the rock and allow the *community* [*ha'edah*] and their beasts to drink.
>
> Numbers 20:8

Moses was thus told by God to assemble the community (*edah*)! However, the text records that "Moses and Aaron assembled the assemblage [*vayakhilu ... hakahal*] in front of the rock" (Numbers 20:10).

What a literal reading of the text is teaching us is that God wanted Moses to look at the motley crew of complainers and see that behind the façade of rabble were to be found witnesses of the divine; Moses was supposed to appreciate the great potential of this people, the fact that standing before him were the children of Abraham, Isaac, and Jacob, Sarah, Rebecca, Rachel, and Leah, and the parents of Yishai, David, and the righteous Messiah. God expected Moses to see through the angry rabble and inspiringly extract from deep within them the faith of their forebears. After all, these same people had declared their willingness to be a "kingdom of priests and a holy nation," had raised their voices and sang as one at the Reed Sea, "the Lord shall be king forever and ever." But Moses, disappointed and disgruntled, personally devastated by their "ingratitude," could only see a congregation of *kvetching* individuals, a mass of fearful and immature freedmen dancing before a Golden Calf, a Datan and an Aviram who even refused to meet with him, a disparate crowd who allowed themselves to become paralyzed before the Canaanites. He had lost sight of the witness community of Israel and could only see the assemblage of Israel; he spoke to what was in front of him instead of to their potential, the great moments and the noble individuals who comprised historic Israel and forged the Israelites in front of him. And so he became incapable of speaking with love; he could only strike out in anger. Such an individual perforce cannot continue to lead the nation towards the fulfillment of its historical destiny.

A Postscript about Recapturing a Sense of Community

Many years ago I had the unique pleasure and privilege of spending an unforgettable Sabbath with one of the great scholars of contemporary times, Rabbi Charles Chavel. I could not resist asking him how, despite the fact that he served as a rabbi of a Jewish congregation, he nevertheless found the time to be so productive in Jewish scholarship, producing special editions of and commentaries on Rashi and the Nahmanides, as well as responses to difficult Talmudic questions asked by Rabbi Akiva Eiger. "I always had small congregations," he told me, "small in number and sometimes even small in soul. And after a difficult board meeting with Mrs. Goldberg and Mr. Schwartz I yearned for the company of profound minds and deep perspectives. Who could be greater antidotes to small-minded and mean-spirited individuals than the Nahmanides and Rabbi Akiva Eiger?" Rabbi Chavel understood the secret; he had the capacity to look beyond the congregation and see the community. That's what every leader must aspire to do if he is to truly succeed.

A Leader Must Educate His People with Love

> *Because you believed not in Me, to sanctify Me in the eyes of the children of Israel, therefore you shall not bring this assembly into the land which I have given them.*
>
> NUMBERS 20:11–12

This Torah reading describes the tragic transgression of Moses, who was told by the Almighty to speak to the rock and instead struck the rock. Because of this, he was punished to the extent that the great prophet of the Exodus was barred from entering the Promised Land, which was his life's goal. Why such an extreme punishment for what appears to be such a minor transgression? Why was it so important to God that Moses speak to the rock? After all, water emerging from a rock after it is struck is also a miraculous happening! And besides, at the beginning of their desert sojourn, when the Israelites had encamped in Rephidim and were thirsting for water, God specifically commanded

Moses to take the rod with which he had struck the Nile River, and to use it to strike the rock at Ḥorev, after which water would gush forth for the Hebrews (Exodus 17:1–7). So can anyone blame Moses for striking the rock at this point?

Maimonides, in his "Eight Chapters" introduction to Mishna *Avot*, maintains that Moses' real sin was his having called the Jews "rebels" ("listen, now, you rebels") immediately before he struck the rock; here he was not merely condemning one of their actions, but he was also denigrating their very personality and character as a nation (much like a parent, who doesn't merely tell a child that he did a bad thing but calls him a bad boy).

Rabbenu Tzadok HaKohen of Lublin, in his biblical commentary *Pri Tzaddik*, fleshes this out further in a striking interpretation which is extremely relevant to every leader of the Jewish people. In almost Freudian terms of dream interpretation, this great Hasidic sage attaches symbolic meaning to the divine command. The rock (*sela*) represents the nation of Israel, a people already described by the Bible numerous times as a "hard-necked nation" (*am keshei oref*), hard as a rock. This description is both positive and negative; hard-neckedness results in stubbornness as well as in stick-to-itiveness. The goal of the leader of Israel is to extract water – or symbolically, Torah – from this very unique nation, to enable and empower Israel to give forth Torah, which is its birthright and ultimate mission. Water is called by the Bible "life-giving waters" and Torah is our eternal tree of life; moreover, our sages teach us that just as human beings cannot live without water for three days consecutively, so the Jewish nation cannot live without Torah for three days consecutively; this is why the Talmud rules that we have a public reading of the Torah at least three times a week, Mondays, Thursdays, and Sabbaths (*Bava Kamma* 82a).

After Rabbenu Tzadok has set down his symbolism, the message of the divine command becomes very clear. God is telling Moses to use his staff of leadership in order to speak to his hard-necked nation, to speak to them and not strike them, to persuade them and not to overpower them. This is an especially poignant message for Moses after the sin of the scouts, when he apparently failed to convince his people concerning the importance of the Land of Israel and to prepare them for the necessity of conquest.

But the Almighty is not only speaking to Moses; He is speaking to every future leader of Israel. We saw in our opening commentary to *Bemidbar* that the Hebrew word for leader is *dabar,* which is built from the verb D-B-R, which means to speak. The Hebrew word *midbar,* translated as desert, is actually the "place of the word," the locus whence the speech of God – the Bible – was communicated to Israel. God Himself spoke to us with words, providing a model of verbal influence rather than physical power – and He did so in a desert, whose stark silence lends itself to the sole and singular sound of the divine words.

The *Pri Tzaddik* goes even one step further. Speech is the medium of the Oral Law, the *Torah Sheba'al Peh* (the Torah of the mouth) as contrasted with the Written Law, the *Torah Shebikhtav*. The sacred Zohar, the mystical interpretation of the Bible, calls the Oral Law the law of softness and compassion (*dina derafia*), whereas the Written Law is the law of exactitude and harshness (*dina detakfa*). Hence, although the Written Law often provides the death penalty as the proper punishment for manifold crimes, the Oral Law insists that no circumstantial evidence ever be accepted in capital cases; two witnesses must not only see the crime itself, but must also warn the would-be criminal about the severity of the act he is about to commit. This leads the Mishna (Oral Law) to exclaim that any Israeli court which put a criminal to death once in seventy years was called a murderous court, with Rabbi Akiva and R. Tarfon both maintaining that they would never give anyone the death penalty (*Makkot* 7a). In a similar vein, although the Written Law states "an eye for an eye," the Oral Law provides for monetary compensation. From this perspective, God's command to Moses that he speak and not strike is a divine dictate that the Jewish leader engage his people with the love of the Oral Law rather than enforce upon them the strictness of the Written Law.

And the teacher of Torah must communicate the Torah of love primarily by loving those he is teaching. "You shall teach the Torah diligently to your children" – these refer to your students, whom you must relate to with the love usually reserved for one's children (Deut. 6:7,

Rashi ad loc.). In the words of our Mishna: "Be among the disciples of Aaron: love peace, pursue peace, love all of humanity and bring them close to Torah" – through love must you teach Torah, and then you will not repel them but draw them ever closer (*Avot* 1:4).

There is one final characteristic of the Law of the Word, or the Oral Law. The Written Law was given by God; it is the divine mandate emanating from above. The Oral Law may be divinely rooted, but it includes the human commentary, interpretations, and enactments of the religio-legal leaders of every generation. It represents a partnership between the divine and the human, the involvement of the committed Jewish people within the process of the development of our jurisprudence. The Almighty is telling Moses that he must use the speech of the Oral Law to involve the people themselves in forging those laws, rituals, and customs which comprise our unique Jewish lifestyle and eternal Jewish values. As every good parent and teacher knows, only when children and students become themselves involved in deciding and developing the ideology and the lifestyle which they commit themselves to follow do they take "ownership" and become truly dedicated. When Moses struck the rock instead of speaking to the rock, he sadly demonstrated that he could no longer lead his people into the next stage of their necessary development: a partnership with God in creating a Torah of love which would bring redemption to Israel and the world.

A Striking Postscript

When may we use the sword, and when must we use the word?

Certainly there are times when necessity demands that the people of the word become the people of the sword – albeit in self-defense. This is the crucial message that Mother Rachel tried to impress upon her husband Isaac: Jacob must have the ability to assume the external trappings and confidently wield the hands of Esau in order to fight for what is rightfully his – otherwise the world will be abandoned to the most heinous forces of evil. The Bible and Talmud do teach the concept of a "commanded" war, a *milḥemet mitzva* (Deut. 20:10 ff., Sota 44).

And therefore Moses slayed the Egyptian taskmaster. But at that time he was fighting the sword with the sword – the only way he could possibly protect the Hebrew victim. Perhaps his very training as an Egyptian prince gave him the necessary ability to use his hands effectively. Indeed, it would appear that the major reason Moses was chosen by God to lead the Israelites was precisely the courage, commitment, and sacrifice involved in his act of smiting.

However, while the power of the sword may be necessary when the Jew confronts the gentile desirous of destroying him, it most certainly has no place when dealing with the Israelites themselves. Jews must attempt to persuade other Jews with the power of the word, with the ideas and ideals of our sacred books, rather than with the might of soldiers' weaponry.

When Moses struck the rock – which symbolized Israel – rather than speaking to it, the very act which had catapulted him to leadership when used against a gentile assailant became the instrument of his necessary fall from leadership in the desert.

Balak

Does God Speak to Us Today? And If So, Can It Be through the Mouth of a She-Ass?

God opened the mouth of the she-ass and she said unto Bileam...

NUMBERS 22:28

Does God still speak to us today, and – if He does – where must we look in order to discover His message? The answer to this question lies in a fascinating Hasidic interpretation to one of the most amazing events recorded in the Bible, that of Bileam's talking she-ass.

Bileam, the central figure in the portion of *Balak*, is generally regarded as a wicked person, possessing "an evil eye, an arrogant spirit, and a greedy soul" (Mishna *Avot* 5:22), a summation easily backed up by the events described in our portion. After all, for the right price and sufficient power, Bileam was willing to sell his soul and curse the Israelites.

And yet another view of Bileam, seemingly contradictory to the Mishna, is found in *Sifrei* where it's stated (*Parashat Vezot HaBerakha*) that in Israel no prophet ever arose like Moses, "but amongst the nations of the world there was such a prophet, and he is Bileam." How does the Midrash place the venal and grasping Bileam on the level of Moses, redeemer of Israel, transmitter of the message of the divine from the foot of Mount Sinai to all generations and all worlds? What can these two figures possibly share in common?

Perhaps by isolating the most unique element of the Bileam narrative, we can perceive what it is that the Midrash wants to tell us. Undoubtedly the magical and mystical moment in our portion is the encounter between Bileam and his she-ass. Bileam set out with Balak, king of Moab, to curse the nation of Israel, but his formerly trustworthy she-ass refused to allow him to continue his journey. The gentile prophet angrily beat his animal, and suddenly: "God opened the mouth of the ass and she said unto Bileam" (Numbers 22:28). The she-ass had seen an angel of the Lord standing in the way with drawn sword, chastising Bileam lest he plan to revile the nation most blessed by God. The gentile prophet's one-word response, "I have sinned" (Numbers 22:34), marks the turning point, and from then on Bileam – to the chagrin of his "sponsors" – rose to poetic heights regarding his praise of Israel which echo Moses' magnificent paean in the book of Deuteronomy. Most significant of all, however, is that Bileam the prophet was brought to a divine vision by the message of a she-ass!

Indeed, the miracle of the she-ass speaking is so profound that the Mishna lists the *pi ha'aton* (mouth of the she-ass) among the ten things created at dusk immediately preceding the first primordial Sabbath of the initial seven days of creation (*Avot* 5:8). We are being taught not to see this event merely as a fable, or a dream, but rather as a miracle built into the very blueprint of creation – an ass's mouth whose voice would be heard not only by Bileam, but would reverberate throughout the generations in the form of Bileam's praise of Israel. The most crucial message of this miraculous mouth is that no gentile leader will ever be allowed to curse and destroy Israel, that those who come to scoff will remain to praise.

But why did the Almighty choose such an unseemly messenger – a she-ass – to convey His message to Bileam? Clearly the mouth of this she-ass – emanating from the very dawn of creation – demonstrates how God's message may emerge from the most unexpected sources. And what is important is not only that a she-ass can communicate the divine will; the most significant message of this tale may be that the individual must strive to develop the ability to hear, to discern from the harsh guttural hee-haws the message that is being sent to him. In effect, God's words may be found in the most unlikely of places – as long as we have the necessary spiritual antennae to receive them.

This principle may be the source of Rashi's explanation of the verse immediately following the Ten Commandments in Deuteronomy. "These words God spoke unto all your assembly out of the midst of the fire, of the clouds, and of the thick darkness, with a great voice, and it did not cease [*velo yasaf*; *Targum* ad loc: *velo pasak*]" (Deut. 5:19). Rashi explains: "and since God did not pause, He did not have to resume, for His voice is strong and goes on continuously." How does God's voice go on continuously? The lesson seems to be that the sound waves released at Sinai are continually and eternally present in the world; we must simply attune our ears to be sensitive receptors.

In his Torah commentary, the *Pri Tzaddik* stresses this idea by citing a tale of the Hasidic master, Reb Zusha who, during one of his journeys, came upon a peasant whose wagon had turned over. Asked to help, Reb Zusha, no longer young and feeling himself too weak to struggle with an overburdened wagon, demurred, saying: "I'm sorry, I can't help you." "You can," said the peasant to Reb Zusha, "You certainly can. You just don't want to." The peasant's words sank into the very core of Reb Zusha's being, resonating with a message from above, as if the *Shekhina* herself was admonishing Reb Zusha for saying "I can't." "You can," he heard the *Shekhina* saying, "you just don't want to." Reb Zusha was able to accept the truth of the peasant's words on more than one level. How often do we say we "can't" when what we really mean is we "won't" or "we do not wish to"? And here, in this world, our Temple is destroyed, the Divine Presence has fallen, and we don't lift her (the *Shekhina*) up. And although it's because we say we cannot, the real reason is because we don't want to! Did the she-ass actually speak? The truth is that that is an irrelevant issue. What is important is what Bileam learned from his donkey, the divine message he perceived from the animal's stubborn refusal to continue the journey, the fact that he, visited with the gift of prophecy, dared not speak out words which were antithetical to the divine will. The she-ass knew not to continue such a sacrilegious journey; Bileam understood that he had better learn from the she-ass!

Herein lies the essence of the teaching set forth in *Avot* (4:1): "Ben Zoma says, who is wise? He who learns from every person." If Reb Zusha can learn a major principle regarding our relationship to the divine from the simple words of a gentile peasant, if Bileam could learn from the she-ass, we must always be on guard to sensitize our ears and our hearts to receive a direct divine message from whoever, and wherever!

The *Pri Tzaddik* reminds us of the Talmud's dilemma regarding R. Meir, who continued to receive Torah from the rabbi-turned-apostate, Elisha b. Avuya (known as *Aḥer,* or "the other one"). After all, does not the prophet Malakhi teach: "The lips of the priest shall preserve wisdom, Torah shall be sought from his mouth, because he is an angel of the Lord of hosts" (2:7), interpreted by our sages to mean that only if a Torah sage is comparable to an angel on high may we study from his mouth? If so, how can R. Meir continue to study from a heretic? The answer in the Talmud is that a truly great individual has the ability and sensitivity to hear God's words even from the lowliest of places (*Ḥagiga* 15b). Hence R. Meir heard it from *Aḥer,* Reb Zusha heard it from a gentile peasant, Bileam heard it from a she-ass, and Moses heard it from the depths of a lowly, prickly thornbush.

In his *Guide for the Perplexed,* Maimonides points out that on Mount Sinai every Jew heard the divine sound, but each person heard only what he was capable of hearing, depending on his spiritual level and human sensitivity. God-waves continue from Sinai and are consistently prepared to deliver the divine word – even from the most unseemly messenger. The question is: are we prepared to receive them?

Why They Hate Us, and Who Will Redeem Us?

Behold, it is a nation that will dwell in solitude,
and will not be reckoned among the nations.

NUMBERS 23:9

Is the biblical statement about our solitude within the family of nations a blessing or a curse?

From the biblical context of this prophecy, it is clearly meant to be a blessing, a vision of the remarkable ability of Israel to live in splendid isolation and ultimately outlast – and ideologically triumph over – the nations of the world. The most classic commentary, Rashi, maintains that our forebears – the patriarchs and matriarchs – have merited us with a unique set of values and a consecrated lifestyle which prevents our degenerative assimilation into the licentious practices of the nations round about (see Ibn Ezra ad loc.); and although every other nation will eventually leave the stage of world history, we alone will emerge victorious.

And so Balak reviled Bileam for this very laudatory vision: "What have you done to me? I hired you to curse my enemies, and behold, you have blessed, yes blessed, them" (Numbers 23:1).

However, when we look upon the last two thousand years of Jewish history, at least the first part of Bileam's words have indeed been fulfilled – but not as a blessing; his prophecy has truly come to pass, but rather as a horrific curse. Until the establishment of the State of Israel we had been hopelessly and helplessly persecuted and exiled from pillar to post by the nations of the world – culminating in the Holocaust, when we truly stood alone in the midst of the Nazis' attempted genocide. And even now post-Medinat Yisrael – when we do have the ability to defend ourselves against the terrorism of Hamas, Hezbollah, and Iran – we (and not the allies of Iran and Al Qaeda) have become the whipping boy not only of the Arab bloc, but also of the European Union, the entire United Nations, and even of the president of the United States. Yes, we stand in isolation – but "stinking" isolation rather than splendid isolation. How can we understand this in light of Bileam's prophecy?

Allow me to take a page from Hitler's *Mein Kampf* in order to understand the mentality of our enemies. Hitler – like his present-day heirs, fundamentalist and Jihadist Islam – sought world domination by the sword. But at the same time that he was building up military prowess to destroy the free world, he was also waging a deadly and diabolical campaign – replete with Kristallnachts and death camps – to dehumanize and decimate the Jewish people. Why the stateless and powerless Jews?

You see, Fascist Hitler believed in Aryan supremacy, in "might makes right," in "to the military victor belongs the spoils," and he, Hitler, belonged to the race of "*uber-menschen*" who had conquered Germany today and tomorrow would conquer the world. But there was one fly in the ointment: the Jews. The Jews believed – a principle of faith deriving from their patriarch Abraham four thousand years ago – that "right would conquer might," that "compassionate righteousness and moral justice" would take over the world (Genesis 18:19), that through the Jews the world would be blessed with peace and freedom, divine ideals that would trump the sword and despotic domination.

Now Hitler wanted to believe that the Jews were "selling" a slave morality based upon their own self-serving need for the world's compassion and righteousness if they were to survive. But he could not deny the fact that they – the most powerless of people – had nevertheless survived the persecutions of Egypt, Persia, Greece, Rome, the Ottoman Empire, and the Catholic Church, giving credence to their claim that they were indeed God's witnesses, entrusted with the mission to enthrone the God of the Ten Commandments as the world's only Führer. And so he became obsessed with the Jews, and was hell-bent on destroying the last Jew, on obliterating Judaism – and its message of love, compassion, and morality – from the face of the world. Only then could he be sure that he would triumph, and would not be subject to eternal damnation.

Hitler is dead, having taken his own life in a Berlin bunker; the final expression of his "Jewish" obsession, a Talmudic tractate *Pesaḥim* (our festival of freedom and redemption) which was curiously found among the few personal effects he brought with him to his suicide sepulchre. The failed Führer probably believed he was burying the last remnant of the Jewish faith, the Talmud; instead, the Talmud buried him. And in his own Germany, a $10 million Jewish Center – replete with synagogue, Hebrew school for children, and adult education classes – has just been completed in Munich. Jews throughout Germany are coming out of the woodwork and declaring themselves as Jews, hundreds of descendants of Jewish fathers are converting to Judaism, and in Hitler's own country Jewish life is slowly but surely being renewed.

Nevertheless, the world is still not ready to accept our morality, hypocritically siding with those who send out suicide bombers and target innocent civilians, with those who repress the rights of their own citizenry (the women, the Christians, the Kurds, the Jews within their own borders); they would rather revile Israel as an apartheid and terrorist state, Israel which enables enemy Arab voices to be heard in its parliament, Israel which avoids aerial bombing whenever possible even at the risk of her own soldiers to prevent the death of innocents, Israel who alone in the world is standing up to the scourge of terrorism, Israel who had an Arab judge serve as chief justice in the trial of its "esteemed" president.

And so the words of Bileam still remain as an eventual promise – but also as a challenge. At the conclusion of our biblical portion, Bileam understands that no external source can vanquish Israel; we can only vanquish ourselves if we fall sway to the immorality round about. But if indeed we continually check our morality not only against the perverted standards of our enemies but also against the morality of the Ten Commandments, then we are guaranteed that not only will we survive, but we will prevail.

Does Judaism Accept Sorcery?

> *There is no sorcery for Jacob, there is no magic for Israel.*
>
> NUMBERS 23:23

What is the true message of an entire Torah portion dedicated to the hiring of a gentile soothsayer to curse the Israelite nation – but who instead becomes inspired to bless Israel and portray the ultimate messianic destiny of Israel in the most exalted and majestic of poetic metaphors? Are there indeed individuals with true power to foretell future events – and ought we seek out such individuals to help us tackle difficult moments in our lives which threaten to overwhelm us? And if indeed Bileam is a superior human being with profound prophetic insights emanating from a divine source, why does the Torah triumphantly record the fact that "Bileam ben Beor the magician" was killed by Israel with the sword amongst the corpses of our Midianite enemies during the conquest of Israel (Joshua 13:22)? And why does our biblical text juxtapose the sublime poetry of Bileam with the seemingly ridiculous tale of the talking donkey?

I believe that from a certain perspective, the entire portion of Bileam is a study in contrasts between the legitimately earned prophecy of Moses and the venally inspired sorcery of Bileam. The Torah understands that individuals may exist who appear to have been born with special powers: superior physical strength, a phenomenal photographic memory, sharp vision which can penetrate the thickest of partitions, intense concentration that can cause physical objects to explode, and perhaps even the ability to bring messages from the dead.

There is even a difference of opinion amongst our sages as to whether such phenomena reflect actual occurrences or are merely sleight-of-hand trickery. When the Bible records King Saul's last-ditch attempt to discover his destiny by asking the witch of Endor to seek the counsel of the dead Samuel – and she indeed provides the true message that "the Almighty will tear the kingdom from your hands and give it over to your friend David" – the commentaries are divided as to the factual truth of the account: Rabbenu Sa'adia Gaon accepts the biblical story as it is written, and Rabbi Shmuel ben Hafni Gaon insists that the witch of Endor deceived King Saul (I Samuel 28 and its Geonic commentaries; see Radak, the end of chapter 28).

In a later generation, the arch-rationalist Maimonides calls all pronouncements emanating from supernatural communications and insights – including the writing and wearing of mystical amulets (*kmeot*) – "false and vain," bordering on idolatry (Maimonides, *Mishneh Torah, Hilkhot Avoda Zara* 1:16 and *Guide for the Perplexed,* I:61). On this basis, Rabbi Yosef Karo similarly dismisses all magical incantations as "not availing in the least," but merely exercising positive psychological influence upon individuals in distress (*Shulḥan Arukh, Yoreh De'ah* 179:6). The Gaon of Vilna, on the other hand, suggests that Maimonides' philosophical study "misled or corrupted him," insisting that there are amulets and incantations, and perhaps even communications from the beyond, which are rooted in the sacred and the divine" (ibid., paragraph 13). Perhaps the most important and representative view on the issue is presented by Rabbi Shlomo ben Aderet (Rashba, *Responsa* 548), when he had to judge the credibility of a Rabbi Nissim who claimed to have received messages from an angel; the great Talmudic scholar Rashba insists that divine communication akin to prophecy can only rest on one who is truly wise and pious, strong and courageous, and sufficiently wealthy as to not be in need of monetary contributions from those seeking his advice. Claims, and even what seem to be empirical facts, of supernatural abilities by individuals who are not outstanding in Torah scholarship and piety dare not be taken seriously – at the risk of flirting with idolatrous and even demonic blandishments.

The truth is that the Bible is indubitably clear when it warns us against seeking after any manner of magic or sorcery and exhorts us to be whole-hearted and pure in our service of the divine (Deut. 18:9–14). Our prophets did not major in futuristic prophecies but rather in inciting more ethical and genuine behavior; they certainly did not take remuneration for their words. Any individual devoid of the proper – and difficult to acquire – intellectual and spiritual prophetic attainments who makes pronouncements which even may appear to be vindicated by future discoveries is no better than the "talking donkey" in our Torah portion; a prophet of God must first and foremost be a model of Torah scholarship and piety.

Hence, the "talking donkey" may serve as a metaphor for all soothsayers devoid of proper qualifications of piety and intellect. Moses was a prophet of God, Bileam was a soothsayer. Moses sought divine truth while Bileam yearned for gold and silver.

Bileam's conclusion is most succinct and specific:

> There is no sorcery for Jacob nor magic for Israel.... Behold the people shall rise up as a lioness, and lift up himself as a lion, he shall not lie down until he eats of the prey, and makes corpses of the wicked.
>
> Numbers 23:23–24

Rashi explains this verse metaphorically:

> When individuals rise early for their Torah study, they triumph like the lion cub, grabbing onto the commandments, wearing the ritual fringes, reciting the Shema, and putting on the phylacteries.

> They do not eat before reciting the Evening Prayer. And they destroy the wicked as when they killed Bileam the soothsayer.
>
> Numbers 23:24, as interpreted by Rashi through the eyes of our sages; see, too, Joshua 13:22

We must search for God by performing the commandments as sincerely and punctiliously as possible; going after wonder-workers or soothsayers is at best a waste of time and at worst flirting with idolatry!

The Difference between Bileam and the Jewish Prophets

This is a nation that rises like the king of beasts and lifts itself up like a lion.

NUMBERS 23:24

One may certainly deduce from a reading of our biblical text that Bileam was one of the foremost prophets amongst the nations of the world, an impressive and poetic personage who demonstrated the universalistic ideal that the Almighty communicates with gentiles as well as with Israelites. But aside from the exalted lyrical cadences of his pronouncements – which were very much in the literary style of Moses' song of *Ha'azinu* and of Isaiah's visions of redemption – there are two fundamental ways in which Bileam parted company from his Israelite counterparts; these differences teach volumes about the unique message of Israelite prophecies.

First of all, while the Israelite prophets chastised their people, Bileam had only the best things to say about the descendants of Abraham and Sarah, Isaac and Rebecca, Jacob, Leah, and Rachel. He seemed even to be playing up to them, greasing their wheels and almost bribing them by exaggerating their positive qualities.

In contrast, King David, the sweet Psalmist of Israel, shouts out, "For forty years I argued [against you] in the desert, and I said, 'they are a nation whose heart led them astray, they do not know [or love] My paths'" (Psalms 95:10); Isaiah the prophet thunders: "My soul detests your New Moons and festival... when you extend your hands in prayer, I hide my eyes from you.... Your hands are replete with blood" (Isaiah 1:14–15).

Bileam, however, expresses fulsome praises: "This is a nation that rises like the king of beasts and lifts itself like a lion" (Numbers 23:24), "How goodly are your tents, O Jacob, your dwelling places, O Israel" (Numbers 25:5).

On one level, this difference may be explained as a logical and necessary outgrowth of the persona who is doing the prophesying. In the words of the Midrash:

> It would have been more fitting had the chastisements emanated from the mouth of Bileam and the blessings from the mouth of Moses, but then the Israelites would have said that their enemy is cursing them... and the gentiles would have said that their beloved leader is praising them. [And their respective words would have fallen on deaf ears.] The Holy One blessed be He therefore decreed, "Let Moses chastise them, because he loves them, and let Bileam bless them, because he hates them. Then Israel will know that both the blessings and the curses are honest and true."
>
> *Bemidbar Rabba* 1

I believe, however, that there is an even more important reason for this difference. The Israelite prophets chastised their people because they wished to instruct them, to improve them, to refine them. As King Solomon teaches, "Those whom one loves, one chastises." The prophet-shepherds cared deeply about their people-flocks and were hurt to the quick if they thought they were backsliding. Bileam, on the other hand, sought the demise, the destruction, of Israel. He importuned the

Almighty to allow him to act as sorcerer for the wicked Balak and went from place to place hoping to find a possible location from which to curse the seed of Abraham. Bileam's intention, upon discovering that God would not allow His chosen and exemplary nation to be reviled, was to fill them with the kind of false praise and conceited hubris which would take them off-guard and render them easy prey for the satanic evil instinct. Then he believed they would become worthy of God's curses; then they would self-destruct!

Along these lines, the Talmud even suggests that Bileam gave devastating and insidious advice to the Moabite and Midianite enemies of Israel. Since the Israelites were desirous of fine garments, he suggested that they set up clothing stalls, with old and wasted gentile women outside and nubile, lascivious women inside. When the unsuspecting Israelite men entered the stalls to make their purchase, they would be seduced by the maidens within (*Sanhedrin* 106a).

Where is there a hint of such dangerous advice from Bileam in the biblical text? Chapter twenty-four concludes the gentile prophet's songs of praise to Israel with the words, "And Bileam rose up and returned home; Balak also went on his way." The very next verse, opening chapter twenty-five, reads, "Israel was staying in Shittim [the name of a place, literally linked to the Hebrew word for licentious foolishness, *shtut*], when the [Israelite] nation began to fornicate with the daughters of Moab." The passage goes on to describe how an "important person [*ish*] from the children of Israel" brought a Midianite woman before his brethren, and in front "of the eyes of Moses and of the entire congregation of Israel" fornicated with her. Pineḥas, son of Elazar and grandson of Aaron the High Priest, drove a spear through the exposed genitals of the indecent pair, arresting a plague which had threatened to destroy the Israelite encampment (Numbers 25:1–9).

This entire incident concludes the portion of *Balak,* immediately following Bileam's last prophecy and departure. Then starts the next portion of *Pineḥas,* which praises the assassin of these public offenders and identifies the names of the immoral couple: Zimri ben Salou, the prince of the tribe of Simeon, and Kozbi daughter of Tzur, aristocrat of Midian. Did not the entire incident belong in the portion of *Pineḥas*? Why break up the story, telling the lurid details in *Balak* and identifying the culprits in *Pineḥas*? Apparently, conjecture the Talmudic sages, this entire tragedy was the outgrowth of a gentile prophet who hoped to bury the Israelites with fulsome praise to his audience and salacious advice to their enemies.

The second distinction between the Israelite prophets and Bileam lies in their ultimate vision. Bileam understood Israel's messianic role, and even foretold the eventual destruction of her enemies:

> A star shall go forth from Jacob and a staff shall arise in Israel, crushing all of Moab's princes.... Edom shall be demolished, his enemy Seir destroyed, but Israel shall emerge triumphant.
>
> Numbers 24:17–19

But Bileam did not see an ultimate world of peace and redemption for all nations, a time when "nation will not lift up sword against nation, and humanity will not learn war anymore" (Isaiah 2:4). To his mind, military success was the ultimate victory, and peace was not at all an ultimate ideal.

Indeed it is only the Israelite prophets – Isaiah, Micah, Zechariah – who understand the true mission of Israel, the perfection of the world under the kingship of God, when "the Torah will come from Zion and the word of God from Jerusalem" (Isaiah 2:3) to all peoples, when "the lamb will lie down with the lion, each individual will sit unafraid under his vineyard and fig-tree, and the knowledge of a God of justice and morality will fill the world as the waters cover the seas" (Isaiah 11:6).

Bileam and Lavan, Rabbi Akiva, and Zimri ben Salou

> *How goodly are your tents O Jacob, your dwelling places, O Israel.*
>
> NUMBERS 24:5

Bileam, the famous gentile prophet of the Bible, is called by our Talmudic sages Bileam the Wicked (*HaRasha*). Why is this so? True, he went along with Balak the king of Moab to curse the Israelites, but at the end of the day he blessed us with the majestic blessing quoted above, which opens our Daily Prayer books. Furthermore, he even prophesied our messianic victory at the end of the days:

> I see it but not now, I look at it, but it is not near. A star has stepped forth from Jacob and a scepter-bearer has risen from Israel.... He [Israel] will pierce and vanquish the nobles of Moab.... Edom will become [Israel's] inheritance.... Israel will emerge victorious....

> Amalek, the first among nations, will ultimately have eternal end of eternal destruction.
>
> Numbers 24:17–20

These stunning words could hardly have emerged from the mouth of an enemy!

To add to the mystery of the negative assessments of Bileam's character by the Talmud, the classic *Targum* of Yonatan ben Uziel identifies Bileam with none other than Lavan the Aramean, uncle of Jacob, who "desired to envelop and assimilate the nation of Israel" (Numbers 22:5, *Targum Yonatan* ad loc.). His source stems from the Talmud, which interprets the "advice" which Bileam says he will give (Numbers 24:14) to have been the suggestion that the young women of Midian and Moab entice the Israelite men (*Sanhedrin* 106a). In other words, just like Uncle Lavan so admired his nephew Jacob that he desperately wished to prevent his return to the land and faith of his father and grandfather by assimilating him into his (Lavan's) pagan Naḥorite clan ("the daughters – your wives – are my daughters, the children – your children – are my grandchildren" [Genesis 31:43]), so did Bileam, a sincere admirer of Israel, wish to head Israel off at the pass by assimilating them into Moab and Midian.

The fundamental question, however, still remains to be answered: when Israelite meets gentile in such close proximity (acts of cohabitation between Moabite women and Israelite men), who influences whom? Bileam apparently banked on Moab's assimilating Israel, although his prophetic vision suggested the opposite, that Israel would eventually trounce Moab; and indeed, the descendant of Moab, Ruth, converted to Judaism, settled in Israel, and became the great-grandmother of King David, progenitor of the Messiah. An interesting model for "the end of the days" and Jewish-gentile relationships is provided by a cryptic comment found in the *Ḥesed LeAvraham*, a marvelous study penned by Rabbi Avraham Azulai (1570–1643), great-great-grandfather of the Ḥida (1724–1807): "Rabbi Akiva was the repair [*tikkun*] for Zimri ben Salou." What possible relationship can there be between the penitent master-teacher of twenty-four thousand disciples who was a major architect of the Mishnaic period and the Simeonite prince who publicly fornicated with a Midianite beauty right in front of Moses?

Rashi (commenting on *Nedarim* 50b) records the following incident towards the end of the life of Rabbi Akiva:

> There was one Roman personage whose name was Rufus, and he would often debate on matters of Torah against Rabbi Akiva; Rabbi Akiva always bested him in argument. The Roman personage became embarrassed, and – upon his return home – told his wife of his defeat. She said to him, "I will tempt Rabbi Akiva and cause him to stumble! [Then you will not have to worry about him any longer.]" She was a very beautiful woman. She came before Rabbi Akiva and, [when they were alone] she revealed her [naked] thigh before him. Rabbi Akiva spat, and laughed and wept. She said to him, "Why do you act in such a [strange] manner?" He said to her, "I will explain to you two out of my three activities.
>
> "I spat, because you came from a fetid drop [of sperm, of which I had to remind myself].
>
> "I wept, because in the end your beauty will decay beneath the earth."
>
> But why he laughed, he did not wish to tell her. Nevertheless, after she entreated him many times, he explained that it was because she would eventually convert to Judaism and would marry him. Whereupon she said to him, "And is there the possibility of repentance?" He said there was. And after her husband died, she converted, married Rabbi Akiva, and brought him great wealth.

Messianic movements all see an end-of-world order in which all of humanity will become unified. True messianism sees this unity under the banner of world peace and freedom for every human being. False messianism, however, sees the same unity, but under the despotic domination of a powerful, totalitarian dictator who will enforce his system – be it religious, economic, or hedonistic – upon all his subjects. Stalinist Communists wanted the world union of workers to unite, but under the banner of totalitarian enslavement; the Islamic-fundamentalist Middle East was and is devoid of individual human rights and has not yet abandoned terrorism; Lavan's only commitment was to wealth and self-aggrandizement, despite his clichés about family togetherness; and Bileam, heir to Lavan, was willing to curse the people of redemption if only he would be paid off in large amounts of gold and silver. Bileam was a messianist, but he was sure that – with the proper sexual blandishments – the Israelites could blend into the woodwork of Moab and Midian.

Rabbi Akiva, on the other hand, believed in true messianism; he was the spirit behind the Bar Kokhva rebellion, and considered Bar Kokhva to be the Messiah; it is quite possible that his debates with Turnus Rufus before the Roman emperor were in order to try to make Judaism the religion of Rome. Rabbi Akiva was a universalist, who taught "Beloved is the human being, for he was created in God's image," and he believed that the cardinal commandment of the Torah is "You shall love your neighbor as yourself" (Leviticus 19:18) – because he, every human being, is like you; every human deserves to be free and all humanity are siblings because each emerged from the womb of the Divine Presence (*Shekhina*). Rabbi Akiva himself came from a family of proselytes, and died with the universal watchword of our faith in world unity on his lips: "Hear, O Israel, [right now] the Lord is [accepted by us as] our God, [but eventually] He will be [accepted by all nations] as the One [God of unconditional love]."

Rabbi Akiva understood that in our meeting with the gentiles, we must love them as we love ourselves because we were all formed in the same womb of the One *Shekhina* – and we must, at the very least, teach them the seven Noaḥide laws of morality. If the gentile is ready to convert all the way – as in the case of the widow of Turnus Rufus – you may then marry her, as Rabbi Akiva did. But their relationship was not one of Bileamist and Zimri ben Salou-ist debauchery which will only lead to the end of the Jewish people and Jewish morality; it is rather the Akiva-ist Song-of-Songs love-sanctity which will usher in the true messianic age, when "everyone will accept the yoke of God's kingship," when "nation will not lift up sword against nation and humanity will not learn war anymore" (Isaiah 2:4).

Public Relations vs. Proper Relationships

My nation, remember now what Balak the king of Moab advised and what Bileam the son of Be'or... answered him in order that you may know the compassionate righteousness of the Lord.

MICAH 6:5

This Torah portion gives us an amazing glimpse into how the nations of the world look upon the Israelites as they emerge from slavery into freedom and seemingly have an invincible army. And the portion of *Balak* does not emphasize the attitudes of Israel's immediate neighbors, not even her frontal enemy, the Amalekites. Our wars with them as well as with the Amorites and other Canaanite nations are described elsewhere. Here we are faced with the attitude of the bordering Middle Eastern nations, the United Nations, and the European Union – maybe even the United States – to this newly-formed people, intending to carve out its destiny within the maelstrom of the Middle East.

Balak, the king of Moab, is frightened of the Israelites, and vastly overestimates their global designs as well as their military might: "this multitude will lick up all that is round about us as the ox licks up the grass of the field" (Numbers 22:4). He therefore turns to Bileam, a magician and a soothsayer, an accomplished poet and master of the spoken word, to curse the Israelites so that they may be vanquished (Numbers 22:6). From a contemporary perspective, Bileam represents the media masters of the world, the newspaper and television magnates who control public opinion, the New York *Times*, CNN, and BBC. (As you might guess, he refuses to deal with Fox News.) Is it not true that these manipulators of minds have the power to destroy a world with a word?

The first message of our Torah reading is that those who speak to the cameras of world opinion – and even the various heads of state themselves – can be bought by promises of monetary gain (materialistic oil interests?). After all, Bileam certainly understood initially that God – or the universal conscience – would not allow him to curse the nation which had suffered so much and was certainly adhering to a higher moral standard than its terrorist and despotic neighbors. From this perspective, the gentile prophet should have sent Balak's delegation packing. But, tempted by wealth, power, and impressive robes, he told them to stay the night; he would seek to assuage God (or his conscience) by importuning and beseeching. And when God said definitely not, Bileam addressed the delegation: "Go home! God refuses to give me leave to go *with you*" (*imakhem,* Numbers 22:13), leaving a door open so that if a more important delegation were to arrive, who knows...maybe he (Bileam) could yet be convinced.

The foreign ministry reported back to Balak that Bileam would not come "with us" and so, without wasting a breath, the next verse records that Balak sent more princes, this time with a larger number of dignitaries.

The higher-ranking officials arrived, showering promises of great honor and the readiness to satisfy any monetary request Bileam might make. Answered the soothsayer: "If Balak would give me his house full of gold and silver, I would not be able to do anything great or small that would violate the word of God, my Lord" (Numbers 22:18).

On the surface, Bileam's answer may sound noble, but there was a hidden message. When Bileam spoke of all the gold and silver in Balak's house which could not get him to violate the "word of God," he again left open the possibility that perhaps an even more generous monetary offer could tip the scales. Rashi suggests (Numbers 22:18) that the expression of "silver and gold" reveals Bileam's real craving for what he seemed to spurn – material wealth! And indeed, Bileam did set out to curse the Israelites. The divine message is indubitably clear: God allows for freedom of choice; in the final analysis, "Towards whatever path the individual [or even prophet] wishes to take, God will lead him there" (Numbers 22:35; Rashi ad loc.; *Midrash Tanḥuma* 8; *Makkot* 10b).

Nevertheless, the Bible goes on to say that the gentile prophet ultimately blessed the Israelites. At first he was struck by his donkey's refusal to take him where he wanted to go – apparently because even a stupid ass must be amazed by the miraculous events which contributed to the preservation and preeminence of Israel who had become energized – from abject slaves to becoming Reed Sea champions – despite their smallness in number and scarcity of power. And then Bileam saw for himself – to the extent that at least this gentile spokesman attempted to record the truth as he stood before the television cameras and wrote his editorial for the press. He may have come to curse, but he stayed to praise. He evoked Jewish destiny in glowing terms, extolling the uniqueness of Israel (Numbers 23:9) and evoking our ultimate Messianic victory (Numbers 24:17–19). He affirmed unmistakably that "no black magic can be effective against Jacob and no occult powers against Israel" (Numbers 23:23) – in the final analysis, evil words spoken by evil people are totally impotent before the modesty and integrity expressed by the Hebrews in their daily lives.

Thus the insight of our biblical text is that, at the end of the day, it is not the speaking donkey – or even the divine will – which will succeed in changing the minds of the many Bileams around us; rather, it is the deeds of the Israelites themselves which will evoke change: "Your deeds will bring you close, your deeds will push you away" (Mishna *Eduyot* 5:7). And so it was then. First of all, Bileam took note of the military success of this fledgling nation against every one of her enemies – Israel had just emerged from a great military victory against the terrorizing Amorites. And, more importantly, it was the chaste and sanctified lifestyle of the Israelites and their commitment to their traditions and ideals which made the greatest impact on Bileam.

"How goodly are your tents, O Jacob, your Sanctuaries, O Israel"

(Numbers 24:5). Bileam was amazed as to how the Israelite encampment (*ohel*) was constructed so that everyone's privacy was reflected, so that no one could see into his neighbor's home. He was moved by the sensitive interpersonal relationships, the love and respect displayed toward one another by family members and the harmony with which neighbors lived together in peace. And when Bileam saw the commitment the Israelites had to their academies and synagogues (*Mishkan*) – their fealty to traditional values and teachings and their faith in divine providence – he understood, and proclaimed the invincibility of this divinely elected people.

But alas, what gentile might and word could not do to the Israelites, the Israelites managed to do to themselves. Bileam and Balak returned to their homes to leave Israel in peace – but the Israelites chose to self-destruct. They themselves chased after the hedonistic blandishments of the pagan societies of Bileam and Balak. The very next chapter opened with "And the people began to commit harlotry with the daughters of Moab... and Israel joined himself to the [idolatry of] Ba'al Peor [Bileam ben Beor]" (Numbers 25:1–3).

We failed in the desert not because of what our enemies did or said, but rather because of our own moral weakness and rejection of the birthright which had initially formed our national definition and mission. Indeed, we are "a people who dwells alone, not subject to the machinations of other nations" (Numbers 23:9); it is not what the nations do, but rather it is what we do or what we do not do, especially in the spheres of ethics and morality, which is of supreme significance.

Pineḥas

How Pineḥas Achieved Peace by Zealous Action

Therefore tell him that I have given him My covenant of peace; and it shall be unto him, and to his seed after him, the covenant of an everlasting priesthood, because he was jealous for His God, and made atonement for the children of Israel.

NUMBERS 25:12–13

Fanaticism, particularly when garbed in the accoutrements of extremist fundamentalism, hardly evokes in us a sympathetic bent. How could it, given its association with uncontrollable zeal and violence for the sake of heaven?!

But when we turn to the opening of this portion, the Torah lauds Pineḥas for zealously killing a Jewish man and a Midianite woman in the very heat of their sexual passion as they recklessly defied God's command. For responding so quickly and decisively, albeit without "due process," we read that,

> God spoke to Moses, saying, "Pineḥas, a son of Elazar and grandson of Aaron the priest, was the one who zealously took up my cause among the Israelites and turned My anger away from them.... Therefore tell him that I have given him My covenant of peace."
>
> Numbers 25:10–12

The biblical summation is certainly one of praise and approbation. Indeed, Pineḥas' full genealogy is presented in this sequence; we are also given the name of his father as well as of his grandfather, Aaron the High Priest, indicating that the Torah wants to underscore his linkage to Aaron, "lover and pursuer of peace" (*Avot* 1:12). Moreover, both grandfather and grandson succeeded in stopping plagues sent by the Almighty to punish the Israelites. Aaron was instrumental in stopping the plague that broke out after the Hebrews raised angry voices against Moses and Aaron when Koraḥ and his rebels were swallowed up by the earth (Numbers 17:6–11), and Pineḥas' act of zealotry arrested the plague which had destroyed twenty-four thousand Israelites who engaged in immoral sexual acts with the Midianites (Numbers 25:9).

When all is said and done it would appear that the Torah wants us to look upon Pineḥas not only as Aaron's grandchild but as his direct spiritual heir. And when Pineḥas received the divine gift of a covenant of peace, it is clear that he was being marked eternally as a leader who fostered peace and well-being, rather than fanaticism and violence.

How do we square this with what appears to have been a flagrant act of zealotry?

In order to really understand the true significance – the purpose and accomplishment – of Pineḥas' act, it is necessary to view it within the precise context and situation of its perpetration. I would submit that had it not been for his quick response, nothing less than "war" would have broken out – and civil war against Moses at that! Pineḥas' aim was not only – or even chiefly – the righteous punishment of flagrant sinners; it was first and foremost the salvation of Moses and Torah as the guides of the Israelites!

The Israelites had begun consorting with the Moabite women (Numbers 25), with harlotry leading to idolatry. They justified their actions philosophically and theologically by claiming that whatever is natural, whoever gives physical relief and "good feeling," was proper and laudatory. This is the idol called Ba'al Peor, who was served by performing one's natural functions before the idol, testifying to a lifestyle which justifies any and every physical expression. At this point, God commanded Moses to "take the leaders and impale them publicly before God" (Numbers 25:4). Only the leaders were targeted, but their death was to be vivid and painful, hanging in the hot sun.

What we have here on the part of the Israelites is a repetition of the Golden Calf debacle – but forty years later and in a far more grievous package. Then it was a panicky return to the comfort of Egyptian idolatry, a search for a Moses substitute; now it was glaring repudiation of both nationality and morality. Nevertheless, the previous time, at the dawn of Israel's freedom, Moses lost no time in exacting punishment. He took the idol of the Golden Calf, ground it to powder, and called for volunteers to execute the ringleaders. The tribe of Levi killed three thousand Israelites on that day. Moses had only to send forth the clarion call – "Whoever is with God, stand with me" – and all of the Levites rallied to his side. Moses was clearly the leader of the Israelites. Indeed, the sinful idolatry at that time was even understandable. It had only occurred because of the people's fear as a result of Moses' absence; they felt like children bereft of their earthly father – and in their despair they turned to the Egyptian father-in-heaven-idol of a Golden Calf.

Now forty years had passed. Long gone were the grandiose hopes of an infant nation on the way to its Promised Land; such an exalted vision had been dashed upon the arid sand dunes of frustration and despair. The only thing this desert generation had to anticipate was dying in the desert! The bright Egyptian gloss on Moses' liberating tunic had become burnished by the hot desert sun and the nagging Israelite complaints. The various rebellions turned Moses' eyes downcast and made his shoulders sag; indeed, the would-be upstarts Datan and

Aviram even refused to give the leader the courtesy of a meeting when they were summoned at his behest.

And now the disgusting Peor idolatry took place before Moses' very eyes, those holy eyes which had a closer glimpse into the divine than any mortal before or after. Moses apparently did not feel himself to be sufficiently in control as to be able to impale the rebel-leaders as God had requested. The best he could bring himself to do was direct the judges to take action. He also felt the necessity to change the divine graphically described punishment of hanging the leaders in the sun to the more diplomatic but far less aggressive command that "each of you must kill your constituents who were involved with Ba'al Peor" (Numbers 25:5).

And then, as a response to Moses' orders, a devastating occurrence followed: "Behold, an important personage (*ish*) from among the children of Israel came and brought... a Midianite woman in the sight of Moses and in the sight of the congregation of the children of Israel" (Numbers 25:6). Moses declared punishment for the idolaters – and a Jew added insult to injury by publicly committing adultery with a gentile Midianite woman!

And who was this Jew who dared defy the divine decree and the authority of Moses? He is biblically identified as none other than Zimri, prince of the tribe of Simeon, second in line of the tribes, between Reuben, the firstborn, and Levi, the priests. He was obviously continuing the rebellion of Koraḥ, demanding his rights as a descendant of the son of Jacob who was born before Levi; he was now claiming for himself an exalted position. Perhaps that is why he chose Kozbi, a Midianite princess – a woman with status and lineage in the gentile world. And even more to the point, he chose a Midianite because he wanted to embarrass Moses as effectively as possible. It is as if he were daring Moses to stop his act of harlotry; after all, how could Moses criticize Zimri if the leader himself had a Midianite wife! No wonder Moses was paralyzed into silence and the people could only weep in impotence: "They were weeping at the Tent of Meeting" (Numbers 25:6). How else can we understand Moses' lack of leadership, his inability to quell this rebellion against him and his God? As the sages of Talmud picture the scene, Zimri ran about taunting the venerated liberator of the Hebrew slaves:

"How can he forbid sexual contact with Midianite women if he himself took a Midianite wife!" (*Sanhedrin* 82a).

Yes, the Israelite world had considerably changed from what it had been forty years earlier, during the period immediately following the Golden Calf. Now the Jews were no longer contrite in the presence of Moses. Everyone was demoralized and disappointed. Zimri now hoped to strike the death knell of Moses' leadership by hitting below the belt, by taunting the supposed guardian of morality with the fact of his Midianite wife!

The Bible records: "And Pineḥas saw" (25:7). What did he see? He saw the people rebelling and he saw Moses weeping. He saw the end of the history of the children of Israel almost before it began, he saw immorality and assimilation about to smash the tablets of stone for the second time – but now without a forceful, fiery, and respected Moses with the capacity of restoring the eternal tablets of testimony once again.

This is when Pineḥas stepped in. In killing Zimri and Kozbi in the midst of their immoral act in front of all of Israel, he was not merely fanatically punishing a sinner without the justice of due process; he was quelling a rebellion against Moses which would have resulted in anarchy at best. He reestablished Mosaic leadership and authority, he enabled Torah to remain supreme. Pineḥas reinstated the covenant between God and Israel, and so he was truly worthy of the covenant of peace.

Pineḥas, A Man of Peace

Pineḥas the son of Elazar the son of Aaron the High Priest turned back My wrath from upon the children of Israel when he zealously expressed My zealousness amongst them…. Therefore tell him I have given him My covenant of peace."

NUMBERS 25:11–12

Covenant of peace?

To pursue why God's gift of peace was bestowed upon Pineḥas the zealot, we need to turn to the book of Joshua, examining an incident from the later history of the Jewish people which highlights Pineḥas as a mediating peacemaker rather than a fanatic zealot – and would confirm our previous commentary.

Many years had passed (Joshua 22); the Bible records that under Joshua's leadership, the major conquest of the land had been accomplished, paving the way for the Reubenites, the Gadites, and half the tribe of Menashe to return to inhabit Transjordan, the land of Gilead on the eastern side of the Jordan River – good grazing land for their cattle requested long ago from Moses before the battles against the Canaanites had begun (Numbers 32).

The two-and-one-half tribes arrived in their desired and apportioned lands and immediately erected an altar near the Jordan, "a large altar, for everyone to see" (Joshua 22:10), a veritable showpiece. The other tribes of Israel were incensed; they saw the erection of a large altar in Transjordan – far from the central Sanctuary in Shilo – as an act of rebellion against the God of Israel, a "declaration of independence" from the rest of the tribes. "And when the children of Israel heard of it, the whole congregation of the children of Israel gathered at Shilo to rise up in battle [against the two-and-one-half tribes in Transjordan]" (Joshua 22:12).

But before they declared a civil war, they dispatched none other than Pineḥas the son of Elazar the priest, together with ten heads of tribes, to attempt a peaceful resolution of the conflict. Pineḥas' delegation brilliantly reminded them of the disastrous plague that had descended upon the entire nation when they had first begun to worship the Peor idol and to cohabit with Moabite and Midianite women, an obvious reference to the idolatry which had led to Pineḥas' own act of punishment which brought about the plague's cessation (Numbers 12:10–18). Pineḥas warned that the building of their altar separate from the central altar in Shilo would cause repercussions, endangering the entire nation of Israel; the remaining ten tribes might be forced to take action against them to prevent a disastrous plague from striking these rebellious upstart idolaters.

The underlying motif of Pineḥas' argument was the integrity of remaining one nation – each responsible for the actions of the other – despite the distance that separated them. In the interest of unity, he told them that if they felt "defiled or contaminated by their distance from the Sanctuary on the other side of the Jordan, then they ought return to mainland Israel," even though it would mean giving up some of their own land in the requisite redistribution of territory which would have to take place (Joshua 22:19).

The response of the two-and-one-half tribes magnified the theme of unity; it was never their intention to use their altar to replace the Sanctuary in Shilo for sacrificial offerings. Theirs was not an act of rebellion, urging religious or civil acts of disobedience. Indeed, they intended their altar to serve as a symbol for future generations of the unity of faith and nationality between the tribes on both sides of the Jordan River. Their actual sacrifices would be offered only in the Sanctuary in Shilo.

His return to the children of Israel in Canaan marked Pineḥas as a successful mediator and peacemaker, revealing the essence of his personality as a true kohen and lover of peace who, when younger, had been forced by extreme circumstances to step out of character and punish without due process in order to prevent Moses and his directives from becoming marginalized.

Or perhaps there is an alternative perspective: that in fact Pineḥas had acted upon his emotions of zealotry, but since, in a fateful moment for Israel, his action actually saved the nation, God granted him the gift which is truly the goal of Israel, the gift of peace and the covenant of compassion. And now we see from the book of Joshua (22) that Pineḥas learned his lesson and eventually became a successful mediator of peace!

Whatever may have been the initial character of Pineḥas, one message is clear from the test: even if a momentary act of zealotry is called for in an unusual circumstance, fanaticism must neither be our national norm nor our national goal. Our norm and our goal must always be God's covenant of peace!

Do What Comes Naturally

Do battle against the Midianites and smite them. They are your enemies because of the plot which they plotted against you concerning the matter of Peor and the matter of Kozbi the daughter of the Prince of Midian.

NUMBERS 25:17–18

Why was Kozbi killed? Was it because of her immoral sexual seduction of an Israelite or because she and her Midianite clan worshipped the idol Peor? Rashi (ad loc.) is aware of the textual problem, and suggests that the end-goal of the Midianites, and the reason for which they sent their daughters to tempt the Israeli men, was to get the Israelites to worship Peor. And there seems to be a strong linkage between blatant sexual immorality between Jew and gentile, and Peor as the Mother of all idolatries; but what exactly is the nature of the transgression on the table, sexual immorality between Jew and gentile or the Peor idolatry?

A careful reading of the biblical account of Pineḥas' act clearly emphasizes a seeming confusion concerning the nature of the transgression, or a fusion of two transgressions which are intermingled. In the previous Torah reading, the introduction to the story of public cohabitation begins:

> And the Israelites dwelt in Shittim, and began to whore after the daughters of Moab. And it happened that the Israelite nation served their idols… and Israel became joined to Ba'al Peor; the anger of God waxed hot against Israel.
>
> Numbers 25:1–3

Again, what was the sin? Was it whoring, or the idolatry of Peor?

And finally, this same seeming confusion appears in our rabbinic commentaries. Bileam is identified as "ben Beor" (Numbers 22:5) which might be identified with Peor, son of the idol Peor, and when the narrative continues to describe how "Balak took Bileam to the top of Mount Peor" (Numbers 23:28), Rashi comments, "Balak was a great magician, and he saw that the Israelites would eventually be punished because of Peor," which apparently applies to idolatry. However, when the Talmud attempts to describe the evil counsel which Bileam offered the nations who wished to vanquish Israel, the picture presented is one of sexual seduction by the young, nubile, gentile women (*Sanhedrin* 106a).

And so we must ask the fundamental question: was the more heinous crime the sexual immorality or the worship of Peor? And what is the real transgression of this idolatry? The answer becomes clear when we attempt to understand the nature of Peor worship. The Mishna in tractate *Sanhedrin* teaches that Peor was worshipped by defecating in front of him – hardly the kind of appetizing religious cult which one would think would attract masses of adherents. But apparently Peor was very popular, at least with Midian and Moab. And I would suggest that the means of serving Peor provides a blatantly antithetical message to everything Judaism stands for and is attempting to teach the world. Yes, defecation is a perfectly normal human function, and the individual who relieves himself feels relieved! Hence, that is how god is to be served! Do whatever is natural to do, do whatever makes you feel good, "Let it all hang out"; if this is your nature, if the act is natural for you to do, then it becomes correct to express it, and thereby to express yourself.

Is this not merely a re-statement – or cultural precursor – of much of contemporary, post-modern thought, of Norman O. Brown's *Eros and Civilization* and Herbert Marcuse's attitude toward life?! Discipline has become the "hobgoblin of little minds," and self-expression takes precedence over duty to family, to country, and to ideal. It is a ramification of Koraḥ's "we are all holy" as is, without the necessity of sacrifice and striving, and a precursor of post-modernism, that there are no absolutes with regard to morality or to what is proper or improper conduct. Everyone has the right to his or her feelings, and everyone is right from his or her point of view. Ethics are "situational," dependent upon one's situation, and every individual is a genius when it comes to justifying the realization of his desires in his subjective situation.

This is a far cry from Freud's *Civilization and Its Discontents* which presumes the price of limiting one's desires in order to form a civil society; it is the very antithesis of the biblical directive (at the pre-dawn of human history in the Garden of Eden) for self-control and self-limitation – not eating forbidden fruit and not defining good and evil based on one's subjective drives. Peor denies absolute morality. For Peor, human is no different from animal; he is a creature of instinct, who may defecate publicly just as animals defecate publicly, and he has no innate responsibility – not before God and not before any other being.

What was the greater crime, worshipping Peor or indulging in public fornication? They are one and the same. Peor teaches that if one feels like fornicating one fornicates, when and with whom one wishes to do it. After all, sex has nothing to do with love and sanctity, and everything to do with a natural physical urge, much more in line with defecation than a sacred union.

From this perspective, the rabbinical voices like the Meiri were absolutely correct: idolatry has little to do with theology and much to do with the "disgusting, immoral practices" of those who follow the teachings of the likes of Peor. And Zimri ben Salou was not only expressing a desire; he was rebelling against Moses, against God, and against the very foundation of Torah.

Women's Rights Express Righteousness

And they [the daughters of Tzelofḥad] stood before Moses, and before Elazar the priest, and before the princes and all the congregation, by the door of the Tent of Meeting, saying: "Our father died in the desert and he was not in the company of them that gathered against God in the company of Koraḥ; but died in his own sin, and had no sons. Why should the name of our father be done away from among his family, because he has no son? Give to us a possession among the brethren of our father."

NUMBERS 27:2–4

The story of the five daughters of Tzelofḥad, whose insistence to Moses upon their right of inheritance is recounted in the Torah portion of *Pineḥas*, resonates with contemporary issues of women's rights. The Bible had already stipulated that land was to be inherited only by the male progeny. But what if there was no male progeny, only daughters?

Moses had apparently not received a prior teaching in this regard so he turned to a higher authority, God Himself, who declared: "The daughters of Tzelofḥad speak right. You shall surely give them a hereditary portion of land alongside their father's brethren" (Numbers 27:7). A surface reading of the text indicates that here we have an early and most striking example of a divine commitment to enhance the legal and economic status of women. And whether the motivation of these women to receive an inheritance in the absence of male siblings was based on economic needs or the desire to "keep the land in the family" is not as important as the fact that the daughters of Tzelofḥad argued the case for women's rights under biblical law. And because they won the first bona fide example of feminist legislation "on the books," it certainly seems that theirs was a landmark victory for women and the feminist cause.

However, it is fascinating that the Midrash calls the daughters of Tzelofḥad *tzidkaniot*, which means virtuous and pious women (*Midrash Rabba*, ad loc.). One could well understand our sages referring to them as persevering, courageous, and aggressive. But why call them virtuous and pious? On what basis term them *tzidkaniot*?

A *tzaddeket* is someone generally perceived as a peacemaker rather than a trailblazer, a do-gooder rather than a crusader, one who moves anonymously garnering help for others rather than one who insists on her own rights, one who shuns the spotlight rather than one who merits biblical headlines.

Do the daughters of Tzelofḥad sound like *tzidkaniot*? Isn't their struggle essentially a legal battle requiring a willful and dynamic personality, a crusading spirit that won't give up until the gavel rules in favor of a specific right and cause?!

In order to understand their piety and virtuousness, I believe we must be mindful of the mood and mentality of the desert Hebrews at the time as well as of the process involved in getting a case heard in the court of Moses. We know that once Moses' father-in-law Yitro (at the very beginning of the desert experience) transformed the time-consuming, frustrating system in which every single problem came to Moses' attention, and suggested in its place a system of lower and higher courts, Moses' life became far more normal. But this meant that each claimant had to start at the bottom.

Like everyone else with a grievance, the daughters of Tzelofḥad first had to approach the captains of tens. Then if they couldn't handle the case, they would approach the captain of fifties, then on to the captain of hundreds, and finally to the captain of thousands. By the time one even got to see Moses, the petitioner had to invest an enormous amount of time, energy, determination, persistence, and what then probably passed for money – a process not dissimilar to what it takes Joan Q. Public (Joan Q. Tzibur) to be heard by the Israeli supreme court (*Bagatz*). No matter how just the case may be, many give up along the way, their nerves and pockets unable to bear the burden of "fighting city hall."

In addition, since the previously transmitted laws of inheritance apparently excluded or made no particular provision for women, there must have been an endless chorus of voices who tried to discourage the daughters of Tzelofḥad from pursuing a lost cause. How many people on the sidelines must have told them to forget about it, that they were wasting their lives; instead of wrestling with the law they should be thinking about getting married! (And according to the Midrash, none of these women got married before the age of forty.) Moreover, the Israelites had already sinned the sin of the scouts, and had been told that the entire generation would die in the desert. So even if their claim proved to be a landmark decision of victory, what good would it do? Remember, the rebellion of Koraḥ had occurred before these women began their battle against the establishment. The nation was filled with frustration, disappointment, and despair, uncertain as to whether any Israelite would ever enter the Promised Land! Why fight so hard for a patrimony in a land on which neither they nor their progeny would ever live, for a mirage? Most of the people believed that the Israelites would live out their historic life in the desert anyway – and the followers of Koraḥ rejoiced in that probable eventuality.

This scenario, I believe, is behind the midrashic perception of the daughters of Tzelofḥad as being virtuous and pious – *tzidkaniot*. When Abraham believed in God's promise to give him and Sarah a son despite the biological impossibility, "God accounted it to him as an act of righteous piety [*tzedaka*]" (Genesis 15:6). The daughters of Tzelofḥad are considered pious because of their extraordinary faith – faith in God, faith in the Land of Israel, faith in the ultimate equity of the Torah of

Israel. By their struggle, they in effect testified to that faith, declaring that although the generation would die in the desert, and perhaps even the next generation would engage in seemingly endless battles for Israel, the time would come when God's promise would be realized; they understood the necessity of fighting for one's children and grandchildren, and not only for oneself. They understood that although the Land of Israel may be denied to a particular generation of Israelites, it belongs to historic Israel of the eternal generations; God does not promise falsely, or repent of His pledges! Moreover, they believed in the rightness and righteousness of the laws of Israel, so they were certain that ultimately their claim would be vindicated! Because of the steadfastness of their faith, they were indeed pious women, *tzidkaniot*!

Postscript regarding Elijah the Prophet

Fascinatingly enough, the story of Tzelofḥad occurs in the Torah portion which opens with the zealot Pineḥas, who is midrashically identified with the zealous prophet Elijah. It is most instructive to point out the significant contrast between these righteous daughters and the zealot Elijah. After forcing an encounter between the false priests of Ba'al and the true Lord of Israel, Elijah had to escape the wrath of Jezebel the queen. His journey brought him to Ḥorev, all the way down in the Sinai desert, a great distance from the Carmel Mountains. Disappointed, bitter, he spoke disparagingly about the Israelites, who did not seem to have been at all affected by Elijah's miraculous victory against the idolaters: "I have been very zealous for the Lord God of hosts, but the children of Israel have forsaken Your covenant" (1 Kings 19:14). Shortly thereafter, Elijah left center stage of Jewish history, bestowing the prophetic mantle upon the shoulders of Elisha. The sages of the Midrash, however, grant him an eternal mission: Elijah has a special seat of honor at every circumcision ceremony and comes to drink the fifth cup of wine at every Pesaḥ Seder.

Perhaps the sages are suggesting that the Almighty chooses Elijah for these supernatural feats not so much as a gift but rather in order to teach him a lesson: you, Elijah, accused the Israelites of abandoning their covenant! Now see with your own eyes how, in every generation, the

Israelites maintain their covenant, circumcise their sons, and celebrate the Exodus from Egypt. In effect, the Almighty is reproving the zealous prophet, is taking him to task for charging the Israelites with having abandoned their covenant. He is forcing Elijah to see Jewish commitment and Jewish faith, the Jewish willingness to pass on from generation to generation, in the very organ of propagation, the command to give our blood for our future and our land (the commandment of circumcision was given by God to Abraham as the seal of His covenant guaranteeing our eternal inheritance of the land in Genesis 17:8–14), and our belief in the impossible dream of redemption, welcoming Elijah every Seder night while crying out, "Next year in Jerusalem" from the cellars of the Inquisition and the dark, dank hiding places in Auschwitz.

Elijah had to be reminded to have faith; the daughters of Tzelofḥad were the very embodiment of that faith. They believed – in a period no less difficult than that of Elijah – in the God of Israel, in the Land of Israel, and in the Torah of Israel. They knew that "the Eternal one of Israel will never promise falsely."

May We Learn Torah from Women?

> *The daughters of Tzelofḥad speak right. You shall surely give them a hereditary portion of land alongside that of their father's brethren.*
>
> NUMBERS 27:7

One of the most fascinating aspects of the entire Torah is the portion which deals with the case of the daughters of Tzelofḥad, an incident considered of such significance that it is repeated at the conclusion of the book of Numbers as well (Numbers 36). How much faith we learn from these resourceful and irrepressible women!

But a most interesting secondary question may be pondered from the midrashic study of the incident of these five women: is it indeed permissible for men to learn Torah from women in the first place? In this particular instance the Talmud (*Bava Batra* 119) pictures Moses giving a class on the levirate marriage, with the five Tzelofḥad sisters in attendance. They raise a question before Moses: Is a daughter considered significant issue, to be respected as progeny and heir to her father's estate, or not? If not, then you must allow our widowed mother to marry her deceased husband's brother and be supported by him as the respected wife of a levirate marriage, just as though she hadn't had issue or progeny at all. But if we daughters are considered progeny enough to exclude our mother from a levirate marriage, then you must allow us to inherit our father! And God decides in favor of the argument of these women. Hence it would seem that we certainly can learn Torah from women!

The Bible refers to two fundamental Jewish ideals, Torah and the Land of Israel, as *morasha,* a heritage, rather than *yerusha,* an inheritance (see Exodus 6:8 and Deut. 33:4). From a literal perspective, the unique word "heritage" (*morasha*) connotes more than the usual "inheritance"; it has the additional directive that it must be handed over from generation to generation. An inheritance can be cash money, and may be squandered away; a heritage is an heirloom, like candlesticks or a Kiddush goblet, and is meant to be passed down to one's children. And Torah study applies to women as well as to men: "And Moses went up to God, and the Lord called to him from the mountain saying, 'Thus shall you say to the house of Jacob [Rashi: this refers to the women] and shall you declare to the children of Israel [Rashi: the males]'" (Exodus 19:3). Therefore, the commandment of *hak'hel,* to gather the Israelites once every seven years and establish a reaffirmation of the covenant via a public study of Torah, includes the women as well as the men (Deut. 31:12). And if women must learn and accept Torah (at least the portions of Torah necessary to properly observe the commandment of God), then they must likewise be responsible to pass Torah down to the next generation – parent to child, teacher to student.

It is for this reason that Deborah is praised as one of the first judges in Israel (Judges 4:4–5), that Bruriah disagreed halakhically with her father Rabbi Ḥanina b. Teradion and her view is recorded (*Tosefta Kelim* 4), and that the *Sefer HaḤinukh* rules (Negative Commandment 152) that a learned woman fit to render religio-legal decisions may do so. (Similarly rule the Ḥida, *Barki Yosef Ḥoshen Mishpat* 7:12, and the Rishon LeTzion HaRav Bakshi Doron, *Binyan Av* Siman 65.) To cite only one anecdotal example amongst many, when a difficult *eiruv* question came up before a number of scholars, the grandmother of Rav Shneur Zalman of Liadi adjudicated the matter, and everyone acquiesced to her decision (*Sefer HaZikhronot,* Rabbi Yosef Yitzchak Schneerson, Part 2).

The practical Torah that we learn from the daughters of Tzelofḥad is that women do not only have a portion of Torah, but that they also have a portion in the Holy Land of Israel. Their particular case, which was ultimately adjudicated by the Almighty Himself because Moses did not have the answer, was that they were correct in insisting that since their father had no sons, they – the five women – were to receive their rightful portions in the Land of Israel (Numbers 27:7). As a direct result of their vindication, the Almighty conveyed all of the laws of inheritance to Moses and Israel (Numbers 27:8–11). Indeed, women's inheritance rights developed from this case to such an extent that if a father bequeaths only a small amount of property, the daughters' sustenance and dowries must be provided for – even if nothing will be left over for the sons (*Ketubot* 108b).

But what we really learn from the daughters of Tzelofḥad is the true love of the Land of Israel, as we have seen in our previous Torah commentary.

It is on this basis that Rabbi Ephraim of Lunschitz, known as the *Kli Yakar*, gives the following "feminist" spin to his interpretation of the first verse of the sin of the scouts: "And the Lord spoke to Moses saying, 'Send forth your men that they may scout out the land'" (Numbers 13:2). Writes the *Kli Yakar*: "Since our Sages teach that it was [only] men who hated the Land [of Israel] and said 'let us return to Egypt,' whereas the women loved the land, as they [the daughters of Tzelofḥad] said 'Give us an inheritance,' the Holy One blessed be He, who knows the future, said it would be better to send women, but [unfortunately], you [Moses] trust [your] men." God understood, however, that only tragedy would result from a reconnaissance mission consisting only of men!

Inheritance in the Land, Our Ticket to Eternity

Why should the name of our father be lessened [reduced] from the midst of his family... ? Give us a permanent holding of land [an inheritance] among the brothers of our father.

NUMBERS 27:4

What was the fundamental underlying motivation of these five outstanding daughters of Tzelofḥad, whom the sages of the Talmud praise as women of "wisdom, analytic ingenuity, and righteousness" (*ḥakhmaniot, darshaniot, tzidkaniot*; *Bava Batra* 119b)? Was it their inheritance rights to land in Israel that they were after or was it their father's rights to land in Israel for his progeny that they were after?

Let us analyze the biblical text in an attempt to understand their true motivation. According to the complaint which they brought before Moses: "Why should the name of our [deceased] father be lessened" by not giving us the inheritance rights to his land (Numbers 27:4)? They were focusing not on an injustice being perpetrated against them, but rather on an injustice being done to their father: without an heir to his land, their father's name was somehow being lessened, being reduced, while he was buried in his grave! What do these words actually mean?

It has truly been said that almost every individual has three names: the name that his parents gave him, which usually expresses in some way the aspirations they had for him; the name by which his friends call him, which expresses how his contemporaries see him; and the name which he gives to himself, which expresses the degree to which he has succeeded in overcoming limitations and even in recreating himself.

But there is yet a fourth name, which is perhaps the most important name of all: the name which the individual leaves behind after his death. The most obvious manner in which one's name is transmitted and continued into the future is through a child, a son or a daughter, in Hebrew *ben* or *bat* (*bant*), which are derived from the verb B-N-H, to build; we build ourselves up into the future through the children we leave behind, or the students, the people, the sundry individuals we may have nurtured and supported, influenced, or significantly touched in our lifetimes, even if we never had biological children. In the words of our sages, "'and you shall teach Torah to your children,' which refers to your students, who are considered like your children" (Deut. 6:7, Rashi ad loc.). Those who because of us continue the values and lifestyle of that legacy we have received from our forebears and which we are responsible to pass over to the next generation become the further stories of our joint building, our gateway into future, our continuity into eternity.

One of the blessings under the nuptial canopy praises God for having made each Jewish couple "an eternal building." Indeed, the very Hebrew word for stone, *even* – the stuff of which buildings are made – is derived from two Hebrew words, *av* and *ben*, parent and child, according to the Midrash. This eternal building had its origins in the Cave of the Couples (*Ma'arat HaMakhpela*) in Ḥebron, in the desert no-man's land and every-man's land at Sinai, and anticipates its fulfillment in the universal acceptance of God's peace which will emanate from Jerusalem. Every individual mortal Jew yearns to be a stone in the immortal building of eternal Israel, a musical score in the unfinished symphony of Israel.

And there is one more aspect to this building of Israel: its foundations must be deeply rooted in the soil of our eternal homeland Israel.

Only in the Land of Israel is there continuity between Jews today and their ancient origins in Ḥebron where our patriarchs and matriarchs began their journey and chartered their destiny – and where their burial place still remains a place of Jewish prayer. Only in the Land of Israel is there continuity between Jews today and the holy city of Jerusalem, where Abraham took Isaac to the *Akeda* and where Jews still pray at the Western Wall, remnant of our Holy Temple which will yet be rebuilt – and will eventually stand as a beacon of peace for all nations. It was in the City of David that our two commonwealths were established and flourished, in the Galil that the Mishna (the literary basis for the Talmudic literature and our Codes of Law) was written down, that the Jerusalem Talmud was completed, and that the mystical lore of the Kabbala was revealed and incorporated in our prayers and rituals; it was in the Negev where Abraham and Isaac grazed their sheep, that David Ben-Gurion, first prime minister of our Third Commonwealth, returned to live out the final years of his life, and established institutions of higher learning dedicated to the scientific progress of humanity.

On the other hand, in Babylon – today Iraq – for example, where the Jews experienced a golden age of creativity with the great yeshivot of the Talmudic *Amora'im* and the post-Talmudic Geonim during the first thousand years of the Common Era, there is not the slightest remnant of the once-proud Jewish community which flourished in that land. No wonder the Talmud insists that only in Israel can the Jewish residents consider themselves a *kehilla*, a real and eternal community (*Horayot* 3b). No wonder that Jews who lived in the furthest areas of the globe were often buried in Israel or – at the very least – provided with earth from the Land of Israel to be placed upon their final remains. "Generations go and generations come, but the land remains forever" (Ecclesiastics 1:4). And so Jews throughout history have wished their last physical remains to be merged with the eternal soil of our eternal homeland.

Hence the Bible tells of the tragedy of an individual who dies childless; ideally, his brother is to marry his widow, and the first son who is born shall assume the "name" of the deceased and received the patrimony – portion of the land in Israel – of the deceased, so that the "name" of the deceased not be blotted out of Israel (Deut. 25:6). Jewish eternity is predicated upon the continuation of the name of the deceased, expressed by the maintenance of his values and traditions, as well as upon rootedness in the Land of Israel. And so Jacob blesses his grandchildren, even when they were in Egyptian exile, "And my name and the name of my forebears Abraham, Isaac, and Jacob shall be called through them, and they shall multiply into multitudes in the midst of the land [of Israel]" (Genesis 48:16).

Yes, the daughters of Tzelofḥad made a great stride forward on behalf of women's rights to inheritance by receiving their father's patrimony. But their major motivation was familial and national: to secure their father's eternity, to see to it that his "name not be reduced" in the building of Jewish eternity by his ability to give over (*morasha*) both his traditions and his portion of land to his progeny after him. Jewish eternity means having children true to the values and traditions of historic Israel (*Knesset Yisrael*) living in the eternal Land of Israel.

Precisely What Did Moses "Hand Over" to Joshua, and Why?

> *And the Lord said to Moses, "Take for yourself Joshua the son of Nun, an individual who has spirit within him,* and lay [or lean] your hand upon him. Stand him up before Elazar the Priest *and before the entire congregation and command him before their eyes.* And give of your glory upon him *in order that the entire congregation of the children of Israel may obey him."*
>
> NUMBERS 27:18–20

In these three verses we see the "passing of the guard," the succession of leadership from Moses to Joshua. Embedded within the three different actions which God commanded Moses to perform are profound insights into three different aspects of traditional Jewish leadership. Firstly, Moses was to "lay his hands" upon Joshua, an act which expressed a conferral of rabbinic authority, *semikha* (literally a laying upon or leaning upon), from master to disciple (Mishna *Sanhedrin* 1:3). Since Moses was traditionally known as *Moshe Rabbenu,* Moses our religious teacher or our rabbi, and since Joshua is biblically and midrashically pictured as Moses' devoted disciple, it is perfectly logical to assume that the first transference from Moses to Joshua was that of religio-legal authority to rule on religio-legal issues. Moreover, Moses was a great prophet who conveyed the divine word to his nation and who was responsible for the spiritual and ethical well-being of his nation; as such, his charisma derived not only from his intellectual acumen, but also from his ability to religiously inspire and elevate. Hence Moses was here bestowing upon Joshua his own authority as religio-legal master as well as spiritual guide and mentor.

Moses was then commanded by God to "stand Joshua up" before Elazar the High Priest. The *Kohen Gadol,* or High Priest, was certainly a leader in ancient Israel – but his divine service was formal, ritual, and external, very much limited to the Sanctuary or Holy Temple. It was necessary for the rabbi-scholar-teacher to be recognized and respected by the High Priest, and vice versa; however, whereas the former had to constantly bring the living word of God to the people, had to interpret it and make it relevant for each generation and its needs, for each individual on his or her level and in accordance with his or her personal situation, the latter merely had to perform the precise Temple ritual so that the continuity of the divine service from generation to generation would be maintained. The rabbi-scholar-teacher had to be a person of the people, a *posek* very aware of the temper of the times and the personal needs of the individual he was dealing with; the *Kohen Gadol* was more like the classical Rosh Yeshiva, who lived within the Torah tower of timeless eternity and whose task was to protect and preserve the laws and rituals which linked the generations and the peoples together, as part of an eternal nation. The two had to respect and complement each other, despite the natural tensions which their respective responsibilities were likely to engender.

And finally, Moses was to "give of his glory [*hod*] upon [Joshua] in order that the entire congregation of Israel may obey him" (Numbers 27:20). In addition to being the religious rabbi-scholar-teacher (and prophet), Moses also served as authoritative king (Deut. 33:4–5), the chief executive office of the Israelite nation, a rabbi-king or prophet-king. This is the aspect of authority which is referred to as the glory which Moses conferred upon Joshua. Rabbi Jonathan Sacks, chief rabbi of the United Kingdom, sees the first aspects of Moses' leadership – rabbi, teacher, prophet – as expressing *influence*, and this *hod* aspect of Moses' leadership as expressing *power*! Moses, after all, acted in the capacity of halakhic prophet-king, a singular advance over Plato's philosopher-king.

My revered teacher Rabbi Joseph Soloveitchik went one step further when he interpreted the biblical text of the "laying of the hands" at the celebration of my class' rabbinical ordination (*Ḥag HaSemikha*). The "laying of the hands" is usually interpreted as an intergenerational conferral of authority: the master from a former generation is "handing over" the authority of our ancient tradition (*trado* in Latin means to hand over) to the younger generation. In this regard the disciple is "leaning upon" his master-teacher, who taught him the traditions and is now qualifying him to teach them to the next generation.

However, says Rabbi Soloveitchik, that is not the picture presented by the biblical text. The Hebrew *smokh* (*semikha*) principally means to lean on, so that the picture being conveyed is that of an elderly Moses leaning with his hands upon a younger Joshua. The message seems not to be that of a young Joshua dependent upon the authority of an elder Moses; it rather seems to be that of an elder Moses dependent for his support upon a younger Joshua. Rabbi Soloveitchik looked at us, his student-rabbis, with great yearning and expectations. "It is I who am dependent upon you. Without you, my Torah and my unique teaching, indeed all of the traditions which I imbibed from the previous generations, will all die with me. You are my insurance policy. It is through you and your teaching that my Torah will continue to live." Power barely lasts for one generation; influence can continue into eternity.

This is why Moses had to put down Koraḥ – who wanted to usurp power for a false end – but encouraged Eldad and Medad, who were influenced by a divine spirit. And this is the true meaning of our sages' adage that a father is never jealous of a child nor is a teacher ever jealous of a disciple. Politics yields power, which disappears in the sand dunes of time; learning and piety breed influence, which lasts for all time. The Israelite kings are scarcely remembered while the Israelite prophets and sages are still being studied and interpreted today. Lust for power is ultimately consumed by fiery flames, while the influence of Torah education will enable the light of the menora to emblazon the path to the tree of eternal life as we progress (halakha) on the road to messianic redemption.

The True Task of Leadership: Unity in Diversity, Not in Uniformity

If only our rabbinic leadership would understand that kashrut *is supposed to unite our people rather than divide us.*

May the Lord God of the spirits of all flesh appoint a leader over the witness community [edah].

NUMBERS 27:16

After the Almighty commanded Moses to ascend Mount Avarim (Mount Nebo) and gaze at the Land of Israel – to which he had been denied entry because he struck the rock – Moses proposed: "Let the Lord, God of the spirits of all flesh, appoint a person over the community who will go out before them, come in before them, and who will lead them out and bring them in." The Almighty responded: "Take for yourself Joshua the son of Nun, a person in whom there is spirit, and rest your hand upon him" (Numbers 27:12–18).

It is fascinating that Moses referred to the Almighty as "God of the spirits of all flesh." Rashi sees this as a ringing endorsement of pluralism – the necessity of a leader to be sensitive to different attitudes and ideas: "[Moses] said before Him: Master of the Universe, it is clear to You that each individual's understanding is different from that of their counterparts. Appoint over them a leader who will be tolerant of everyone, each in accordance with his understanding" (Rashi, ad loc.).

Rashi's commentary is based on the *Midrash Tanḥuma*, which links this idea to the rabbinic enactment that if one sees a gathering of six hundred thousand Jews or more, one is to recite the blessing "Praised be God, the Wise One of Mysteries"; "just as the facial features of each individual are different, so are their mindsets."

This special blessing is a practical expression of the Mishna (Mishna *Sanhedrin* chapter 4) which contrasts the Lord God, King of all kings, with a human mortal king; the mortal king takes one mold from which he mints millions of coins, each exactly alike; the divine King took "one" person, Adam and Eve, from whom came many billions, each one *different*! And it is the different ones which emanate from the one which are the truest glory of the God of Creation.

Rabbi A.Y. Kook, the first chief rabbi of Israel, explains in his *Olat Re'iya*:

> And in accordance with the secret mysteries known and revealed only to the Almighty, praised be He, even antithetical notions may be joined together and synthesized, until a harmonious result emerges from the combination of different ideas.... Their views do not begin as convergent, but ultimately the different strains and strands will merge as one. And it is certain that this ultimate unity is not evident from the beginning, because then the dispute as well as the fine-tuning of the differences would not continue.... And so we are taught by the Talmudic sages: "Scholars increase peace in the world."

The word "increase" is a plural form (*marbim*); through the multiplicity of ideas in a dispute for the sake of heaven, an ultimate peace and unity can be formed, a peace and unity which unites not from the obliteration of differences, but rather from incorporating part of what is different within the ultimate unity – as a synthesis, and sometimes even as a dialectic.

Rashi and the Midrash both explain the phrase "God of the spirits of all flesh" as referring to differences of opinion, first and foremost in halakha – as expressions of "these and those are the words of the living God" (*Eruvin* 13b), which teaches us to preserve minority opinions in halakhic discourse because they may become admissible, and even vital, for another individual in another situation or in another time period. This also and perhaps especially holds true in the realm of beliefs, opinions, and attitudes.

Contemporary Judaism is a great deal richer as a result of the differing approaches of Hasidim and *Mitnagdim*. Even secular and less halakhic forms of Judaism have contributed rituals which have become integrated within more traditional expressions of our faith, such as the bat mitzva, preaching sermons in the vernacular, and the synthesis between Judaism and socialism which characterizes the religious kibbutz.

A perfect and ultimate unity, a true synthesis, can only emerge from the creative tension which is a by-product of a sincere clash of ideals and opinions.

What has all this to do with leadership? Moses asked God that his successor be sensitive to the "manifold spirits of all flesh"; that Moses' replacement not lead as a despot who silences all differing voices, but rather as a conductor who produces harmonious euphony from distinct instruments. The leader must recognize that what unites is much more significant than what divides, and so his major task is to unify without squelching individual creativity. He must produce unity but not uniformity, harmony but not a monotone.

The *Magen Avraham*, in discussing the various traditions in our prayer liturgies (Sephardic, Ashkenazic, Yemenite, and variations on the theme), suggests that they all hark back to the varied tapestries of "flags" of each of the twelve tribes; each tribe had its gate to the divine throne of glory, and "all the gates to heaven are gates of holiness."

If only we would all learn to love and respect the other, rather than to fear, delegitimize, and dehumanize. After all, the truest Other is the Almighty Himself, to whom we must cleave, and whom we must emulate; the Master of the Universe is the One who can bring together sun and clouds, fire and water, and fashion from these two opposing forces the ineffable and supernal peace and harmony of the heavens above (*oseh shalom bimromav*).

Matot

The Unique Prophecy of Moses

This is the thing [or word]
which God has commanded.
NUMBERS 30:2

How was Moses different from the many other prophets recorded in the biblical tradition? Was there a distinction only in degree, or was there a much more fundamental difference, a difference in "kind" between Moses and those who came after him?

The opening verse in the portion of *Matot* may well provide us with an insight concerning this issue. We read, "And Moses spoke unto the heads of the tribes of the children of Israel saying: 'This is the thing [or "word," *zeh hadavar*] which God has commanded: when a man vows a vow unto God …'" (Numbers 30:2–3).

In his commentary, Rashi cites a midrash (*Sifrei*) which makes the following distinction between Moses and the other prophets: whereas the other prophets consistently introduced their prophecy with the word, "*Thus* said God," (koh *amar Hashem*), the expression "*zeh hadavar asher tziva Hashem*" (*this* is the thing which God has commanded) is unique only to Moses (although *koh* also appears in Mosaic prophecies), and so *zeh* represents Moses' additional and superior prophetic status.

Rashi is apparently lifting Moses above the other prophets; he does not seem, however, to flesh out the substance of this superiority. One of the most important supercommentaries – or commentaries on the primary commentary Rashi – Rabbi Eliyahu Mizraḥi, the Re'em (1448–1526, chief rabbi of Constantinople), suggests that the phrase "*koh amar Hashem*" (thus said God) expresses the intention or the essence of the vision, although not necessarily the vision itself; after all, the other prophets only see "through a glass darkly" (*aspaklarya she'eina me'ira*). Moses' prophecy, however, is through "a glass brightly" (*aspaklarya me'ira*), and therefore he had the power to express precisely what was given to his eye or communicated to his mind, word for word: "*zeh*," this is (precisely) the thing, or word.

In *Emek HaNetziv*, the classic commentary on the *Sifrei* written by Rabbi Naftali Tzvi Yehuda Berlin, the author questions any interpretation which could possibly suggest that the vision of the other prophets could be anything less than an exact transmission. Moreover, the Netziv proves that the use of the word *koh* elsewhere in the Torah is taken by the Talmudic sages to indicate something absolute and exact: for example, when the priests are commanded to bless the Israelites, we read the following words, "And God spoke unto Moses telling him to speak to Aaron and to his sons, saying: 'This [*koh*] is how you must bless the children of Israel'" (Numbers 6:23). And our sages insist that the blessing is to be recited exactly as presented in the text, twenty-two words, no more and no less, in other words, "*This* is how you must bless...."

The Netziv therefore explains that what makes the prophecy of Moses unique, and what is the true significance of "*this*" rather than "*thus*," is the fact that Moses communicated the divine word immediately upon his having received it, whereas the other prophets could only process their message after a delay of a period of time; after all, the prophetic state had a paralyzing and debilitating affect on the other prophets, weakening their physical condition, while Moses received the Godly message naturally, without the requirement of time-in-between for recuperation. It was that in-between time which caused the delivery of the message by the other prophets to be less exact.

Rabbi Isaac Bernstein, the late erudite rabbi of London, called my attention to another commentary of Rabbi Yitzḥak Zev Soloveitchik (*Ḥidushei HaGryz*) which can truly illuminate our distinction between *koh* and *zeh*. When the young shepherd Moses is confronted by a burning bush which is not consumed, the Almighty attempts to convince him to accept the responsibility of Jewish leadership. Moses is hard to convince: "Who am I that I should bring forth the children of Israel out of Egypt?" (Exodus 3:11). But God counters Moses' resistance: "Certainly I will be with you" (Exodus 3:12).

The *Gryz* points out that the real significance of this dialogue is more profound than Moses merely seeking assurance and God guaranteeing "back-up." Moses is questioning the efficacy of human involvement altogether in what he thinks ought to be a divine mission. After all, did not the Almighty promise the patriarchs that He, God Himself, would act as the redeemer (*Midrash Rabba* 15)? The interpretation must be that the divine response "I will be with you" is God's explanation that indeed He will act as the redeemer, but that God acts through human instruments. God requires, as it were, human beings to be His full partners; the ground rules with which the world is governed require divine objectives to be realized through human agency. Hence, God must insist that He and Moses go to Pharaoh and redeem Israel *together*; God is choosing Moses to redeem the Israelites alongside of Him!

I would suggest that herein lies the truest distinction between Moses and the other prophets, as well as the significance of the differences in phraseology in the Hebrew text. The other prophets succeeded in receiving and transmitting a divine will; Moses succeeded in living a life and doing deeds which were the human extension of the divine plan, "this is the thing which God commands." *Davar* is more than a "word"; it is a *thing*, an objective and substantive reality. The other prophets conveyed words in accordance with the divine message; Moses, however, changed reality in accordance with the divine plan, in accordance with his actions. The other prophets spoke words which were a transmission of the divine; Moses lived a life which was an extension of the divine. And the Hebrew word *zeh* can also refer to a human being (*ha'ish hazeh*, this man), and not only to a word, *koh tomar* (thus shall you say).

Perhaps this is why the *Sifrei* chooses to point out this distinction between Moses and the other prophets in the context of the opening verse of our biblical portion *Matot,* in the context of the laws of oaths and promises. Human beings have the power to alter reality by the oaths and words which they utter, as well as to effectuate forgiveness and absolution by words which they express (Numbers 30:3). The realm of oaths and promises unmistakably points out the almost God-like powers of human beings, the ability of humans to serve in an almost divine capacity as God's helpers, as God's partners. It is indeed the most exalted goal of every person to become a vehicle for the expression of the divine will. Rabbi Samson Raphael Hirsch so interprets the biblical words *zeh Eli ve'anvehu* sung by the Israelites after the splitting of the Red Sea: "This is my God, and I shall be His sanctuary" (Exodus 15:2). Most translators render the verse, "This is my God and I shall glorify Him" from the Hebrew *na'eh,* to beautify, but Rabbi Hirsch derives the meaning from *naveh,* which means "home" or "sanctuary." The human being, his very body acting upon the messenger of his brain, his heart, and his soul – must become the vehicle, the expression, for God's will in its every word and action.

Moses' physical being, Moses' every act and word, was indeed a *sanctuary,* an extension of the divine. Moses is therefore the greatest of all prophets and the highest human achievement in world history.

The Power of the Word

This is the thing which God commanded. When a man vows a vow unto God, or swears an oath to bind his soul with a bond, he shall not break his word; he shall do all that proceeds out of his mouth.

NUMBERS 30:2–3

At first glance, the inclusion of the law of vows and oaths in the portion of *Matot* seems puzzling and out of place.

Why here, why now? We have been dealing with desert wanderings and land distributions, conflicts and narratives, rebellions and wars, transgressions and punishments – but not legal codes and prohibitions. Moreover, at the conclusion of this segment of vows, we resume the saga of the Midianite struggle with the Israelites, a conflict which initially broke out when Balak hired the services of Bileam to curse the Hebrews in the previous portion. And everything that follows in our portion deals with aspects of war, including the final section wherein Gad and Reuben, their eyes fixed on the rich grazing land, petitioned Moses to remain on this side of the Jordan where they could easily feed their abundant cattle. Moses insisted that their request could not be honored until they agreed to join with the rest of their compatriots in the war of conquest.

Hence, given the themes of the portion as a whole, the subject of "vows and oaths" serving as the introduction to our Torah reading seems stunningly inappropriate.

I would maintain that a reading between the lines of the Bible will reveal a profound contrast between the word and the sword, the power of the voice and the power of the fist – a contrast which will clearly explain the placement of "oaths and vows" as a most fitting bridge between our victory over Bileam and our impending battle with Midian in the desert.

If we turn back a few chapters to the portion of *Ḥukkat,* we are confronted with a glaring contradiction between verbal communication and physical aggression: Moses' transgression which results in a dire punishment. The context of this tragedy was the whining complaint of the Israelites thirsting for water, leading God to instruct Moses to speak to the rock after which water would emerge from the lifeless stone. Moses, however, had exhausted his tolerance for the nation's constant *kvetching*. Instead of addressing the rock with words, he used his staff to hit the rock with strength, not only once but twice. Water did emerge, enough for the entire nation. Nonetheless, God deemed Moses' act of physically striking the rock so sinful that He punished the great leader-prophet by preventing him from ever entering the Promised Land, from ever realizing his life's goal.

And why such harsh punishment? Perhaps the reason is because Moses didn't grasp the moment which would enable him to express the ultimate mission of Israel: there is no power as great as the word – by means of which water can spring forth from a rock. And the word symbolizes verbal communication – the "Ten Words" we received from Sinai; the Torah, a book of words. The physically aggressive rock which was Rome, Babylon, Egypt – all these have turned to dust over the ages. No remnant of these once-proud civilizations stands as a beacon of inspiration – indeed, is constantly influencing the world round about – as do our Ten Words of the Divine revealed at Sinai. The word is the symbol of Israel just as the sword is a symbol of our gentile enemies.

The fact that this contrast is indeed the essence is underscored by the biblical text, which – immediately after Moses' sin – records how Moses sends messengers from Kadesh to the king of Edom, declaring:

> This is what your brother Israel says: "You know all the sufferings that we have experienced. Our fathers went down to Egypt, the Egyptians afflicted us and our fathers. And when we cried out to God, He heard our *voice,* and sent an angel, and brought us out of Egypt."
>
> Numbers 20:14–15

The prophet concludes with the plea that the Israelites be permitted to pass through their land, promising neither to touch any object nor drink any of their water.

Edom's answer cuts to the quick. "You better not pass over my land lest I go against you with the *sword*" (Numbers 20:18).

Rashi's comment emphasizes the clash between two incompatible values, Edom's sword and Israel's word. He writes:

> [Edom taunted]: "You take pride in your voice [*kol*], which your fathers [specifically Jacob, whose distinctive voice always invokes God and sanctity] bequeathed to you; therefore you said, 'And we cried out to God and He heard our voice.' Nevertheless, I will come out against you with that which my father bequeathed to me. 'And by your sword shall you live!'" [from Isaac's blessing to Esau, ancestor of Edom]
>
> Rashi on Numbers 20:18

Rashi is also implying that when Moses opted to strike the rock rather than speak to it, he was stepping outside the boundaries which God had chosen for His people: a people of the word, a people of the Torah, a people committed to resolving conflicts by "words" and not by "swords."

Indeed, Rashi again discerns this theme of sword vs. word in his explanation of the first text that follows the subject of oaths and vows in our portion. We read of an army of twelve thousand gathered by Moses to fight the Midianites, finally to put an end to their constant attempts to seduce the nation with harlotry and idolatry. "And they warred against Midian…and they slew every male. And they slew the kings of Midian" (31:7–8). And then we read that "Bileam they killed by the sword" (Numbers 31:8). Of all the thousands killed, why does the Torah stress the instrument of death used to kill Bileam?

Explains Rashi:

> Bileam came against Israel, by exchanging his expertise for the expertise of the Israelites. After all, the victory of the Israelites is only from their mouths, by means of their prayers and beseeching. But he [Bileam] came and used their expertise to curse them with his mouth. So now they [the Israelites] exchanged their expertise with the expertise of the nations by coming against [Bileam] with a sword.
>
> Rashi on Numbers 31:8

One might even argue that on a certain level Rashi is rebuking the Israelites for resorting to the sword. However, it seems to me that in a deeper sense Rashi is soberly acknowledging that until "words" alone are recognized by all of humanity as the true element of persuasion and teaching, we have no choice but to face sword with sword. Jacob must wear the outer skins of Esau, the voice of Jacob must learn to utilize the hands of Esau, in order to make certain that the good and the true are not destroyed by our enemies. However, although behaving in such a manner may be necessary, it is never our ideal. The Almighty wanted Moses to speak to the rock, and the words of Torah have proved mightier than the hordes of soldiers, and more eternal than the tallest of pyramids. And in the messianic age, the prophet declares about the Messiah, king of Israel: "With the spirit of his mouth will he slay the wicked" (Daniel 11:4).

Hence, the introduction to our battle with Midian and the postscript of our victory over Bileam are the laws of oaths and promises, laws which demonstrate the enormous power of words, laws which emphasize how "life and death are in the hands of the tongue"; these laws prove that words are much more than a movement of the mouth, but rather they create in their wake new realities. The proper word at the right moment can bring an errant lost soul back to his roots and moorings, but a wrong word or even inflection can alienate and drive away. A positive response to a particular individual's name can earn him a livelihood as well as a place in the community, whereas a negative response can literally destroy a life. The Almighty created and destroyed worlds through His usage of speech – and so do we. "A slap goes away, a word is here to stay," declares an old Yiddish proverb (*a patch dergeht, a vort basheteht*). This is why we open the most solemn and fateful day of the Jewish calendar – Yom Kippur (The Day of Forgiveness) – with *Kol Nidrei,* the absolution of oaths. And this is why our Torah reading mediates between Bileam's blessings and the Midianite battle by reminding us how words are more powerful than swords and must be used only with caution and sensitivity.

Different Tribes within a Central Ruling Government: Unity with Diversity

> *And Moses spoke unto the heads of the tribes of the children of Israel, saying: "This is the word which God commanded."*
>
> NUMBERS 30:2

Our Bible develops from the story of a family in the book of Genesis to the emergence of a nation in the book of Exodus. And the bridge between family and nation seems to be the twelve tribal divisions enunciated by Jacob, especially in his final blessings of his twelve sons before his death.

However, the tribes did not disappear with the development of the nation. In the incident of the twelve scouts, princes of each tribe were specifically chosen, and this Torah portion begins with Moses presenting the commandments regarding the laws of promises and oaths to the "heads of the tribes" (Numbers 30:2). Indeed, the very division of the Land of Israel was established along tribal lines. The biblical book of Judges is filled with tribal rivalries and murderous tribal conflicts, and even after King David united the nation under one monarch with a single capital city of Jerusalem, the enmity of Judah and Ephraim persisted until the destruction of the Holy Temple. Maimonides goes so far as to legislate separate courts of law for each individual tribe. Even to this very day, kohen descendants of Aaron from the tribe of Levi rise to bless the congregation (daily in Israel, on the festivals in the Diaspora), and descendants of the tribe of Levi are called to the Torah immediately following the first-to-be-called kohen. Why retain a tribal system which seems to have only contributed to the internecine strife which prevented the united period of Kings David and Solomon from becoming the norm of Israel's government?!

The Hebrew word generally used for tribe is *shevet*. When grandfather Jacob concludes his blessing-descriptions of his twelve sons, certainly highlighting the differences and even the tensions between them, the biblical text states "all of these are the tribes [*shivtei*] of Israel, twelve [in number]" (Genesis 49:28). Similarly, our Torah reading speaks of "half the tribe [*shevet*] of Menashe" (Numbers 32:33).

However, there is another Hebrew word used for tribe, *matteh*, and it is precisely this noun which is found in the opening verse of our Torah portion: "And Moses spoke unto the heads of tribes [*matot*, translated by *Targum* as *shivtaya*]"(Numbers 30:2). The very book of Numbers, which opens with a census count of each of the tribes, provides for a representative of each tribe, "one man per tribe" (*lamatteh*; Numbers 1:4). Indeed, in the book of Numbers the Hebrew word *matteh* (and not *shevet*) is used for tribe no less than ninety-one times! What is the reason for these two different Hebrew nouns for the very same concept of tribe? And what is the precise distinction between *shevet* and *matteh*?

According to most of our classical commentaries, *shevet* is to be defined as a ruling rod whereas *matteh* is a supporting staff. When grandfather Jacob blesses Judah, he declares, "The rod [*shevet*] shall not depart from Judah" (Genesis 49:10). The Talmudic sages interpret, "the rod refers to the exilarchs of Babylon, who strong-handedly [tyrannically] rule the nation with a rod; they derive their authority from the gentile governments" (Genesis 49:10, Rashi ad loc.). The Hebrew word *matteh*, on the other hand, is a supporting staff, as in the modern Hebrew position of *ramatkal*, or chief of staff, with staff referring to a support group of knowledgeable and experienced individuals. In our book of Numbers, when Koraḥ challenged Aaron's leadership as High Priest from the tribe of Levi, each tribe was asked by God to take a staff and write upon the staff the name of the prince of each tribe; on the staff of the tribe of Levi was to be written the name of Aaron. "And behold, the staff of Aaron of the tribe of Levi flowered, a flower arose, a bud blossomed and almond fruit matured" (Numbers 17:23). The staff (*matteh*) of the tribe (*matteh*) of Levi "supported" Aaron's appointment as High Priest, *Kohen Gadol.*

The best Hebrew translation of *matteh* is *mishenet*, a word used for the support staff of an elderly person with difficulty walking, which is also a Talmudic idiom for the son of a widow who serves as her aid and benefactor. This is likewise how many commentaries understand King David's Psalm (23): "The Lord is my shepherd, I shall not want. He leads me through green pastures.... Your rod [*shivtekha*] and your staff [*mishantekha*], they comfort me." The Psalmist is saying that sometimes he feels God's punishing rod, and sometimes he feels God's supporting staff; in both cases they give him comfort, because he knows that God means for his well-being! (In this context, *mishenet* is a synonym for *matteh.*)

In effect, the Torah is teaching us that a nation comprised of different and distinctive tribes has both negative and positive possibilities. On the one hand, a particular tribe can be desirous of unilateral control (*shevet*), initiating a rivalry and even a civil war. The United States of America – the individual states being analogous to the various tribes – underwent just such a fierce and threatening internecine struggle, the great and infamous Civil War.

But too centralized a governmental power can turn unity into uniformity and produce all of the tyranny of a totalitarian Tower of Babel. Different tribes – each with its own cultural flavor, temperament, and specific point of view – can provide a unity with diversity, an orchestra comprised of many individual instruments, as long as there is one conductor who recognizes, respects, and knows how to "orchestrate" the different sounds into one magnificent symphony. Obviously, the tribes must subscribe to a united goal and agree upon basic values, ideals, and rules of conduct. But differences which are respected and which respect others can provide the breadth, depth, and growth possibility, which is the best defense against stagnation and tyranny. Such a system of inclusive leadership will also leave room for many more individuals to express themselves and for special interest groups to contribute and flourish.

Hence the world must have different nations, nations must have different cities (tribes, *edot*), cities must have different communities, and communities must have different families. It must be, in my grandmother's words, a *"velt mit veltelakh"* – a large world with little worlds – as long as each little world, as well as the greater world, remains committed to the integrity and inviolability of every individual and does not countenance fanatic bigotry in any form. As the prophet Micah teaches, as long as "humanity does not learn war anymore.... Every individual can call upon his god and we will call upon the Lord our God forever" (Micah 4:3–5).

Revenge: Yes or No?

Take revenge against the Midianites.
NUMBERS 31:2

What is the biblical attitude towards revenge? On the one hand, the biblical portion of *Matot* unequivocally states that God commands Moses to "rake revenge for the children of Israel against the Midianites" (Numbers 31:2). On the other hand, the Torah declares in Leviticus, "Do not take revenge nor bear a grudge" (19:18). Indeed, when it comes to revenge, the Israelites were always cautioned to keep a healthy distance. For example, in the event of an accidental killing, the Torah commanded the Jewish people to establish cities of refuge where the one seeking revenge was prohibited to enter and the one who killed accidentally would be provided with a "sanctuary"; in such a way, family members were prevented from the usual "code of honor" to avenge the blood of a relative.

Why then does the Torah command revenge against Midian when revenge clearly goes against the Torah's own standards of morality?

Secondly, what compounds this issue of revenge is the seeming inequality between the Moabites and the Midianites. After all, both nations were involved in their female seduction of the Israelites to attempt to destroy us from within, both created the licentious atmosphere that led to the idolatrous worship of Ba'al Peor on the part of Israel. If anything, it was the Moabites, and not the Midianites, who were at the forefront. They were the ones who initiated the entire series of events from the very beginning of the portion of *Balak*. Balak was king of Moab, and he contacted the gentile prophet Bileam to curse the Jews; when Bileam was forced by God and the morality of Israel to turn his curses into blessings, he suggested the ploy of the Moabite women to secure Israel's demise (*Sanhedrin* 106a): "[let them] commit harlotry with the daughters of Moab, who invited the nation to the sacrifices of their gods, and the nation feasted and worshipped the false gods, and Israel joined itself to Ba'al Peor" (Numbers 25:1–3).

The women were Moabites! The Torah never denied their role in seducing the Israelites to fall into a pit of lust and idolatry that led directly to a plague in which twenty-four thousand died. And lest a mistake be made that the command to take revenge against Midian included Moab, the Torah drives home the very opposite point: "And God said unto me: 'Do not harass Moab, nor contend with them in battle'" (Deut. 2:9).

Our second question is asked and answered by Rashi himself (on Numbers 31:2). He explains that although Moab and Midian may have committed the same acts, nonetheless revenge was commanded against one and not the other because of their different motivations. When Balak, king of Moab, went out to try to curse us, he was genuinely afraid lest we conquer him and plunder his wealth. The portion of *Balak* opens with this explicit fear: "When Balak ben Tzippor saw all that Israel had done to the Amorites, the Moabites became deathly afraid because the Israelites were so numerous." Dreading the Israelites, Moab said to the elders of Midian, "This multitude will lick up all that is round about us as the ox licks up the grass of the field" (Numbers 22:2–4).

Somehow, according to Rashi, God can understand a nation striking out against Israel because they fear us. But Midian wasn't afraid; nevertheless, when called upon to join Moab they did so with a zest and delight merely because they reveled in murdering Hebrews! And Midian became much more than a mere secondary accomplice; Midian assumed active leadership. They taught their black magic to Moab, and it eventually became the Midianite women who seduced Israelite leadership and caused the Jews to betray God in the Ba'al Peor episode (Numbers 31:16 and *Sanhedrin* 82a). Midian's stain was dark and deep, with their only motivation being the obliteration of Israel at any and all cost, not because they feared what Israel would do to them, but only because they hated Israel!

But what about the issue of revenge? In addition to the commandment of revenge against Midian, do we not declare, after mentioning the name of an individual who dies in sanctification of God's name: "May the Lord revenge his blood"? The Bible exults: "Sing aloud O ye nations, of His people; for He doth avenge the blood of His servants, and doth render vengeance to His adversaries" (Deut. 32:43). And the sages of the Talmud teach: "Revenge is great, even praiseworthy, because it exists between the two names of God" (*Berakhot* 33a).

How do we square all of this with our earlier-cited prohibition against "taking revenge or bearing a grudge" (*netira* and *nekima*; Leviticus 19:18)?

A deeper understanding of the concept of revenge comes to light in a Talmudic discussion of the differences between the two terms expressed by the Bible, usually translated as revenge and grudge, *netira* and *nekima* (*Yoma* 23a): "If a person asks another to lend him his scythe, and he refuses, and the one who refused turns around the next day and asks the other person to lend him his axe – if he answers, 'Since you didn't lend me your scythe yesterday, I'm not going to lend you my axe today' this is an example of *nekima*, revenge," which is prohibited. *Netira*, bearing a grudge, goes one step beyond *nekima*. "If a person says to his neighbor, 'Lend me your axe,' and the neighbor refuses and then, on the following day, the one who refused to lend him the axe asks to borrow a shirt, to which the other person agrees, but adds, 'Here's the shirt, because I'm not like you,'" the additional remark is called *netira*, and is also prohibited.

When the Torah gives us the basic commandment against taking revenge in Leviticus (19:18), Rashi cites the entire Talmudic passage we've just quoted concerning the axe, the scythe, and the shirt. When we examine all of the examples given, they involve an issue of borrowing and lending various objects of monetary value. From this perspective, the Torah is teaching us that in the realm of material goods – borrowing and lending to others – an individual dare not base his moral and ethical standards on the standards of anyone else. I ought not desist from lending you an object because you refused a similar one when I made the request and I ought not lend you an object merely in order to teach you how superior I am to you. My standards must be absolute – and not dependent on your actions at all. In the brilliant words of the Kotzker Rebbe, "If I am I and you are you, then I am I and you are you. But if I am I *because* you are you, then I am not I, and you are not you." The individual must live by his God-given ethic – regardless of society around him! "Do not take revenge or bear a grudge." Perhaps in that way we might teach others to eventually accept our standards.

However, when it comes to issues beyond money, beyond property, but issues that reach down to the existential core of our being, when we are confronted by a nation which is out to destroy us no matter what – then we dare not be naïve and cry out "thou shalt not murder," allowing our enemy to continue his evil murders as we "turn the other cheek." Since the enemy is "playing for keeps," such "tolerance" will only lead to an abandonment of morality and a "give-away" of the world to the darkest forces of evil. We must then play by their rules and destroy them before they have an opportunity to destroy us! In such an instance, we are commanded to take revenge!

Moab was frightened lest we would steal their money; they didn't want to lend us their axe, their scythe, their shirt, and they even refused us a little bit of water when we were wandering in the desert. They wanted us cursed only so that we could not "lick up their produce." The Bible therefore commands that we let them live – and we attempt to teach them that they need have no fear, that our design is not to "clean them out," but only to cleanse them with our God of Purity.

But the Midianites sought our destruction because they wanted to see us drown. Money or fear was not the issue; Hebrew genocide was. Hence the Midianite attack strategy was not merely a curse to weaken us, but was rather assimilation to uproot us at our very foundation through the right combination of wine, women, and blood on the altars of Ba'al Peor.

To chart a course of action for ourselves as a people, we have to determine if the party facing us is a Moabite or a Midianite. Moabites did what they did out of desperation and fear, and deserve another chance. Remember that the righteous convert Ruth, and therefore the Messiah, is destined to emerge from Moab. But if those who face us are Midianites, hell-bent on our destruction, any sign of pity will only be used to destroy us, God forbid – and then "Revenge is great… because it comes between the two names of God."

Whence the "Half-tribe of Menashe"?

And Moses gave to them, to the children of Gad, and to the children of Reuben, and to the half-tribe of Menashe... the kingdom of Siḥon, king of the Emorites, and the kingdom of Og, king of the Bashan.

NUMBERS 32:33

Out of the blue, the half-tribe of Menashe?! Where did they come from? Initially Moses was approached by the tribes of Gad and Reuben to allow them to remain in Transjordan where there was ample grazing lands for their abundant cattle (Numbers 32:1–2). Moses explained to them that only after they participated in the battle for the conquest of the rest of the Land of Israel together with all their tribal brothers would they be permitted to receive Transjordan as their inheritance; they agree to Moses' conditions. And then, when the "West Bank" was conquered and Transjordan given, we suddenly find one-half of the tribe of Menashe entering as a partner in the Transjordan land-parcels. When exactly and why did the half-tribe of Menashe enter the scene?

Nahmanides is sensitive to this issue, and suggests that although Moses had initially been approached only by Gad and Reuben, it soon became apparent that the land in Transjordan was plentiful enough to include another partner. Moses called for volunteers, and members of the tribe of Menashe responded to his call, "perhaps because they were also herdsmen seeking grazing lands" (Nahmanides on Numbers 32:33).

I would submit that perhaps Menashe had an altogether different intention: perhaps they were materialistic opportunists, seeking lush farmland and desiring to be distanced from the more spiritual tribe of Judah, from the more centralized location of the Sanctuary, from the eventual divinely-centered capital city of Jerusalem. In this regard the people of Menashe were acting true to their namesake and tribal forebear. Remember that Joseph said about the name he chose for his eldest son Menashe, "God has enabled me to forget [*nase*] all of my toil and everything involved in my father's house" (Genesis 41:51), including perhaps many of the Abrahamic traditions. Moreover, Menashe was the politically adept, linguistically fluent son who aided his father in his sale of grain to the various representatives of various countries of the world; he was not like his younger brother Ephraim, who studied Torah with his elderly grandfather, Jacob. And indeed, it would seem that these two-and-one-half tribes did attempt to build an altar to idolatry in their land in Transjordan during the period of Joshua, until they were dissuaded from doing so by a delegation composed of Pineḥas together with representatives from the rest of the tribes (Joshua 22:12–19). Apparently geographical distance from Jerusalem creates ideological difference as well – until this very day.

A different scenario and a blessedly more spiritual intention is suggested by the Netziv, Rabbi Naftali Zvi Yehuda Berlin, in his late-nineteenth-century biblical commentary *Ha'amek Davar*. He insists that Moses specifically chose half the tribe of Menashe to join together with Gad and Reuben in Transjordan precisely because Moses was concerned lest "far from the eye makes one far from the heart" – since absence often makes the heart grow absent. After all, the ancient and persistent enemies of the Land of Israel and the Torah of Israel were Datan and Aviram, scions of the disgruntled and "disinherited" tribe of Reuben;

leaving the tribe of Reuben so far away and isolated from mainstream Israel was certainly asking for trouble.

The tribe of Menashe, on the other hand, contained perfect "religious supervisors" (*mashgiḥim ruḥani'im*) for the less trustworthy Reuben. Did not the wise, the righteous, the committed lovers of Israel, the daughters of Tzelofḥad, come from the tribe of Menashe? And Yair (literally "he will shine forth light"), the son of Menashe, is considered by our Talmudic sages to have been equal to the majority of the Sanhedrin (*Bava Batra* 44a).

Hence the sincerely Zionistic and learned tribe of Menashe were the perfect individuals to religiously influence the suspect tribe of Reuben who, together with Gad, were to be far from the spiritual center of the Land of Israel and so removed from the majority of the Israelite tribes. One-half of Menashe was to serve in a capacity very similar to Chabad emissaries, Strauss rabbis, Beren educators, or Torah MiTzion emissaries to Jews in far-flung places to bring the traditional religious message to those who are distanced from it, geographically as well as ideologically.

And this will also explain why only half the tribe of Menashe. When people are sent to a far-flung community, the hope is that they will influence the community – but the danger always exists that they will be influenced instead. But if half the tribe still has another familial half – uncles, aunts, brothers, sisters, cousins – closer to the religious center, chances are that the emissaries will make frequent visits to, and receive familial visitors from, the more religiously involved central area. This situation of frequent communication between family members of the tribe of Menashe enhances the chances that the emissaries will remain unchanged and firm in the commitment with which they must inspire their neighbors in Transjordan.

Masei

To Advance by Going Back

> *These are the journeys of the children of Israel… these are the starting points towards their [destination] journeys… and these are their [destination] journeys toward their starting points.*
>
> NUMBERS 33:1–2

Undoubtedly the Exodus from Egypt stands unparalleled as the central event of our nation's collective consciousness, the very epicenter of our history, an event we invoke daily in our recitation of the Shema, on the Sabbath, festivals, and after each and every meal. Still, when we consider the painstaking detail that our portion of *Masei* devotes to recording all forty-two stops along the way during the forty-year sojourn, we're somewhat taken aback at what seems to be a largely inconsequential travelogue.

Starting with verse 5 in chapter thirty-three of the book of Bemidbar, and continuing until verse 49, the Torah lists all of the forty-two locations, and since each location is not only a destination to encamp but also a location to journey away from each place-name is mentioned twice. So for forty-four verses the Torah challenges us with its geographical accuracy, reminding us to what length the Torah goes to in order to name names and construct maps – not only in time, which is what the genealogies in Genesis do, but also in space, as we find in our portion. But forty-two place names must be a record; even if we count Adam to Noaḥ, and Noaḥ to Abraham, and Abraham to Moses, we're still a far cry from forty-two generations. Why such details now?

Different commentators take different approaches to this question, from Sforno's argument – that the plethora of locations is a way of highlighting the merit of the Jewish people, who, in the lovingkindness of youth, followed after God in the desert, a land not sown – to the *Sfat Emet* (*Masei* 5753) who speaks of each location in the desert as a potential for *tikkun olam*, transforming the barrenness of the wilderness into a singing garden by means of divine words. But I would like to concentrate on the commentary of Nahmanides. Apparently he is not only troubled by the delineation of the forty-two stages, but also by the additional declaration in the verse that "Moses inscribed... their destination journeys towards their starting points [of origin]" (Numbers 33:2). How may we understand the significance of such detailed travel stations and this very strange formation?

In approaching the issue, Nahmanides first quotes Rashi's comment (who cites the words of Rabbi Moshe the Preacher) that Moses "set his mind to write down the journeying. It was his intention thereby to inform [future generations] of the loving kindness of God"; after all, He protected His nation throughout their manifold travels and way stations, despite their *kvetching* complaints.

After quoting Rashi, he then turns to Maimonides (*Guide for the Perplexed*, III:50), who understands the necessity of detail as a means of corroborating the historical truth of the narrative. Moreover, later generations might think "that they sojourned in a desert that was near to cultivated land, and in which man can [easily] live... places in which it was possible to till and to reap or to feed on plants that were to be found there... or that it was natural for the manna to always come down in those places, or that there were wells of water in those places...." Hence the enumeration of all these way-stations lacking the amenities delineated above is in order to emphasize the extent of the miracle of Israeli subsistence under such difficult physical conditions.

After quoting these views, Nahmanides concludes with a most intriguing and esoteric comment: "Thus the writing down the journeying was a commandment of God, either for reasons mentioned above, or for a purpose the *secret* of which has not been revealed to us."

By speaking of "*secrets*" Nahmanides seems to be telling us – if not beseeching us – to probe further. And I would submit that the secret may be the secret of the Jewish survival. After all, the concept of *ma'ase avot siman lebanim* (the actions of the fathers are a sign of what will happen to the children) is well known to the sages, and is one of the guiding principles of Nahmanides' biblical commentary. It may very well be that the interior, hidden message of this text is the fact that we are being given an outline as well as an assurance of what we should expect over the course of Jewish history. From the time of the exile after the destruction of the Temple, the "goings-forth" of the Jewish people – until our present arrival in the Land of Israel – would certainly add up to at least forty-two distinct stages: Judea, Babylon, Persia, Rome, Europe, North Africa, and the New World. And each particular Diaspora was important in its own right, made its own unique contribution to the text (Oral Law) and texture (customs) of our Jewish civilization, of the kaleidoscope which is the Jewish historical experience; and each is worthy of being recorded and remembered. Are not the Holocaust memorial books, these heroic remains of survivors trying to preserve what little that can be preserved of lost, destroyed worlds, examples of our sense that God commanded us to "write" things down – to remember?! Perhaps the Jews didn't invent history, but they certainly understood that more important than those hieroglyphics which exalt and praise the rulers in their battles are the places of the Jewish wanderings, the content of the Jewish lifestyle, and the miracle of Jewish survival.

Furthermore, the "secret" that Nahmanides refers to may not only be a prophetic vision of the children of Israel throughout our history, but – even more importantly – a crucial lesson as to how to survive and even overcome the long night of Jewish exile.

If we look at the verse where Moses writes down the journey

according to the command of God, we find two phrases that appear like mirror images: first we read that Moses writes "their starting points towards their journey-destinations [*et motza'aihem lemasa'eihem*] at God's command," and then, inexplicably, the verse continues with the exact opposite direction, "their journey-destinations towards their starting points [*masa'eihem lemotza'aihem*]." What do these two "opposite antithetical formulations mean"? Let us examine this difficult verse again.

"*Motza*" (as in *motza'aihem*) means a starting place, a place of origin. *Masa* (as in *masa'eihem*) means one's travels or journey-destinations – the end-game, the purpose of the journey. When the verse opens with the declaration, "Moses wrote their places of origin for their travels," it makes sense: after all, setting forth means that we set out from a certain place of origin to certain place of destination. But what does it mean when the verse concludes with "Their journey-destination towards their place of origin?" Isn't this contradictory? You don't go backwards!

But I believe that is precisely the point: the Jews have always traveled – backwards!

Fundamental to our history as a nation is that we are constantly traveling – in all of our wanderings – on the road to the Promised Land, on the journey towards redemption. Our traveling is not an aimless wandering; it is with a clear compass and a purposeful direction, to return to the place where we began.

That direction was given to us at the dawn of our history: in Ḥebron, with the Covenant between the Pieces as well as in Jerusalem, at the binding of Isaac, and then again at Sinai, with the Divine Revelation.

As we move down the road of time, we must always keep in front of our eyes the place of our origin. When Shai Agnon received the Nobel Prize for Literature, he was asked about his birthplace; to the interviewer's surprise, he answered that he was born in Jerusalem. The interviewer pointed out that everyone knew he was born in Buczacz, a town in Galicia. Agnon corrected him: "I was born in Jerusalem more than three thousand years ago. That was my beginning, my origin. Buczacz in Galicia is only one of the stopping off points along my way back home."

Only two princes of tribes who serve as scouts reach the Promised Land: Caleb and Joshua – Caleb because he visited the graves of our patriarchs and matriarchs in Ḥebron, and Joshua because God's name, the Author of the Revelation, was added to his name. Only these two set out for the Promised Land with their place of origin at the forefront of their consciousness; only those with a proud past can look forward to a glorious future. This is the true secret of the delineation of our wanderings: as long as we wander with our place of origin as our compass, we will assuredly reach our goal and bring redemption. When our points of origin – and the Torah lessons and experiences we glean from them – continue to inform and direct our destinations, we give higher meaning to our travels and transform our destinations into our highest destiny.

The Prerequisite for a Return to Zion: A Belated Letter to My Communist Grandfather

And you shall conquer all the inhabitants of the land and you shall destroy all of the idols. And [then] you shall make the land your heritage and dwell in it.

NUMBERS 33:52–53

Efrat, Israel

Dear Grandpa Shmuel,

Remember Murray Bershad's *shvitz* (steambath) on Myrtle Avenue? After a good amount of time in the steamroom where we sweated, poured buckets of cold water over each other, and took massages with leafy brooms, did you have any idea that the grandson with whom you publicly debated – while a crowd of listeners would gather around us, listening intently while eating schmaltz herring and baked potatoes and drinking wine with seltzer – would end up a rabbi?

You, the passionate communist standing up for everyone's rights, and me, not even at the age of bar mitzva, trying to match your Marx with my Moses; even thinking about those debates makes my adrenalin rise. Your anti-religious views forced me to begin clarifying my thoughts about God, Judaism, Torah. You didn't agree with my yeshiva ideology, but I could tell you were proud of my ability to debate, to speak with passion and commitment. And I was proud of you, a public speaker and writer, a Yiddish communist intellectual, who took his pre-adolescent grandson seriously and treated him very much like an adult.

Before I knew it, you had me reading Marx, Engels, and Lenin. Since you hadn't stepped inside a synagogue since your own bar mitzva, and had taken an oath, you said, never to attend synagogue again, attending Sabbath services when I turned thirteen proved a moral dilemma for you. "But who did you make the oath to?" I tearfully wanted to ask, but couldn't get out the words. Apparently, however, even though religion for you may have been the opiate of the masses, a grandson is a still a grandson and family trumped ideology. You resolved the conflict in a most unique fashion. How many other yeshiva students that year received the *Communist Manifesto* and the Constitution of the Soviet Union as bar mitzva gifts? At the last moment you entered the synagogue to hear my Talmudic discourse in Yiddish! You entered after the morning prayers had been concluded, and you left before the additional prayers began. But you didn't leave without kissing me on the forehead and giving me the two books which assuaged your conscience.

Grandpa, I received much more from you than books on communism. What I really received was the spirit of a man who sought answers and worked to share with others, an idealist who wished to redeem the world. If anyone in the family understands my move to Israel it should be you, even though as a communist you had no room for a Jewish homeland. "Nationalism," you called it, as you were swept along by the gods of a new world order, which sought to banish God and greed forever. You had a tremendous influence on my life. You taught me to read *Shalom Aleikhem* in the original because you wanted me to feel for the Jewish poor and to develop a distinctly Jewish sense of humor. Perhaps you also realized that if I ever seriously tackled Jewish study in the 40s and 50s, Yiddish would be invaluable. And so the words you taught me on your knee ironically enough make it possible for me to study Torah with one of the great Talmudists of the century, Rav Joseph B. Soloveitchik, who gave his unforgettable classes in Yiddish and set me on the path of a life dedicated to Torah and Israel.

One of my most profound memories goes back to the Saturday night right before you suffered your first heart attack. Reports of communist purges had arrived, including the atrocities against the Jewish doctors, and even you – an avowed atheist who had believed God was dead and Lenin was His prophet and proudly kept Stalin's picture on your kitchen wall (along with FDR) – out of your basic humanity and your love for the Jewish people allowed questions of heresy to pierce the ideological iron curtain you had erected in your own mind. You had always been a fervent believer, not just in theory through the articles you wrote for the *Freiheit*, the Yiddish communist daily, but in practice, for you practiced communism in the way that a Jew practices Judaism – on a daily basis. The moment the wood-working shop you set up did well, you began to share profits among the workers. You truly believed, and now you'd been betrayed. As we quietly sat together in the steam room, you reminisced for the first time about the Sabbath in your parents' home during pre-czarist days, the Sabbath you'd rejected in favor of faith in a new world order; you said in a half whisper, more to yourself than to me, "Perhaps I gave up too much too soon for too little."

Why am I writing this letter to you thirty-four years after you've died? Ever since the *aliya* from the CIS began, I have thought of you often. And, more to the point, I recently found myself in Budapest, one of the major European terminals for the Jewish emigrants departing for Israel, together with other members of an Israeli delegation. While there we visited a former army camp transformed into a little Ellis Island for immigrants destined for Israel, in a facility for a thousand people with beds and kitchens and medical facilities.

As I walked through the vast hall, I found myself facing a man who reminded me of you, Grandpa Shmuel. A life-long communist, he was now leaving his dreams behind. He too seemed to be a profound intellectual. Perfectly fluent in English, he explained that communism had failed because it ignored individual human rights, and had miscalculated the tremendous power of nationalism. People cannot sacrifice for a universal ideal whose leaders are a bunch of hypocrites. "And to ask for sacrifice when the government itself denied, destroyed, and derided the human rights of others is intolerable."

While the man spoke, it struck me that if not for your idealism, I too may have been sitting in Budapest, waiting for my name to be called. I grew up in America, became religious, went to yeshiva, and came to Israel only because some ninety years ago you idealistically organized the workers in your own father's factory which produced uniforms for the czars. Arrested, banished to Siberia, you managed – with great travail – to escape to America, where you felt you could freely continue to work towards your dream for humanity. I am American-born because in 1907 you arrived in New York. Had you not been sent to Siberia, there would have been no reason for you to leave Russia. You would have stayed to see Marx's dream become a reality. And your children and grandchildren – had we been fortunate enough to have been saved from the Nazi and communist purges – might well be in Budapest, preparing to immigrate to Israel, after a lifetime of disillusionment and disappointment.

And if that hour had ever arrived wouldn't you have thanked God that there was one place in the world, one land, which accepted Jews with open arms? Grandpa, yours was a false god, but I could never convince you it was false. Before our eyes the Union of Soviet Socialist Republics fell, and we saw how vulnerable your all-powerful, omniscient communist god really was. The Iron Curtain turned out to be nothing more than a fragile veil attempting to hide a forgotten and glorious world of Jewish piety and culture which they tried – but failed – to destroy.

Budapest was beautiful. I walked inside a synagogue from the first half of the nineteenth century which seats five thousand people, with acoustics so clear that a speaker could be heard from one end to the other without a microphone. The Nazis wiped out the vast majority of Jews, and those few who remained behind were worn down by the communists. With the fall of the old regime, Jews began reemerging from the woodwork, awakening to their long-lost heritage. Believe it or not, ex-communist Budapest is going through a Jewish reawakening, and streets which hadn't seen signs of a Jew in decades became a way station for the Jews from Mother Russia on their way to Israel. How is this possible, Grandpa? The Talmud describes it in magnificent, metaphoric terms.

The Talmud in *Avoda Zara* records an amazing episode. Rabbi Ḥanina b. Teradion, one of the Ten Martyrs tortured during the Hadrianic persecutions, was thrown into a blazing fire, his body wrapped in a Torah scroll. As he was being burned alive, his students asked what he saw. He answered that although the parchment was turning to ashes, the Hebrew letters were rising to the sky. No physical force could destroy the spiritual energy of the sacred letters of our eternal Torah.

In Budapest, Rabbi Ḥanina's words were proven true. For seventy years the communists had been trying to destroy Torah, but all they could manage to destroy was the parchment; the letters resisted their efforts. And as I flew back with a planeload of Russians, I saw how letters were literally flying up in the sky – Soviet Jewish letters, souls of proud, Jewish émigrés, who were returning home.

Grandpa Shmuel, the Torah portion *Masei* records the commandment for the Jew to live in Israel, "And you shall make the land your heritage and dwell in it" (Numbers 33:53).

But this verse is preceded by two necessary conditions: "And you shall conquer all the inhabitants of the land, and you shall destroy all of the idols" (Numbers 33:52). The first of these conditions is eminently understandable, from a practical perspective; two nations cannot occupy the same land at the same time, and so the necessary moral and military prerequisites must be met for us to be able to inhabit the land.

The second condition, "And you shall destroy all the idols," is not as readily obvious in meaning. The usual and literal understanding of this text is that once we succeed in possessing the land, we have to destroy the idols that the Seven Nations left behind. But there is an alternative reading. Before the Jews can possess the Land of Israel, before they will truly desire to inhabit the land for the right reasons and thereby be enabled to hold onto the land, they will first have had to destroy their own false gods, the idols they carry with them. They will have to desire a homeland to express their unique Jewish culture and values, so that they may truly be a holy nation and a kingdom of priests to the world.

And we saw this in Budapest. Before this massive *aliya* could take place, the false god of communism had to be destroyed. Before the Jew can accept his own faith and destiny, he must rid himself of the *false gods of the world about him,* the false gods that he himself had mistakenly and tragically espoused. The Land of Israel of God's covenant is not only a safe haven for Israel's physical survival; it must be the vehicle through which Israel would be enabled to teach our message of compassionate righteousness and moral justice to a world which is to be blessed by this teaching. Otherwise, Birobidzhan or Uganda could have provided the same haven to a wandering nation.

There are very few, if any, Jews left on Myrtle Avenue. The *shvitz* has long since ceased to exist; there are no more meeting places where old and young Jews debate together questions of ideology. But when we can meet again, Grandpa, I will greet you with great love and respect, and thank you for showing me that *Moshe Rabbenu* was a far greater teacher than Karl Marx.

Your loving grandson,
Shlomo

To Make Aliya or Not to Make Aliya, That Is the Question

And you shall make the land your heritage and dwell therein, for I have given the land to you to inherit.

NUMBERS 33:53

During a radio interview in New York shortly after my *aliya* to Israel, the interviewer wanted to know why an Orthodox rabbi would continue to celebrate Thanksgiving – an American holiday commemorating the special meal in praise of God set up by the early American colonists after their having survived a very difficult first winter in the New World, a gentile holiday – even after his move to Israel. I could have responded that Thanksgiving is not only a gentile holiday, that expressing gratitude to God for having provided a country which has granted safe haven to Jews for close to three centuries, which is a model for democracy and freedom (two biblically Jewish values) throughout the world, and whose citizens are generously supporting Israel (indeed,

I often feel the necessity to make the blessing "*hamotzi leḥem miḥutz la'aretz*") is a genuinely Jewish obligation.

Nevertheless I opted for another Jewish characteristic (in addition to expressing gratitude): to answer a question with a question. I asked my questioner, an extremely devout Jew whose appearance shunned any compromises with modernity, why *he* continued to live in America, despite the clear biblical command to "Make Israel your heritage and dwell in it" (Nahmanides, "Strictures on Maimonides' *Sefer HaMitzvot*," Mitzva 4). For Nahmanides, in accordance with the explicit meaning of the biblical text, settling the Land of Israel is not merely a *ḥumra* (an additional stringency) but is one of the 613 commandments! (Sometimes I think it is a pity, because were *aliya* to be a mere stringency, then perhaps all of the "pious" Jews of Boro Park, Lakewood, and Stamford Hill would stampede the country in their rush to settle within it!)

Moreover, even Maimonides, who does not include *aliya* as one of the 613 commandments in his *Sefer HaMitzvot* (Book of Commandments), does record in his *Mishneh Torah* (*Hilkhot Melakhim* 5:10–12): "The early sages would kiss the stones of Israel, and roll themselves in its dust.... A Jew must *always* opt to live in the Land of Israel, even if the city in Israel has a majority population of gentiles, and not opt to live in the Diaspora, even if the city in the Diaspora has a majority population of Jews." So, if living in Israel is so cardinal to Maimonides, why doesn't he list *aliya* as one of the 613 commandments?

The most probable explanation is to be found in the first chapter of his *Hilkhot Terumot*. He opens there with the general statement that the command to separate heave offerings and tithes is only applicable in the Land of Israel, and goes on to stipulate that a duly constituted Land of Israel refers to a geographical entity within the boundaries of Joshua's conquest, to which the majority of the world's Jews will return under the leadership of a king, a prophet, or a prime minister (*Hilkhot Terumot* 1, 2, and 26).

Apparently Maimonides felt that an individual could not be commanded to live in Israel without the requisite protection of a sovereign government and the backup presence of a majority of the Jewish population (in order to understand his view of the great importance of a sovereign Jewish government, even a Jewish government that did not adhere to Jewish law, see his *Hilkhot Ḥanukka,* 1:1). It is important to note that since the world's Jewish population is estimated to be thirteen million (of which at least two million cannot be considered to be halakhic Jews) and since the Jewish population in Israel is nearing six million, we probably already have (and will certainly have within the next few years) the majority of world Jewry living in Israel!

At any rate, to return to the New York interviewer, I believe that the Jew from America living in Israel and celebrating Thanksgiving is far less a paradox than the Jew living in the Diaspora who punctiliously attempts to observe the more lenient commands no less than the more stringent commands but ignores the central command – so critical in our biblical passages and so basic in all of our prayers – of settling in the Land of Israel!

Postscript: A Historical Overview which Mandates Aliya

Our discussion of this topic cannot be considered complete without providing a brief historical and sociological overview of the rise and fall of the Jewish Diaspora. The year is 69 CE, Jerusalem – the city of the holy Temple and the seat of Jewish national sovereignty – is surrounded by the Roman armies and appears to be doomed for imminent destruction. R. Yoḥanan b. Zakkai, president of the great *Sanhedrin,* secretly leaves Jerusalem to meet with Vespasian, general of the Roman armies and future emperor of Rome. Apparently the Jewish sage has concluded that the cardinal command "You shall live by these [Torah Laws] – live and not die by them" takes precedence over national sovereignty, and he is ready for an accommodation with Rome. "Give me Yavneh and its sages," he implores; enable us to live with our Torah intact, and we will manage without Jerusalem, without the holy Temple, without Jewish national sovereignty.

History credits R. Yoḥanan with having rescued "historic Israel" (*Knesset Yisrael*) with his wise decision. For the past eighteen hundred years we have witnessed the rise of Yavnehs all over the world – from

Pumpedita in ancient Babylon to Yeshiva University in New York. Nevertheless his successes do not mean that his compromise with Rome was unanimously accepted by his contemporaries.

Professor Gedaliah Alon, a leading Second Commonwealth historian, argues that the majority of the sages remained to continue the war – until the Temple was razed, and they were forced to flee to Yavneh. But they were embittered against R. Yoḥanan; they felt that he had given up too much too soon, and that he had, albeit unwittingly, aided the enemy by weakening the Jewish ranks of opposition to Rome. Rabban Gamliel was appointed head of the *Sanhedrin* at Yavneh, and R. Yoḥanan was constrained to leave for a self-imposed "exile" in *Bror Ḥayil,* where he lived out his last years in relative obscurity.

The ambivalence in his own mind after his fateful meeting with Vespasian could not have been expressed more forcefully than it was by R. Yoḥanan himself on his deathbed (*Berakhot* 28b, in accordance with the interpretation of Rabbi Joseph B. Soloveitchik). When his students came to visit him during his final illness, they were shocked to find this right-hand pillar of the Jewish people weeping, as if fearful of the final judgment before the heavenly throne. The sage responded that if he were to be brought before a flesh-and-blood mortal king, whose punishments were not eternal and who could be bribed by gifts and appeased with words, he would still weep in fear; how much more ought he be expected to weep now that he is about to meet the King of all kings, whose punishment is eternal and who can neither be bribed nor appeased!

Moreover, he continued, two roads lay before him, the one leading to heaven and the other to hell, and he did not know to which he would be directed…. Now why should a pious and selfless leader fear hell? Was it not because perhaps he had made a wrong decision in abandoning Jerusalem at the last, most critical moments of the battle? And he went on to bless his students to fear God as much as they fear mortals. "Is that all?" they asked. "Would that it would be as much!" he responded.

Is it not logical to surmise that R. Yoḥanan was relating to himself, that in his moment of truth he had perhaps feared Israel's facing the hordes of the Roman armies more than he had feared facing the Lord after having given up Jerusalem and the holy Temple? And remember, the sage opened his response to his students by invoking one's fear before a mortal king – an obvious reference to his feelings when he had stood before Vespasian.

And, indeed, one generation later the renowned Rabbi Akiva forcefully condemned R. Yoḥanan and his decision by attributing the verse "[Sometimes God] turns wise men backwards and transforms their wisdom into foolishness" (Isaiah 44:25) to none other than R. Yoḥanan b. Zakkai, who was the teacher of both Rabbis Joshua and Eliezer, the two main teachers of Rabbi Akiva!

Rabbi Akiva himself refused to compromise with Rome, and some sixty-five years after the destruction he gave his spiritual backing to the Bar Kokhva rebellion, claiming that the Jewish general was none other than the long-awaited messianic redeemer. He apparently believed that one must sacrifice one's life on the altar of Jerusalem and the holy Temple, that Jewish national sovereignty in the face of an inimical and cruel world power is a *yehareg uval ya'avor*, an instance of the necessity to die rather than submit to foreign rule.

What followed the tragic and abortive rebellion were the horrific Hadrianic persecutions and an almost two-thousand-year exile. The historical events vindicated R. Yoḥanan b. Zakkai, whose legacy weaves its way down the ages and leaves behind the enormous expansion of Jewish thought and law, the Babylonian Talmud, the Responsa literature, the works of Hasidut and *musar*. The trauma of the abortive Bar Kokhva rebellion engulfed the Jewish people; the dreams of national sovereignty and a holy Temple in Jerusalem were relegated to God – far removed from human involvement. And so Jews made their homes in the farthest corners of the globe and, in the main, waited for God to restore them to their homeland and effectuate their redemption.

The very end of the tractate *Ketubot* encapsulates this mindset of historic Israel following the abortive Bar Kokhva rebellion. There were three oaths to which God adjured Israel and the nations of the world: Israel must not climb the ramparts of Jerusalem, Israel must not rebel against the nations of the world, and the nations of the world "must not subjugate Israel too much." A universal contract: Israel would wait for God to achieve national sovereignty and a holy Temple, and the gentile world would allow us to live and practice our faith in peace.

With the advent of the eighteenth century, the situation became radically altered. The French Revolution ushered in a period of nationalism and secularism; populations were no longer divided into different religious groupings but rather into quickly emerging nation-states, with the sudden possibility of secularism – a by-product of the science-enamored Emancipation – becoming the order of the day. Since the stateless Jews were the "odd man out" in this new scheme of things, anti-Semitism was becoming more and more virulent. Large numbers of Jews identified with an assimilated Viennese reporter and playwright, Theodor Herzl, when he penned the clarion call to Jewish nationalism *Der Judenstaat* (*The Jewish State*) mostly in response to the infamous and Jew-baiting "Dreyfus Affair." At the same time, major disciples of the Gaon of Vilna, the Ba'al Shem Tov, and the Ḥatam Sofer urged *aliya* as a "Custer's Last Stand" against secularist assimilation, and many of them established the Yishuv in Jerusalem.

But the final death-blow to the "three oaths" was struck by the gas chambers of Auschwitz and Treblinka, when the world stood silent while six million Jews – including aged, infirm, and innocent babies – literally went up in smoke. What welled up from these crematoria was neither the "You shall live by them" of R. Yoḥanan b. Zakkai nor the *kiddush Hashem* (sanctification of God's name) *yehareg uval ya'avor* (one must die rather than transgress) of Rabbi Akiva, but was rather the historical *ein breira* (there is no other choice) of the "one nation which dwells alone," of the victim who understands in his soul that unless he gains the wherewithal to defend himself, no other nation will take up the cudgels in our defense. The Nazis and the world at large subjugated Israel too much; the oaths were clearly abrogated.

We realized during those fateful years between 1939 and 1945 that if we wished to continue to live as a people we must have our own nation-state, our own army, our own police force. For this reason, as well as for the eventual realization of our dream to be a "light unto the nations" teaching the message of divine rule and world peace, we must fulfill the commandment of the desert generation – between slavery and freedom: "You shall make Israel your heritage and dwell in it."

During one of my idyllic summers in Kibbutz Ein Tzurim (between 1976 and 1983), I was teaching a group of eight-year-olds about the horrors of the Holocaust on the day of Tisha B'Av. A young boy cried out, "But HaRav, where was the IDF?" I kissed his forehead with tears in my eyes, proud of a generation emerging which had never known Jewish life without an IDF!

God Lives in the Land and within His Nation

> *You must not defile the Land upon which you live and in the midst of which I [God] dwell, since I [God] dwell in the midst of the children of Israel.*
>
> NUMBERS 35:34

The Bible insists that the very Land of Israel is sensitive to immorality committed within its borders, that the very Land of Israel becomes polluted by the shedding of blood within its boundaries; indeed, God Himself is present (as it were) within the midst of the land. What does this really mean?

The sacred Zohar teaches that the nation Israel, the Torah, and the Holy One blessed be He are one; this suggests that the eternal God may be experienced and apprehended through those phenomena in this world which are also perceived to be eternal. Hence, since the covenantal nation Israel is eternal (by divine oath; Genesis 15) and since the

Torah is eternal, Israel, Torah, and God are inextricably linked together by virtue of their common eternity.

The Land of Israel shares in this feature of eternity. The earth's perennial cycles of birth, growth, decay, death, and rebirth, express a movement of regeneration and renaissance which informs the very nature of the most primitive form of life. There are intimations of immortality in the earth's movement from life to life: a fruit falls from the tree when it no longer requires the physical sustenance provided by attachment to the branch, and the tree rebirths (regenerates) its fruit once springtime returns. The trees shed their leaves and fruits onto the earth, and once they decompose and merge with the earth, that very earth provides the necessary nutrients for the tree to continue to grow and bear fruit in the future; plants leave their seeds in the ground, which continue to sprout plant life from the earth after the mother herb has been taken and eaten. And so the cycle of life, decay, death, and rebirth is grounded in the eternal, infinite, and natural dimension of the earth. In the words of the wisest of men, "one generation passes away and another generation arrives, but the earth abides forever" (Ecclesiastes 1:4).

In a more national sense, it is the biblical tradition to bury our dead in the earth, and specifically in the Land of Israel. The biblical idiom for death is, "And he is gathered to his nation, or his family," for if one is buried in one's homeland, one's physical remains merge with the physical remains of one's family members, of those who came and died before as well as of those who will follow in the future.

Furthermore, the Land of Israel is invested with a special metaphysical quality which is inextricably linked to *Knesset Yisrael,* historic Israel. The first Hebrew, Abraham, entered into the Covenant between the Pieces – the divine mission of a nation founded on the principles of humans created in the image of God and the right of freedom for every individual – in the city of Ḥebron, and according to prophecy, God's promise of world peace and messianic redemption will be realized in the city of Jerusalem. The Cave of the Couples – Abraham and Sarah, Isaac and Rebecca, Jacob and Leah – was the very first acquisition by a Jew of land in Israel, earthly resting place for the founders of our faith, but which, at the very same time, is the womb of our future, a future informed by the ideas and ideals of our revered ancestors. "Grandchildren are the crowning glory of the aged; parents are the pride of their children" (Proverbs 17:6).

It is for this reason that the Talmud maintains that only in Israel is there a true and authentic "community" (*kehilla*; *Horayot* 3a) – for only in Israel do we see the footprints of historic Israel, the sweep of the generations, the "common unity" of tradition, from Abraham to the Messiah; Israel formed, prophesied, and taught its eternal traditions and continues to live out its universal destiny within the Land of Israel.

Moreover, the eternal Torah is rooted and invested in the very earth, stones, and vegetation of the Land of Israel. This is true not only in terms of the biblical covenantal promise which guarantees our constant relationship and eventual return to Israel; it is also true because of the myriad of mitzvot embedded in its bedrock, its soil, its agricultural produce. The seventh Sabbatical year provides free fruits and vegetables for anyone who wishes to take them; the "corners" of the field actually "belong" to the poor every day of the year, and they may come and reap their harvests; tithes from the land's produce immediately go to the kohanim, the Levite cantors, and the poor who share in the land of the rest of the nation. The Land of Israel itself cries out to its inhabitants in the name of God: "for the land shall not be sold in perpetuity because the land belongs to Me. You are a stranger and resident [on the land together with Me]" (Leviticus 25:23).

Hence God Himself, as it were, becomes inextricably linked – even "incorporated" or "in-corporeal-ized," if you will – within the peoplehood, the Land, and the Torah of Israel, the very objects and subjects which express God's will eternally and out of which our essence and destiny is formed. Indeed, historic Israel, the Land of Israel, the Torah of Israel, the Holy One blessed be He God of Israel, and the universe are truly united in an eternal bond.

When the Dead Inherit the Living

Command the children of Israel: … This is the land which shall fall to you as an inheritance, the Land of Canaan and its boundaries.

NUMBERS 34:2

But the Israelites to whom Moses was addressing these words were not to inherit the land! With the sole exceptions of Joshua and Caleb, the entire desert generation – the Jews who left Egypt – were all to perish before reaching the Promised Land. The sin of the scouts occurred in the second year of the desert sojourn, when they were all informed that the desert would become their grave. How did the Hebrews have the fortitude to persevere for the next thirty-eight years, knowing that the goal of settling the Land of Israel would not be realized during their lifetime? How does someone persist with the struggles of life knowing that they are suffering from a terminal illness?

On the deepest level, each of us is plagued by this problem as soon as we become aware of our own mortality. Most of us manage to repress such "intimations of mortality" fairly successfully. The Midrash teaches that each year, after the sin of the scouts, Moses ordered every Hebrew to dig his own grave on the evening of the Ninth of Av and sleep in it. The next morning, a significant percentage would not get up (*Bava Batra* 121a, Rashbam ad loc.). Apparently, the desert generation could not repress their impending doom; they lived in the midst of the graves waiting to receive their bodies, which daily stared them in the face. Perhaps the way in which they coped will teach us all an important lesson.

The secret lies in the manner in which the land was to be divided, as described in the portion of *Masei*, but harks back to the previous portion of *Pineḥas*. One verse implies that the land was to be divided according to the number of people entering it (Numbers 26:53), whereas two verses later, the text implies that the division was based upon the numbers of the generation that left Egypt and died in the desert.

The Talmud (*Bava Batra* 117a) orchestrates a solution to the apparent contradiction by means of a practical illustration: Reuben and Simeon leave Egypt; Reuben has one son, Simeon has two sons. The three sons who enter the land receive three portions, representing the fact that this is the number of sons who enter the holy homeland. But in order to give credit to the two fathers who came out of Egypt, the three boys divide their portions in half, with Reuben's one son receiving one and a half portions, and Simeon's two sons sharing one and a half portions. This prompts R. Yonatan to cry out: "How different is this inheritance from any other inheritance in the world; generally the living inherit the dead, whereas here the dead inherit the living!"

The idea behind this Talmudic declaration is a glory to behold. The narrative of Israel is an unfinished symphony, which began with Abraham and will not conclude until the eventual redemption of the world. Every generation owes its accomplishments to the foundations and guideposts established by its forebears. Hence the generation which left Egypt but did not enter the Promised Land must likewise share in the inheritance of the children.

This is the significance of the teaching in the Pesaḥ Haggada: "It is incumbent upon every individual to feel as if he came out of Egypt." Superficially, such an emotion seems impossible. How can one individual traverse four thousand years?

But the first time I sat at the Pesaḥ Seder with my grandchildren and recognized my genetic characteristics – but even more importantly my values and customs – within their words and deeds, I realized how much of me was in them and how much of them was in me. Indeed, I am them and they are me.

At that moment, I ceased being afraid of my mortality, for I realized to what extent it is possible to participate in eternity. As the Talmud says so eloquently: "Father Jacob never died" (*Ta'anit* 5b). As long as his children and grandchildren are alive, and following his customs and values, he too is alive.

And this does not necessitate biological children and grandchildren; anyone who influences the next generation – as a teacher, as an author, as a patron, anyone who makes the continuity of the narrative possible – shares in that eternity.

"Spiritual children" can be even more significant than biological children. What is crucial is to be imbued with the desire to preserve our narrative into the next generation.

It is this interpretation which prompted our sages to declare, "Whoever teaches his grandchild Torah is as if he received it from Sinai," as our sages teach, "The crown of the elders are their grandchildren and the glory of the children are their forebears" (Mishna *Avot* 6:8). The parents and grandparents who died in the desert entered into the Promised Land together with their children and grandchildren. The dead inherit the living!

Who Was Tzelofḥad, and Why?

> *This is what God has commanded concerning the daughters of Tzelofḥad saying: "They may marry anyone they wish provided they marry into a family of their father's tribe. No inheritance of the children of Israel may pass from one tribe to another, for the children of Israel shall cleave everyone to the inheritance of the tribe of their fathers."*
>
> NUMBERS 36:6–7

The book of Numbers, and the biblical portion of *Masei*, concludes with a recap of the earlier ruling of Moses from God that the five daughters of Tzelofḥad would be able to inherit the land of their father – since he left no male heirs – but added that they would have to marry within their tribe of Menashe, so that their familial inheritance would not pass over to another tribe (Numbers 36:1–12). In effect, this final biblical decision was orchestrated between women and familial rights on the one hand – simply because Tzelofḥad had not borne male heirs was no reason to deprive him and his future generations of ancestral property in the Land of Israel – and tribal rights, on the other hand: were the daughters to inherit their father and then marry men from another tribe, that other tribe would benefit the land of Tzelofḥad, who was a Menashite. In biblical history, tribal rights were very zealously guarded (not unlike individual state's rights in early American history). Hence this decision created a win-win solution to what had threatened to erupt into a full-blown conflict. Yes, in the absence of men, the women could inherit their father, but the land would have to remain in the father's tribe by forbidding these female inheritors from marrying into another tribe!

The initial story concerning the five brilliant, learned, and religious daughters of Tzelofḥad is told a few chapters earlier in the portion of *Pineḥas* (Numbers 27:1–11). These five women went all the way up the judicial and political ladder until they stood before Moses himself, insisting upon their rights of inheritance so that Tzelofḥad would have a portion in the future eternity of Israel through his descendants' working and living in the Land of Israel."Why should the name of our father be lessened from the midst of his family, merely because he has no son? Give us [women] an inheritance among the brothers of our father" (Numbers 27:4). And the Almighty granted a ringing endorsement to these brave women "who spoke right" and were therefore "worthy of a portion of the inheritance"; indeed, they won the case for female rights to inheritance, and caused an entire new addendum to be added to the previous inheritance laws of the Bible (Numbers 27:8–11).

But who was this man Tzelofḥad of the tribe of Menashe, who fathered such special women? The Talmud records a fascinating dispute between Rabbi Akiva and Rabbi Yehuda b. Beteyra:

> Our rabbis have taught: "The one who gathered wood [on the Sabbath and was stoned to death as a punishment (Numbers 15:32–36)] – was Tzelofḥad, as it is written, 'and the children of Israel were in the *desert* and they found a man gathering wood,' and later it is written 'our father died in the *desert*' [regarding Tzelofḥad]; just as the second refers to Tzelofḥad, so does the first," these are the words of Rabbi Akiva.
>
> Rabbi Yehuda b. Beteyra said to him, "Akiva, whether or

> not you are correct in your identification [of Tzelofḥad], you will eventually be punished. If it is as you say, then if the Torah saw fit to hide [the identification], why did you reveal it? And if you are mistaken, how dare you cast aspersions on such a righteous person?… But then from where did Tzelofḥad come? From the group of *brazen climbers* [*ma'apilim*] atop the mountain [who defiantly attempted to conquer Israel without God in their midst and without the Holy Ark (Numbers 14:40–45)]".
>
> *Shabbat* 96b–97a

Let us look at Tzelofḥad, and the character of his daughters, from the perspective of this Talmudic discussion. Rabbi Yehuda b. Beteyra sees Tzelofḥad as one of the *ma'apilim*, the brazen would-be conquerors of Israel, and this identification would assume three distinct political parties of Israelites in the desert: all of them together were opposed to Moses' leadership, but each had its own unique platform. The first is Datan and Aviram, who saw the fleshpots of Egypt as the real land flowing with milk and honey, and that's where they wanted to be; the second is Koraḥ, who, like *Neturei Karta*, wished to remain in the religious "Kollel" of God outside of Israel, so as not to become sullied by the stench and struggle of a new startup state; and the third are the *ma'apilim*, the non-religious Zionists, who storm the ramparts of the Land of Canaan with neither God nor the Holy Ark of the Torah in their midst. This third party is akin to *Hashomer Hatza'ir* secular Zionists; they may have failed at their attempt in the desert, but it was apparently their passionate love for the land of Zion that produced these very special five daughters, who learned their love for the land from their father, but added to it an indomitable faith in God and in the equity of His Torah.

That is in accordance with Rabbi Yehuda b. Beteyra. But why did Rabbi Akiva identify Tzelofḥad with the culpable gatherer of wood, a wicked Sabbath desecrator who was condemned to death? I believe that Rabbi Akiva was stressing a crucial foundation stone of Judaism: we are both a nationality as well as a religion, with each of these critical compartments of our faith having been worthy of a divine covenant, a national covenant with Abraham "between the pieces" in which He guaranteed the first patriarch progeny and a homeland, and the religious

Revelation at Sinai, a divine covenant to the entire nation of Israel. And even though Tzelofḥad, in desecrating the Sabbath, may have "lapsed" in terms of his religious obligations, this dare not detract from his national status as a member of *Klal Yisrael*, the historic Jewish nation. "An Israelite, no matter how much he transgresses, still remains an Israelite," teach our Talmudic sages. And remember that the daughters' claim was that "the name of their father not be diminished" by his inability to bequeath a portion of land in Israel because he lacked male heirs. Certainly there were some "sages" who may well have claimed to the five sisters that they were not entitled to any land, to any parcel of the Israel patrimony, if their father had been a transgressor of the law, if he had desecrated the Sabbath publicly. Perhaps Rabbi Akiva specifically identifies Tzelofḥad as the culpable wood-gatherer in order to stress that even though a Jew may tragically cut himself off from the religious covenant, he still remains an inextricable member of the national covenant, the historic nation of Israel. And although his five brilliant, indomitable, and righteous daughters reestablished a profound relationship with the Hebraic laws and traditions, they undoubtedly received much of their Zionistic fervor for the land from their father! Therefore, his share in the land was indisputable, and deserved to be bequeathed to his daughters.

About the Author

Rabbi Shlomo Riskin is a widely respected spokesman for modern Orthodox Judaism and the State of Israel.

He is chancellor of Ohr Torah Stone in Israel, a network of educational programs that includes high schools, university programs, a rabbinical seminary, and a center for training women as Torah leaders. He also serves as chief rabbi of the town of Efrat, Israel, and was the founding rabbi of Lincoln Square Synagogue in New York City.

Rabbi Riskin has published many works, including *Torah Lights* (biblical commentaries), *Listening to God: Inspirational Stories for My Grandchildren, Siaḥ Shulḥan* (*Around the Family Table*) and *Yad L'Isha* (*Women and Jewish Divorce*), all available from Maggid Books.

The fonts used in this book are from the Arno family

Other works in the Torah Lights series

Bereshit: Confronting Life, Love & Family

Shemot: Defining a Nation

Vayikra: Sacrifice, Sanctity & Silence

Other works by Shlomo Riskin
available from Maggid Books

Listening to God: Inspirational Stories for My Grandchildren

Siaḥ Shulḥan (Around the Family Table) [Hebrew]

Yad L'Isha (Women and Jewish Divorce) [Hebrew]

Maggid Books
The best of contemporary Jewish Thought from
Koren Publishers Jerusalem